SPAIN 1923–1948

CIVIL WAR AND WORLD WAR

SPAIN 1923–1948

CIVIL WAR AND WORLD WAR

ARTHUR F. LOVEDAY, O.B.E.

ANTELOPE HILL PUBLISHING

Third printing 2022.

Originally published in England, 1948.

Cover art by Swifty.
Edited by hospitaller.
Formatted by Margaret Bauer.

Antelope Hill Publishing
www.antelopehillpublishing.com

Paperback ISBN-13: 978-1-953730-00-8
EPUB ISBN-13: 978-1-953730-01-5

TABLE OF CONTENTS

FOREWORD

By Sir R. M. Hodgson

It is a real pleasure to write a Foreword to Mr. Loveday's book and that for the best of reasons. In the first place he has a knowledge of Spanish mentality and of Spanish affairs generally such as few foreigners succeed in acquiring. As chairman of the British Chamber of Commerce in Spain and as correspondent of the *Morning Post* he has had contact with persons in all walks of life and, besides being singularly well-informed, he is most reasonable and objective in his outlook. Then at the present moment we are all chattering about the vital necessity of achieving Western Union. Surely this is the time for challenging the justice of Spain's continued exclusion from U.N.O.; of her persistent black-balling whenever the question of canceling the decision of December, 1946 is raised, as well as of the refusal to allow her to adhere to E.R.P., though her need of Marshall Aid is unquestionably urgent, and all other candidates, the Soviet Union among them, were cordially welcomed. Mr. Loveday is eminently qualified to argue the Spanish case in a manner which promises to dispel the atmosphere of ill-informed hostility by which it is still surrounded. And now is the moment for doing so.

This is no place for raising the various issues that must be studied if a dispassionate appreciation of the Spanish enigma is sought. I would, however, stress most strongly that, despite the belief to the contrary prevalent in England at the time, the movement in which in July, 1936, General Franco took the lead, had the support of the majority of the Spanish people; further, that our antagonism to it markedly increased its standing in a xenophobe Spain. Even in the Basque provinces, believed to have been in alliance with "The Loyalists"—sympathy with the Nationalist cause was in fact general. Navarre and Alava nearly to a man were in favor of Franco, while in Vizcaya and Guipuzcoa important minorities were of the same way of thinking. A region which had produced Ignatius Loyola, Francis Xavier and other eminent ecclesiastics could not have much in common with an atheistic dispensation which murdered priests and destroyed its churches.

Spain 1923–1948: Civil War and World War

Another point to be borne in mind is that our condemnation of the Nationalists for having recourse to German and Italian aid in the field—for which, incidentally, they paid heavily in cash—is grossly illogical in face of the very considerable assistance rendered to "The Loyalists" by other countries, notably by France. Not only were the International Brigades organized and equipped with the sanction of the Blum Government—sire of nonintervention—in French territory, but some 20,000 to 30,000 trained French soldiers took part in the civil war. Our participation was numerically unimportant, though Mr. Attlee lent distinction to it by giving his name to the British unit, while Germans, Americans and other nationalities contributed considerable quotas. The Russian contingent was small but was composed of "technicians"—airmen, motor-mechanics, drivers and so forth, while Soviet propaganda was incredibly active. In all, the International Brigades numbered at least 70,000 and—a fact which we are prone to forget—they arrived in Madrid a month or two before the Germans and Italians arrived in Nationalist Spain. The second event was the logical sequence to the first. There are other grievances which Nationalists can quote to our detriment. Our refusal to concede to them belligerent rights was in contradiction to the accepted principles of international law, while the terms of the nonintervention agreement which we substituted for them were flagrantly disregarded by nearly all the signatories. Again, our tardiness in granting *de jure* recognition to the National government was a fruitful source of soreness, for it entailed the prolongation of the war to no purpose. Nor was our insistence in styling the Nationalists "The Insurgents" at a time when practically the whole of Spain was in their hands the embodiment of tactfulness.

Turning to subsequent events—to the days of the World War—"Wartime Mission in Spain," by Mr. Carlton Hayes, American ambassador in Madrid, is a book which all should read who wish to have a balanced view of the behavior of the Spanish government in those difficult days. It confirms that the wish of the great majority of the Spanish people was to abstain from involvement in the World War, to avoid the recurrence of civil war and to reach a friendly understanding with the English-speaking democracies, especially with the United States. Another tribute was paid by Mr. Churchill in the shape of the "kindly words" he spoke in the House of Commons, on May 25th 1944. Surely it is time we abandoned the contention that the continuation of the present regime constitutes "a potential menace to world peace" and made up our minds to reach agreement with a state which entertains friendly dispositions towards us and whose cooperation may be a useful factor in the achievement of Western Union. As for the projects of creating Spanish governments in exile headed by Republican leaders of the caliber of Martínez Barrio or José Giral, which received a measure of support here, it is hard today to believe that anyone should have taken them seriously. The vital fact that we have to bear in mind in relation to Spain is that Franco on his own initiative refused to listen to Hitler's remonstrances and to plunge the country into the world holocaust. Had he done otherwise, Spain would have been overrun, Gibraltar taken and our access to the Mediterranean cut off.

The position today is that, by the inevitable process of events, a gradual modification in the unreasoning hostility of public opinion here towards the present Spanish regime is coming into being. That it has the support of over 70 percent of the population is now freely admitted. Lord Hinchinbrooke's speech in Madrid on October 21st, with its statement that, "[t]he majority of the British Conservative Party would like to see a normal diplomatic situation resumed between Spain and Britain. The whole Conservative Party would welcome Spain's inclusion in the Marshall Plan, provided other countries allocations are not cut," is evidence that a more sensible frame of mind in regard to the Spanish problem is coming into being. So, especially in view of the relatively broad-minded attitude the American authorities are adopting, we can look forward confidently to a continued improvement in public opinion here.

With this background, Mr. Loveday's book promises to appear at a moment when it will exercise a salutary influence on the development of events. Lack of understanding in the past has been largely responsible for our antagonism towards a system of administration which was no concern of ours and which the majority of Spaniards approved. Today we have plenty of troubles of our own to bother about and elementary principles of commonsense demand that we allow Spain to work out her own salvation, and indeed that we lend her a kindly hand when possible. It is my firm belief that Mr. Loveday's book will aid potently in bringing about a relationship which both parties will applaud.

*R. M. HODGSON**
The Athenaeum, November 3rd, 1948

---

* Sir R. M. Hodgson K.C.M.G. K.B.E. late *Chargé d'Affaires* and Agent in Russia and Nationalist Spain.

I

OUTLINE

Though a considerable number of books, both historical and journalistic, have recently been written about Spain, the Spanish Civil War, its causes and its repercussions, and Spain's behavior during the Second World War, yet there are few subjects about which both the reading and non-reading public are still so confused or so misinformed, or about which so many egregious falsehoods have been written. The result of the civil war, though it was confined to the Iberian Peninsula, is as important to the Christian world and to the Mediterranean civilization, of which Spain, the U.S.A., the British Empire and many other countries are common inheritors, as was the defeat of Islam by Spain at the battle of Lepanto in 1571. It is immensely important that its history, its antecedents, its after effects and the subsequent history of Spain's neutrality in the Second World War should be accurate and accurately understood.

The Spanish Civil War was in reality the opening of the struggle between those two forces and theories which are increasingly in conflict in every country in the world, whose civilization for centuries will depend on the outcome of that conflict. It can best be described in general terms as a struggle between those who follow the tenets and ideas of Karl Marx and those who hold to the Western civilization of which I have spoken, a struggle between the totalitarians, whether of the Communist, Nazi or Socialist breeds, and the believers in the individual dignity and freedom of man, and of his divine origin and destiny. Most Spaniards are uncompromising individualists and Christians, and in 1939 they won a resounding victory over the Communist type of totalitarianism, a victory which was partly spoilt by the adoption, temporarily, of a semi-authoritarian form of government quite contrary to their Spanish character and tradition.

In the chapter on Hispanidad it is pointed out how a false history grew up around Spain and Anglo-Spanish relations of the Elizabethan period, which is beginning to be corrected after more than three centuries of error by modern research, and it is further pointed out that a new false legend has been built up under our eyes around the Spanish Civil War, its causes and effects.

A false legend such as that described contains the seeds of international misunderstandings and dislikes and of future wars. It is in the cause of historical accuracy and of Anglo-Spanish understanding and friendship that this history has been written.

Among the many books published there has not so far appeared any short comprehensive history of the period 1923–1948, which is easy reading for the public and which can also act as a handbook to students, and as a reliable book of reference; it is the object of this book to fill that want. The author ventures to claim that he has the prerequisites necessary for accurate observation and knowledge in his long residence in Spain, intimate contact with Spanish people, knowledge of their language and considerable study of their history and culture. To obtain accurate information about Spain and, when obtained, to appreciate its relative bearing and importance is always immensely difficult for a foreigner, for Spain is a country of great and apparently irreconcilable contradictions. Even for one possessing the prerequisites, it is difficult, and without them it is impossible, to discern what is happening; misapprehension and false history are the natural consequences of newspaper articles and books written by people who have not got them. Blind religious prejudice and devotion to some particular political creed or ideology have often been fruitful elements in creating false history and in this case they aroused a passion of partisanship for one side or the other during the Spanish Civil War, which obscured the truth. When all is said, there cannot be two true versions of one historical fact; the events happened or did not happen and it is the duty and object of the historian to study and sift the evidence objectively, and instruct his readers with the result.

Partisanship is right when it is the result of knowledge, of the study of the history and of the facts of both sides of a question—in fact when it is objective. But it is a rank weed when it is the fruit of ignorance and prejudice.

The present history is believed, by its author, to be honest and objective and he has made no statements of facts which have not been proved by documentary and well-sifted evidence or by his personal knowledge and observation, which he had great opportunities of exercising during a long residence in Spain.

The author is no politician but a business man, who carried on business in Spain for many years; he is only secondarily a historian and became one because, after many years of residence in Spain and of study of her people, history and institutions, he learned how twisted was the average Englishman's knowledge about Spain and Spaniards and how very badly informed about them England was by her daily press. Seeing this, he sought and found a London newspaper (the *Morning Post*) which was prepared to publish his dispatches, which depicted truly (as subsequent events proved) the trend of events and policies in Spain leading up to the civil war. Those dispatches, some of which appear in this history, are incontestable evidence of the truth of much that is set forth in it. During the course of the Spanish Civil War an extensive tour of Nationalist Spain and of the battlefront and his correspondence or conversations with British and Spanish friends from Republican Spain assisted the author to paint what he believes to be a true picture of what happened in Spain during that period.

It is one of the great illusions of what is called the modern mind that truth is relative and not absolute, as all the great philosophers of all ages have previously held. That illusion is at the root of many of the troubles of the present day and of the chaos and decadence in religious faith, science, literature, art, and morals. Absolute truth must be one of the bases of all true sciences, as indeed the word denotes, and that is especially the case in the science of history; if truth be relative, the writing and reading of history are wastes of time.

The present history has been written on the following plan. First a short outline of the Spanish character and then short historical notes on the Catalan and Basque questions, without which backgrounds an understanding of Spanish modern history is impossible. This background is followed by a series of chapters describing in chronological order the history of Spain from 1923 to 1948 as regards both internal and foreign affairs. There are also special chapters on King Alfonso XIII, the Monarchy, General Franco, the labor organizations, the Communist origins of the civil war, the religious persecution and other subjects, which on account of their historical importance require separate and comprehensive reviews.

In 1945, at the end of the World War, Spain found herself the victim of a persecution on the part of governments and the daily press of a great part of the world, at that time filled with admiration for and adulation of Soviet Russia. This, together with her own mistakes, resulted at the Potsdam Conference in her express exclusion from the world security organization as long as her existing regime should last. This persecution and ostracism was continued by the United Nations throughout the conferences of that organization, from San Francisco to Lake Success, and still continued at the beginning of 1948, when this history comes to end, but with visible signs of weakening as the Western nations gradually awoke to the aims and dangers of international Communism and Soviet Russian imperialism.

It is very important for future peace and security that the world should know the historical truth and the events leading up to this position, and thereby be able to understand how such problems have arisen for Spain and their possible repercussions. It is hoped that this book will provide the necessary material for such an understanding by giving Spain's history from 1923 to 1948, the period which saw her pass through her own civil war, the Second World War and the first years of the aftermath.

II

HISPANIDAD, OR THE ESSENCE OF THINGS SPANISH

In order to be able to understand and appreciate the great struggle that took place in Spain in 1936–1939, some knowledge of the Spanish character is necessary. Just as there are definite British characteristics, of which we are justifiably proud, which have resulted in our great Empire and its power and wealth, so there are equally definite Spanish characteristics, which were responsible in the past for the building of that equally great Spanish empire and which still inspire the fine qualities of the true Spaniard of today. These characteristics have been given by Ramiro de Maeztu the name of "Hispanidad" or the soul of things Spanish.

This "Hispanidad" is such a penetrating and dominant factor that, wherever Spain went in her colonizing or empire-building days, her language, customs, religion and ways of being became and remained those of the countries she conquered.

In the whole of Central and South America, except Brazil, where the language is the kindred one of Portugal, Spanish is the language of the people and the impress of Spain is so great that it is evident everywhere and in every activity, and even seems to have caused a similarity of landscape.

Many an old town or village of Colombia, Peru or Bolivia could be planted down in Castile or Andalusia and would so completely fit into the surroundings and atmosphere as to create no comment; the donkeys with their panniers, the mules with their alforjas and the riders perched between them, the peasants in the fields, their hats and clothes are all redolent of Spain. So are the music, the guitar, the mantón de Manila, and a thousand and one other things.

One of the chief features of Spain itself is its unchangeableness in some of its aspects. A traveler or resident in Spain at any time during the last few years could read Richard Ford's travels written in 1845 or George Borrow's *Bible in Spain* written some ten years earlier, and find there was little change except that he travelled by car and train instead of by the diligence or horse of Ford and Borrow. And if he got away from that car or train and from the busy town, the traveler would find himself still further back, seeing the sights and thinking the thoughts of Cervantes's masterpiece. Then, if he had vision and had caught the right feel of things Spanish, he would understand something of "Hispanidad." It is this changelessness, united to other great Spanish characteristics— Christianity, chivalry, conservatism and traditionalism—that gives the hope that the finer qualities of Spanish character have not been greatly affected by the civil war and by the attack of Communist and anti-religious ideas; the poison will have had its effect on many young minds, but the evidence of its inevitable results were so glaring in massacre, terrorism and misery, that these may well provide an antidote.

All natures have their contradictions and one of the most confusing of these in Spaniards is that, in spite of their strong conservatism and traditionalism, they are procrastinators and as great lovers of change in some things as they are unchangeable in others. It is this love of change that was perhaps the chief factor in bringing about the fall of the dictatorship of Primo de Rivera, notwithstanding that under his regime the country and people had reached a state of prosperity with a spiritual and material progress, such as they had not seen for centuries. Spanish unpunctuality and procrastination are exasperating to every Englishman and they are, with the beggars, agricultural methods and architecture, a tribute to the eastern connection of Spain; these failings are not, as with us, matters of manners for which the fault lies with the procrastinator and for which apology is required, his mental attitude is typified in what the Spaniard says when he has missed his train; "*Me dejó el tren,*" "the train has left me behind," he says, not "I have missed the train." It is no fault of his!

The true picture of Spanish character has been and is still lamentably obscured by the suppression or falsification of Spanish history in this country and especially of the history of the height of Spain's greatness, which reached its peak when Philip II, husband of Queen Mary of England, was king of England and Spain. The emphasizing of the cruel methods of the Inquisition without any word to explain that such methods were the universal custom of the times or to give the political situation, which in the eyes of Spain's statesmen made the policy necessary, the relating of the facts that Jews and Moors were expelled, again without giving the reasons for the policy, and in fact the emphasis on every bad motive or procedure and the omission of every statesmanlike motive or good deed have created in every Englishman's mind the legend of a Spain that is "inquisitorial, ignorant, fanatic, the same today as yesterday, always inclined towards violent repression, the enemy of progress and innovation." Some of these characteristics exist in Spain as elsewhere, but it is a false picture which sees only these and forgets the others of intense religious faith, physical courage, individuality, kindness and chivalry.

Gradually the English misunderstanding of sixteenth century Spanish history is being dispelled by the researches of historians and by such publications as Walsh's *Philip II* and E. M. Tenison's *Elizabethan England*. The late Marqués de Castel Bravo (Alvaro Alcalá-Galiano) wrote in the Madrid newspaper A.B.C., shortly before he was murdered, that this history (whose author is a member of the Academy of History of Spain) was "completely reconstructing the historical perspective by showing England in relation to Europe, especially Spain. Some of its manuscripts translated from Spanish have not hitherto seen the light even in Spain." This refers particularly to the Alba MSS., which Tenison is the first English historian to use.

The standard injustices to sixteenth century Spain have been largely due to ignorance, but a new falsification of history is taking place under our eyes which will, unless it is curbed, not only obscure and misrepresent the facts of the Spanish Civil War but revivify the false legend.

It is not the purpose here to discuss the pros and cons of the Inquisition, the expulsion of Moors and Jews or Spanish fanaticism, nor does the author defend them, but he merely desires to point out that there is more than one side to these questions and that most of our school and other histories have misled us about them, as is being proved by the discovery and translation of contemporary evidence.

A study of the contemporary publications, which will supply future historians with their facts about the Spanish war, show that for the first year of the war the news came almost entirely from one side and that, though not never retracted, it was often proved to be notoriously false and that, throughout the first part of the war there was a notable tendency to bend the news in favor of the Republican side, to accept their statements and to reject those of the other side. One of the most commonly held fallacies is that all Spaniards are cruel. This has arisen partly because of that callousness or disdain for death and pain which is depicted below; it also arises because the national sport of Spain is the bullfight, a fine sport from the point of view of the bullfighter, who risks his life in matching his cunning and courage with that of the bull, but, from the point of view of the crowd of spectators, one which offends

English ideas of sport. It is a gladiatorial show in which neither the quarry nor the horses have a chance of escape, and in which the sight of blood excites some primitive passions in the least cultured of the mass of spectators.

It might have been expected that this national recreation would have produced a brutal and cruel race; people, who know nothing about the Spaniard from personal contact, have jumped to the conclusion that it is so. Generations of sportsmen have not trained these people to that fineness of kindness to animals which exists in this country, but the average peasant or cartman in Spain treats his horse or mule with kindness and animal pets are common among all classes. Cruelty of course exists, but it must be remembered that it still takes a wealthy and powerful S.P.C.A. in this country to keep it down and punish it, and that no society for the prevention of cruelty to children is required in Spain.

There are variations of Hispanidad in the various regions of Spain; the highest and noblest is found in Castile and Navarre, and a weaker one in Catalonia, which can be explained by its industrialization and by the cosmopolitanism of Barcelona.

Personal courage and endurance are essential features of most Spaniards. Proof of this is given throughout the history of the discoverers and conquistadores of America and, in our day, in the war on Morocco, the civil war, and episodes in that war such as the sieges of the Alcazar, of Oviedo and of the Sanctuary. Hand in hand with this personal courage there goes what appears to the Englishman to be a callousness towards human life, but this characteristic has this feature about it, that the Spaniard is just as callous about his own life as about the lives of others. A drive behind a Spanish chauffeur on the hairpin bends and precipitous roads of the Spanish highways is an illustration of this, which any traveler who wishes may experience. On the other hand, it may be that the Spaniard places the value of life lower and the value of other qualities higher than does the Englishman; it is not at all certain that modern England has not over-accentuated the value of life to the detriment of the value of far more important things.

Perhaps the greatest of the defects of Hispanidad are an excessive pride and an individuality, which is so great that it sometimes amounts to selfishness. Some modern Spanish philosophers attribute the fall of Spain from her high place in Europe in politics, literature and art, to the Spaniard's diffidence or lack of confidence in himself, resulting in his adopting foreign, and especially French, ideas of politics and life. Though the liberal ideas propagated by the French revolution and the adoption by Spain of an Anglo-French democratic parliamentary system have doubtless been big contributing causes to the decline of Spain, yet they would not have gained root and prevailed unless the Spanish character had provided a fertile soil for their exploitation. This soil was fanned by the individuality and selfishness which has prevented the Spaniard from accepting discipline or from acting with his brother Spaniard in the common national weal.

A deep Christianity and devotion to the Christian Church is one, and perhaps the most dominant, of the Spaniard's characteristics; it is seen throughout his history and is prevalent throughout all classes. The Spaniard believes himself, and with reason, to have been the chief bulwark of the Christian faith throughout the centuries. His part in the crusades, which resulted in the kings of Spain right up to Alfonso XIII holding the title of King of Jerusalem, is a relic of this; he remembers that it was Spain's fleet that broke the power of Islam and stopped its encroachment on Europe at the battle of Lepanto. He now believes that it is Spain that has checked the anti-Christian onslaught on western civilization of the forces of communism. Who will dare to contradict him? With such a historical background and the stimulant of an acute religious persecution, it is not surprising that an intense and all-pervading religious revival took place throughout the country as it was progressively conquered by General Franco.

It is curious that Lenin in 1920 should have chosen Spain, probably the most Christian country in the world, as the object for a communist attack, but on the other hand it is always the policy of Marxism to attack the strategic points, in politics, religion, education, literature, science, and art, and it may be that for this very reason he attacked Christianity at one of its strongest points, where it coincided with a great political weakness.

Appreciation and creation of things beautiful is a feature of Spain in overwhelming proportions. The architecture, literature and painting of Spain are equal to or finer than those of all other countries.

The architecture of Spain is chiefly demonstrated in its cathedrals and churches, of which there is not a bad one to be found in the length and breadth of Spain, unless it be the cathedral of La Sagrada Familia in Barcelona, but that is a thing in itself, an excrescence on Spanish architecture of the middle of last century. Many of their cities, such as Salamanca, are complete gems of architecture and coloring, and it is only where modern industrial conditions have caused the building of cheap suburbs that ugliness is reached. The evident appreciation of things beautiful, and most of Spain's modern buildings and houses are either beautiful or pleasing, provides another of those difficult contradictions, for it runs side by side with the excessive drabness of the plains and hills of Castile, Aragón, La Mancha and other provinces, and the similar drabness, combined with dirt and disorder, of villages and country towns almost everywhere. Much of this is due to lack of rain as is proved by the better aspect of the village in northern Spain, but more is due to the endemic disease of untidiness.

It is nothing less than an impertinence to refer to the architecture, literature and painting of Spain in a few short paragraphs, but, as the object is merely to illustrate that appreciation and creation of things beautiful are an essential part of Hispanidad, the reader will perhaps excuse it. The wealth of literature of the sixteenth and seventeenth centuries—the golden age of Spanish literature—is unsurpassed in any other country for its magnitude and diversity; the names of its authors are legion, but one may mention the greatest, Cervantes, as the best known in this country—unfortunately, better known in the eighteenth century than he is today; as already stated he is still a guide to the Spanish character of today. Modern and ancient Spanish literature are fortunately becoming more known in this country through our universities.

The painting of Spain is far better known in England than her literature, for all know the masterpieces of Velázquez, Murillo, El Greco and Goya, and a few know of the wealth of pictures of all the different Spanish schools which exist in every cathedral and innumerable churches and convents in Spain. Many of Spain's art treasures were lost to Spain and the world, owing to the destructions and depredations of the mob and their leaders during the course of the civil war, but Spain's churches, public galleries and religious houses provide eternal testimony that things beautiful and of merit are appreciated and valued by the true spirit of Spain.

All these features of Hispanidad, many of them necessarily contradictory one to the other, as must be the case with all human beings of whatever nationality, must be remembered and taken into account when reading and judging the history of the civil war in Spain.

The word Hispanidad was subsequently much misused and its true meaning perverted by an attempt on the part of the Falange to utilize what was a purely cultural and spiritual idea as a political slogan and weapon. It is, of course, one of the methods of modern propagandists to make unscrupulous use for their own political ends of originally innocent intellectual movements.

III

THE CATALAN QUESTION

The great difficulty about the Catalan problem is that there are two schools of thought that cut right through Spanish and Catalan opinions, whose respective protagonists are each equally sure of their ground and strong in their convictions, which are shared by foreigners according to their political and sentimental tendencies. These two schools of thought can be described as follows:

1. That Catalonia possesses, and has possessed throughout her history, a separate and distinct personality and language apart from Castile, which, notwithstanding four centuries of effort on the part of successive dynasties and governments, refuse to be assimilated, and that she longs for political separation from the rest of the Iberian Peninsula.

2. That the Catalan's wish for separation from the rest of Spain has been exaggerated and inflamed by politicians and revolutionaries, and is not the desire of the majority, and that the close political unity of Spain is essential to the prosperity, safety and happiness both of Catalonia and of the rest of Spain.

It can be said that in recent times General Primo de Rivera was the outstanding protagonist of the second theory, while Don Francesc Cambó was that of the first, but that, after the advent of the dictatorship, Cambó modified his program of separation to one of a confederation of all the various parts of the Iberian Peninsula including Portugal, an idea which has not been welcomed by any party in that country, nor is it likely to be; this can be said to rule out the possibility of such a solution.

The dispassionate student cannot deny that both of these theories are based on undeniable facts, but it is not necessary on that account to accept either completely, for both either overemphasize or under-emphasize one or other of those facts, and the truth is probably somewhere between the two. It is not possible, in the scope of one chapter, to give any but the merest shadow of the outline of Catalan history, of the assimilation of Catalonia into the body politic of Spain, and of her differences with Castile, but a knowledge of the main facts of that history is necessary for the comprehension of this complicated question.

Catalonia first jumps prominently into history when her Count Ramon Berenguer married Petronila, the heiress of Aragón, in 1137. The grandson of these was the great Jaime I, who came to the throne in 1213 at the age of six years, and was surnamed "the Conqueror"; he drove the Moors out of Valencia and the Balearic Islands, and at the time of his death was monarch, not only of these conquests, but of Catalonia, Aragón and Roussillon. Among other benefits Jaime the Conqueror gave the world its first maritime code, and the basis of all such codes, the *Llibre del Consolat de Mar*, which was written in the Catalan language. This period was perhaps the highest peak of Catalonian individual importance. The next 200 years, after the death of Jaime the Conqueror in 1276, saw the gradual welding together of the whole of the Iberian Peninsula, except Portugal, into one kingdom, out of the originally separate kingdoms of León, Castile, Navarre, Aragón, Catalonia, Valencia, and the kingdoms of the south and east conquered from the Moors.

The uniting of Castile with Aragón and Catalonia through the marriage of Ferdinand and Isabella in 1469 completed this period, and then followed the discovery of America, and the building up of the great Spanish Empire, the largest except the British Empire that the world has ever seen, which was only made possible by the assimilation under one crown of the various kingdoms.

Throughout these periods and until 1626, there seems to have been no Catalan problem, but it must be remembered that, though united under one monarch, the separate regions had their own privileges and almost complete self-government. Especially was this the case in Catalonia, and it was the tampering with these, more than anything else, that sowed the seeds of Catalan regionalism and separatism, which were watered and cultivated throughout the nineteenth and twentieth centuries by the agents of revolution, until by 1931 they had become one of the chief weapons of the Comintern and oriental masonry in their creation of the Spanish revolution and of the civil war.

But this is to anticipate, and we must return to the year 1626 when King Philip IV and his minister Olivares quarreled with the Cortes of Castile and Catalonia over the provision of money and men for his armies, which the latter refused to vote. The quarrel continued and in

1640 Catalonia revolted against the oppression of Olivares, and allied itself with France, then ruled by Louis XIII and Richelieu. This war with France dragged on until 1659 and sowed lasting seeds of bitterness between Castile and Catalonia.

The next violent clash between Castile and Catalonia took place over the War of the Spanish Succession. The Bourbon candidate (Philip V) was supported by the greater part of Spain, while the Austrian candidate (Charles III) was supported by Aragón, Valencia and Catalonia; the French were for the former, and England and her allies for the latter; the war raged up and down Spain from 1702 until 1707, when the victory of the Duke of Berwick at Almansa finally decided the conflict in favor of the Bourbon. Catalonia, and especially Barcelona, had suffered severely in the war, and was the last to surrender. Then came that act which, according to some views, did more than anything else to create the Catalan problem, and is always quoted by the politicians and agitators who wish to inflame Catalan nationalism: Philip V abolished almost all the ancient privileges of Catalonia after a most cruel siege of and massacre at Barcelona, which fell on September 11th, 1714.

Apart from some minor risings the tenacious and turbulent Catalans made no serious rebellion against the central government for close to two centuries. There was fighting and participation in the Carlist wars, and in July 1835, a terrible outburst took place in Catalonia, where the mobs burnt churches, attacked religious houses and murdered priests, but these do not appear to be primarily manifestations of Catalanism against Castile, and indeed it almost seemed as if the assimilation of the whole Peninsula by the culture of Castile had taken place.

However, at the end of the nineteenth and the beginning of the twentieth centuries a new Catalanist political movement began, first under the guise of regionalism (local self-government), which later developed into separatism. During this period, the principal leaders of the movement were Prat de la Riba, Puig i Cadafalch, Francesc Cambó, and Juan Ventosa, all men of great ability and great position, and the last two held office as ministers of state during the reign of Alfonso XIII. These men and their party, called first the Lliga Regionalista and then the Lliga Catalana, gained great favor and prestige up to the time of the dictatorship, 1923-1930, and secured the return of some of the ancient privileges of Catalonia, but, after the dictatorship of Primo de Rivera, the movement swept past its original leaders and doctrines, and "separatism" was stolen by and became the policy of the revolutionaries, who used it as a successful stalking horse in their efforts to disrupt Spain. The Lliga then became a minority party representing the extreme right. The dictatorship of Primo de Rivera was hailed with joy by the majority of Catalans, who were then passing through a period of industrial stagnation and disorder, caused by the revolutionary workmen's syndicates and their gunmen. They benefited enormously by the period of six years' great prosperity, tranquility, and progress both spiritual and material, which the dictatorship provided, but the effect was spoiled owing to the ill feeling aroused by the suppression of the Catalan flag and language, thus arousing afresh all the old jealousies, and giving that opportunity to the malcontents and the Comintern of Soviet Russia for which they were waiting.

On the fall of the monarchy, power in Catalonia fell into the hands of the, then, extreme revolutionary Francesc Macià, who, by forming a political alliance with the left parties in the Cortes of Madrid, obtained the Statute of Autonomy of Catalonia, of which he became first president. But the anarchist, syndicalist and communist elements, who were inspired by the Comintern, and whose votes had put the Republicans into power, gradually dominated the government of Catalonia, as they did that of Madrid. As is described in a subsequent chapter, finding themselves in a minority, the socialists, anarchists, and communists attempted a proletarian revolution in August 1934, in Asturias and Barcelona. The failure of this cost Catalonia most of the privileges of her Statute, which were only returned when the Popular Front came into power in February 1936.

After this the Catalan president (Companys) and parliament continued to function and ostensibly govern Catalonia, though the power was mainly in the hands of the committees of the F.A.I. (Iberian Anarchist Federation), C.N.T. (National Labor Confederation), and U.G.T. (General Workers' Union), the second anarchist, and the last socialist-communist.

When the Madrid government, then very largely controlled by Soviet Russia, moved to Barcelona, the reality of government passed almost entirely into their hands and those of the syndicates, and the Catalan government and Statute became merely a facade.

The political action of the Catalanist movement fomented naturally the use of the Catalan language and flag. No one can doubt the antiquity of either, but they were made to appear as antitheses or opponents to the Castilian language and the flag of Spain instead of, as they had been in previous centuries, their associates. The inhabitants, except in retired agricultural regions, were bilingual, but it seemed senseless to impose bilingualism in the courts and the universities, with all the consequent loss of efficiency and time. Primo de Rivera appreciated this, but he did not appreciate that because a thing is logical it is not necessarily expedient, and his prohibition of the Catalan language and flag was one of the causes of the fall of his regime, and gave a weapon to the disruptive forces which they used with great efficiency. The Catalan language is a variant of Provençal, the language of the troubadours, and spoken in its different dialects in all the Mediterranean country from Provence to Valencia, in the Balearic Islands, in Roussillon, Cerdanya, and all along both slopes of the eastern Pyrenees. It was the language of Jaime the Conqueror, in which he spoke and wrote his diaries and the famous maritime code; in it, at the same period, wrote the poet and mystic Ramon Llull, but it and its literature are pygmies compared to the giants of the Spanish language, spoken by more people in the world than any other language except English, and of Spanish literature. There is, and there has been throughout this century, a remarkable increase in literature of all sorts in the Catalan language, and in Catalan music, painting and sculpture, to which every lover of art must pay tribute but the various pseudo-cultural movements, such as *Palestra, Renaixença*, and *Occitania*, though started honestly enough by politically myopic students and intellectuals, were exploited by the revolutionaries to show that Spanish and Catalan cultures were hostile to each other. The revolutionaries merely followed the technique of all revolutions by using the "intelligentsia" of their day as tools to serve their political and selfish objects.

The movements Palestra, Renaixença, and Occitania were intimately connected and are worthy of study. Palestra was the name of the society for the propagation and development of the ideas typified in the Renaixença (Renaissance) and Occitania movements, both containing true historical and traditional elements. Both were based on the lingual affinities of Southern France and Eastern Spain, the ancestry of whose local languages and dialects are the *langue d'oc*, the language of the troubadours, of which Provençal is the best known. According to the supporters of these movements, a Catalan literary renaissance began with the Catalan poet Aribau in the year 1833 and was further inspired by the Provençal poet Mistral, who lived and wrote in the middle of the last century; it was only about 1933, when the movement had become political and it was thought necessary to provide another prophet, that Sir Walter Scott was adopted as the great inspiration of the renaissance; as the discoverer of the Romantic novel and the period of the troubadours he was a very suitable figure, though there is not the slightest record to support the idea that he had any knowledge of or interest in a Catalan renaissance.

In this connection an amusing ceremony took place in 1933, when revolutionary politicians were making much of the movement, near the monastery of Montserrat, an especially holy shrine of the Catholic Church, which is the object of yearly pilgrimages for tens of thousands of the faithful. Notwithstanding the especial sanctity of the spot in the eyes of Spanish Catholics, an ill-informed English Protestant clergyman was induced by the leaders of the renaissance movement to organize a ceremony and to plant on the spot a plant of white heather brought especially from Sir Walter Scott's home at Abbotsford. The ceremony took place in the presence of the president of Catalonia, and speeches of political significance were made in English and Catalan, and the press and politicians made much of the incident. The sequel was that the next morning, when the man charged with watering the plant went to fulfill his job, he found no heather but in its place a cabbage; however, as white heather is one of the common indigenous plants of that region, the situation was saved by tearing a plant from the hillside and substituting it for the cabbage.

The political tendency of the Renaixença became still more evident when the Occitania movement was launched and developed rapidly into the idea of one national entity under that name of not only Catalonia, Valencia, Roussillon and Provence, but including also the French provinces of Languedoc, Gascony, Limousin and Auvergne, thus comprising the whole of Southern France from the Atlantic to the Mediterranean.

Pamphlets and maps of this new nation were published and a poem by Mistral called "La Copa Santa" was adopted as the hymn of a united Occitania. The political implications and dangers of this movement are easily seen. It may appear to be unimportant but it illustrates the methods by which a local provincialism was forced by exterior revolutionary elements for its own objects into a separatist movement, which was in reality purely a minority desire, and not the wish of the majority of the Catalans.

The treasures of the golden age of Spanish literature and painting are as much the heritage of Catalonia as of the rest of Spain, and Catalan culture has its roots deep in them. Barcelona possesses in the Archivo de la Corona de Aragón what is probably the finest medieval library in the world, but it is chiefly composed of Spanish and not Catalan literature.

The protagonists of the first theory propounded at the beginning of this chapter, would have the world believe that the conflict between Catalonia and Castile is a struggle to the death between self-determination and political slavery, and that it is the only thing that matters to the vast majority of Catalans. If it were so, then Catalonia would have to decide between self-determination and economic decay, for Spain is Catalonia's only market of importance, whereas the rest of Spain can buy her requirements from twenty other countries or set up industries in other parts of Spain in competition with Catalonia, as she began to do as a result of the Catalan Statute. But the theory is an overemphasis of one phase of Catalan character. Every student of Catalonia will agree with the statement that he would be an exceptional Catalan who quarreled with his bread and butter, and that business and profits are almost certainly the Catalan's chief preoccupation, and the inspiration of his renowned industry and commercial efficiency.

Another factor to which emphasis is seldom given is that one-quarter to one-third of the population of Barcelona—and Barcelona is Catalonia—is non-Catalan, but that these people dwell in perfect harmony and unity with their neighbors, intermarrying freely with the Catalans, without any sign between them of the political slavery, which the theorists would have you believe is the chief preoccupation of every Catalan. Such is a very short outline of the Catalan problem as it existed on the outbreak of the civil war, and it remains to be seen if the hands of Spain, as represented by the industry and efficiency of Catalonia, will in future continue to quarrel with the belly of Spain, as represented by the rest of Spain, which is Catalonia's most important market.

IV

THE BASQUE QUESTION

The Basque question has many similarities with that of Catalonia, but also many differences. The true Basque is far more separated both in race and language from the rest of Spain than is the Catalan, but, like Barcelona, Bilbao is a center of industry and of an industrial people drawn from all over Spain and not all by any means natives of the particular region in which they live. The history of the Basques does not show the same turbulence or so much conflict with Castile as does that of Catalonia, and their ancient privileges or *fueros* had not been taken from them as had those of Catalonia in the early eighteenth century.

On the other hand, the Basque provinces were the center and heart of Carlism throughout the Carlist wars of the nineteenth century. Guernica and its sacred tree were the shrines of Carlism and, throughout the reign of Alfonso XIII and right up to the civil war, the traditionalists and legitimists, as the followers of the pretender were called, represented the soul of Basque-land, and especially of Navarre. Ardent support of Christianity and of the church was their distinguishing feature, and an exclusive nationalism.

How then was it that a section of them became identified with the Socialist-Republican government of Madrid and with the Anarchists, Syndicalists and Communists in the civil war? The answer is that the machinery of government in Bilbao was captured by a socialist minority with the assistance of the votes of anarchists, syndicalists and communists, most of whom came from other parts of Spain, and had no Basque blood in their veins. In accordance with their published program of action, and with their procedure in all other countries, communism continued to work under the surface towards revolution and civil war, while rendering lip service to constitutional procedure and successfully gulling the public to think that they represented an undefined blessing called "democracy" against an equally undefined evil called "fascism." As in the case of Catalonia, the nationalist tendencies of the people were exploited and irritated by the revolutionaries for their own ends.

There had existed for a long time a Basque nationalist party, but it was only with the advent of the Republic that an autonomous Basque state or separation became a question of importance.

From the start the Navarran Basques showed their hostility to the statute of autonomy, which it was proposed should be granted to the Basque provinces; at the plebiscite held in November 1932, the delegates of Vizcaya and Guipúzcoa gave a big majority in favor, Álava was half for and half against, and Navarre almost unanimously against the Statute. Parliamentary opposition in the Cortes prevented the granting of the Statute because, notwithstanding the figures of the plebiscite, there was stern opposition, not only in Navarre and Álava, but also in the other two provinces, which made it doubtful that the figures of the plebiscite really represented the wishes of the majority. Even had they done so in 1932, the continued anti-religious legislation of the socialist majority in Madrid more and more shocked the sentiments of this keenly Christian people, and alienated an ever-increasing number from the *Euzkadi* party (the separatists), though this party still continued to hold the support of the small number of the Basque clergy, who had strong separatist leanings. It should be remembered that the Basque representatives in the Cortes had withdrawn in a body from the house in 1932 as a protest against the anti-religious legislation of the Republic.

In the summer of 1934, a conflict took place between the municipalities and the central government, over the question of taxation and the prerogatives of the Basque provinces, and several mayors were deprived of their offices and arrested. This conflict coincided significantly with an alliance between the Basque and Catalan separatist movements and with the agrarian dispute between Madrid and Barcelona, culminating in the revolt in Barcelona and the attempt to set up a soviet in Asturias, which cost so many lives and so much destruction in the city of Oviedo. The defeat of this first attempt to substitute a soviet for the legal, constitutional and democratic government then existing in Spain will be described in another chapter. In the second attempt in 1936 the Popular Front, the very same revolutionaries under a different party name, chose as one of their most effective cries that they were "legal, constitutional and democratic."

In 1936 an alliance was formed, chiefly through the instrumentality of Sr. Prieto, between the Basque nationalist party and the Madrid government, by which the former gave their support to the latter in return for the passing of the Statute through the Cortes. On October 1st, in a very short session, the Statute was passed by the Cortes, which then consisted of the extreme left parties only and was merely a rump parliament, for the majority had either been murdered, or were in exile, or did not attend.

Consequent on the passing of the Statute, the *Euzkadi* government was set up in Bilbao under the presidency of Sr. Aguirre and continued to rule part of the Basque provinces until the fall of Bilbao to General Franco's armies in June 1937.

Able propaganda on the part of the Madrid and Bilbao governments for some time made the world believe that an oppressed and united Basque nation was fighting for its existence against General Franco. The truth was that the nationalist and separatist movements only represented a doubtful majority of two of the Basque provinces, Vizcaya and Guipúzcoa, while Navarre was solidly, and Álava mostly, fighting for him; there were more Basques fighting for General Franco than against him. In fact, the Basque provinces were the home of the scarlet beret and the Requetés, who flocked in their thousands as volunteers to the support of General Mola at Pamplona at the outbreak of the war, who provided General Franco with some of his best and bravest troops, and whose political party was throughout one of his greatest supports and bitterly opposed to the communists and socialists. In May, 1937, the Requeté party was amalgamated with the Falange in the one great national party *Falange Española Tradicionalista y de las J.O.N.S.*

After the final conquest of the North, General Franco signalized the different behavior of the four Basque provinces by canceling the *fueros* or local privileges of taxation in Vizcaya and Guipúzcoa and confirming them in Navarre and Álava. Reconstruction of the destructions caused during the war, and a reorganization of commerce and mining began immediately after the conquest.

The rapidity and tranquility with which these processes were carried into effect was conclusive evidence that the great majority of the people supported General Franco, and that the manifestations of joy with which they welcomed his entry into Bilbao were genuine. Within a few months, coal and iron ore productions, which had fallen to a small percentage of their capacity under the Republican regime, had reached and surpassed the usual normal figures.

President Aguirre and most of the leaders of the *Euzkadi* government were able to escape from the country to France and Barcelona, while a great deal of loot from the Bilbao banks and houses had been previously loaded in steamers and shipped to France.

The *Euzkadi* government, linked up with communist international organizations, flooded the world with propaganda, and used as one of its chief weapons the export of thousands of children to Russia, Mexico, England, France and Belgium, in order to prove that they were being saved from massacre, bombardment and starvation.

In reality the Nationalists had already offered a safe haven of refuge to these children, far from the battle zone, in their own country, under the direction of the Red Cross Society, but the propagandists preferred to take them from their people and country, to which many of them, especially of those sent to Russia and Mexico, could never be expected to return. Though described as "the Basque children" a large proportion of them were not Basques at all but children of Spaniards from other regions who had settled in Bilbao.

Further reference to President Aguirre and the loot shipped to France is contained in Chapter XXII.

V

THE DICTATORSHIP OF PRIMO DE RIVERA

AND THE FALL OF THE MONARCHY, 1923-31

On September 13th, 1923, General Primo de Rivera, Marqués de Estella, issued his manifesto, and carried out that bloodless revolution, or coup d'état, which brought to an end temporarily parliamentary government in Spain and substituted for it a military dictatorship, subject in theory, if not in fact, to the king, which gave the country a short period of stable government, during which she showed such rapid material and spiritual progress as has seldom, if ever, been exhibited in history by any other nation in six short years. In order to appreciate this fact it is necessary to paint the background of the situation of Spain as it was then, for that will give ample reason for the fact that the manifesto was acclaimed enthusiastically in all parts of Spain and especially in Barcelona, where primarily the movement was launched.

Law and order were continually being flouted, terrorism was rife in all industrial and in many other centers, a cardinal, an ex-governor, professional men, employers, and government officials had been murdered; while in Barcelona, the chief industrial center of Spain, the gunman was almost completely in control, and assassinations or fights between rival gangs took place almost daily. Both in the matter of law and order and in most of its functions, the Cortes and successive political governments had proved their incompetence to govern. Public finances were in a state of chaos, with big budget deficits. The war in Morocco, begun in 1919, was threatening to end in disaster, while the sufferings of the troops owing to inefficient organization were causing an ever-growing discontent. The railways were disorganized, with rolling stock and permanent ways in a lamentable condition; one would be justified in saying there were no roads fit for automobiles, and probably right in saying that what roads there were, were the worst in Europe. Public buildings, schools, etc., were generally in a ruinous state. Industry and public works were almost at a standstill owing to the rule of the gunmen.

Such was the situation in 1923, when Primo de Rivera issued his manifesto, and it would be well here to outline the conditions of Spain in those respects in 1929, when he was driven from his country with contumely. Law and order were reestablished and maintained without bloodshed, while agitators were either driven out of the country or in jail. Industry was more tranquil and prosperous than ever it had been before, or for that matter has been since the war in Morocco had been ended satisfactorily for Spain and with prestige to her arms. Public finances were in order and there was a budget surplus according to the budget statements of the Finance Minister, Calvo Sotelo. The railways were in good order and condition, and Spain had a network of what were universally acknowledged to be equal to the best roads anywhere in Europe. These results of good government, stability, and tranquility have been taken out of their sequence to serve as a comparison to the situation existing in September 1923, to which we now return.

The public and the military garrisons enthusiastically welcomed the news of the rebellion and Primo de Rivera's manifesto. The king, who was at San Sebastián, according to the evidence available did not know of the movement; and Primo de Rivera stated afterwards that he did not know what attitude His Majesty would take up. He summoned Primo de Rivera to Madrid, and the first military directorate was then formed, consisting of General Primo de Rivera, Rear-Admiral Marqués de Magaz, General Gómez-Jordana of the General Staff, General Hermosa of the artillery, General Ruiz del Portal of the cavalry, General Mayandia of the engineers, and Generals Navarro, Rodriguez Perré and Muslera of the infantry. It was this directorate of nine soldiers who took over the functions of all the ministries. They began the work and were subsequently succeeded by a ministry composed partly of civilians and partly of soldiers, under the presidency of Primo de Rivera. There can be no doubt, for everyone in Spain saw it, that, between them, these ministries or directorates turned chaos into order and ruin to prosperity. Why, then, did they fall?

The answer is by no means easy, though one can indicate several of the contributive factors. Perhaps the first is the Spanish character, for Spaniards love change and become restless without it, even under prosperity. This may seem a strange statement, but history confirms it. Then there come the mistakes of Primo de Rivera and his directorate. Though he was so successful, who can deny that he made mistakes? Probably he was too merciful to be a completely successful dictator. Then he caused Catalonia, his jumping-off place, to become hostile to him, by trying to suppress her language; but, above all his schemes, that to build up a national party (*Unión Patriótica*) on the basis of patriotism and unity, and that to create a national assembly, to take the place of the Cortes, though logically sound, were failures. Then again there were the constant intrigues of the old expelled politicians and of the socialists, aided by the untiring propaganda of the Communist International of Moscow and of freemasonry of the Grand Orient, in both of which organizations a certain section of Jewry played an important role. Even before 1923, and throughout the subsequent years, the publications of communism, and above all the minutes of the meetings of the Third International (Comintern) prove what an active and studied part it was playing in sowing the seeds of revolution and discontent in Spain. A study of this period in conjunction with the history of the French revolution gives surprising examples of the similarity, and sometimes of the identity, of the organizations and methods employed; thus, while Grand Orient and a section of Jewry inspired both revolutions, the Comintern and the international intelligentsia took the place in the Spanish revolution of the Illuminati and Encyclopédistes of the French revolution.

Another factor contributing to the overturn of the directorate was the continued fall in the value of the peseta; various reasons are given to account for this phenomenon at a time of increasing prosperity and improved credit.

Primo de Rivera himself attributed it to the machinations of the oil interests, which he had dispossessed by making the sale of oil a government monopoly; others claimed that it was due to the international or Jewish bankers, with the double purpose of making profit and of discrediting the dictatorship, basing their allegations on the fact that the chief centers of speculation in the peseta were Zurich and Amsterdam, where Jewish banking is so prominent. A further and important cause of discontent with Primo de Rivera was his quarrel with the artillery, whose officers had for some years past constituted a "junta" or committee, independent of the Ministry of War, which made its own regulations as regards promotion and other matters, and to whose regulations every new subaltern had to swear allegiance. This obvious anomaly the dictator determined to remove; but he collided with established interests and with the most conservative element of the army. The quarrel was fanned and fomented by all the other hostile elements and thus became, undoubtedly, one of the causes of his fall.

During the years 1927 and 1928 those hostile elements became more vocal and, in January, 1929, the rising of the garrison of Ciudad Real, the capital of Don Quixote's La Mancha, took place, with, simultaneously, the arrival in Valencia of Don José Sánchez-Guerra, the refusal of the garrison of that place to revolt, and Sánchez-Guerra's subsequent imprisonment and trial by court martial. The revolt of Ciudad Real was led by the artillery. It was undoubtedly intended to be part of a general revolt to take place all over the country, but the rising went off at half cock, as fortunately risings often do in Spain, and the garrison of Ciudad Real with Sánchez-Guerra, who was to have been the political head of the movement, were left to bear the consequences of failure. The garrison surrendered without fighting, and the leaders were arrested and committed to court martial, as also was Sánchez-Guerra, on whom at his trial all eyes were fixed, for he was an interesting and curious figure in an inexplicable position. A strong conservative leader and formerly a prime minister in a conservative government, he had voluntarily exiled himself to Paris on the advent of the dictatorship, where he joined the group of agitators and Republican malcontents, such as the novelist, Blasco Ibáñez and the radical politician, Santiago Alba, and proceeded to risk his life in this venture.

The trial went on throughout the year, until in November, to the surprise of the Government and the astonishment of the public, he was acquitted by the court martial. All sorts of rumors as to the reason of this acquittal and the influences that had brought it about sprang into life; and whatever their truth, the result was that, though the rebellion had been squashed, a severe blow had been struck at the dictator and his colleagues, shaking them fundamentally, as it showed that the army was divided and in part was hostile to them.

On December 31st of that year, 1929, there was a historic cabinet meeting, presided over by the king, at which the dictator prepared a far-reaching program comprising general elections for a one-chamber parliament and the gradual return to a modified form of constitutional government under a new constitution. The king refused his approval and then Primo de Rivera made his great mistake. Instead of asking the king if he still had his confidence, he turned to the army and navy without consulting the king, by sending a note to all the higher commands, asking them at once to reply as to whether or not he had their confidence and support. This caused a breach with the king, between whom and Primo de Rivera a violent quarrel took place. In addition, the answers of the army and navy commands were in many cases unfavorable to the dictator. The note was dispatched on January 26th, 1930; on January 28th, Primo de Rivera had resigned and General Berenguer had been asked to form a new government. Primo de Rivera retired to Paris, where he died suddenly on March 16th, a wearied and disillusioned man.

The next year and three months were passed under the vacillating rule of General Berenguer and his ministers; the date for the proposed general elections and the return to parliamentary government was repeatedly postponed, and the government was carried on by royal decrees as it had been during the dictatorship. In February, a general amnesty was declared, and gradually the exiled politicians and agitators returned and began to show their influence, reflected in the condition of the country. Throughout that year Spain proceeded to gallop down the hill towards the chaos and terrorism from which she had climbed laboriously through six years of order and increasing prosperity. In July and in August again general strikes broke out in Málaga, Seville, and Granada, also in Barcelona, Bilbao, Zaragoza, and Madrid. Riots were frequent in the universities of Madrid, Barcelona, and other cities. Meanwhile the value of the peseta fell—a sharp fall usually synchronizing with every riot or strike.

In November and December came the rebellions of Cuatro Vientos and Jaca, the former by the air force and the latter by units of the army. In the rebellion of Cuatro Vientos, the leader, Commandant Franco[1], escaped to Portugal; but the leaders of the Jaca revolt, Captains Galán and García Hernández, who were merely disloyal and mutinous subalterns and the instruments of others, were shot. It is difficult to see how their fate could or should have been any other, for they had attacked and fired on their commander, wounding their general Las Heras, who subsequently died of his wounds; but the Republic made of them martyrs and national heroes. These two rebellions were intended to be part of an extensive revolution, which, however, like that of Ciudad Real, went off at half cock. A revolutionary provisional government was proclaimed, consisting of Alcalá Zamora as president with Indalecio Prieto, Alejandro Lerroux, Miguel Maura, Fernando de los Ríos, Manuel Azaña, Santiago Casares, Álvaro de Albomoz, Largo Caballero, Martínez Barrio and Nicolau d'Olwer, which subsequently became the first socialist government of the Republic. Several men were arrested, but though at first condemned by the Tribunal, they were set free, on March 24th, 1931, as were also those condemned for their share of the Jaca rebellion. These acts of weakness disclosed the tottering state of the government,

---

[1] Ramón Franco, brother of General Franco and holding a high command in the Nationalist Air Force during the civil war.

and riots took place at Madrid and elsewhere.

On April 12th, the municipal elections, which it had been decided should precede the parliamentary elections, took place. In Madrid and all the provincial capitals there was a landslide, resulting in large socialist or Republican victories, though in the country districts the majorities were conservative and monarchical. It can be asserted without danger of mistake that all were astounded by the result, not least of all the Socialist caucus. Everything seemed to fall to pieces like a pack of cards. On April 12th, the king and his family were in their palace, and he was apparently firmly established on the throne of Spain; the ministers were transacting business and the functions of the State proceeding as usual. Yet on the evening of April 14th, there were no government and no ministers; the king had fled from Madrid to a Spanish man-of-war in Cartagena, which took him to France. The king throughout acted with the greatest dignity and courage; he refused to abdicate and consented to depart to avoid a civil war and the bloodshed of his people. After an anxious night in which their lives were in danger, the queen and her children were obliged to leave the palace secretly and drive to the Escorial, where they said a sad goodbye to the friends who had accompanied them and then took train to the frontier.

When the total results of these municipal elections, which had suddenly and unexpectedly changed Spain from a monarchy into a republic, became known, surprise was even greater than it had been before. The king had departed on the advice of his ministers, because the first election results, which came in from the big towns only, showed a majority against the monarchy. When, however. the results came in from the smaller towns and country districts, it was seen that, far from having a minority, the monarchy had the majority of the people in its favor, the figures were juggled with at the time to such an extent and there was so much controversy, that it is probable that the true figures can never be proved. In one thing, however, all authorities agree and that is that the majority favored the king. De Madariaga in his history gives the figures as 34,368 Republicans and 41,224 monarchists and states that "the Republican triumph of April, 1931, was in fact... no Republican triumph at all"; other authorities gave a much larger majority in favor of the king.

But by then the king had already gone, and the Republic caucus had seized the machinery of government and was in the saddle. What was the explanation of this astounding state of affairs? Did the king's ministers and soldiers get into a panic on hearing the first results? Was the whole thing a successful plot on the part of left wing politicians and their allies?

Who can tell?

What is certain is that the true account and figures of the election were only allowed to filter into the public mind in Spain after much delay and are scarcely known in foreign countries.

But though the elections, as far as the whole country was concerned, showed that the monarch was popular, some explanation is necessary for his unpopularity in the large towns, shown by the adverse votes at the elections. It is probable that the disasters in Morocco and his political activities, to which reference is made in the chapter on King Alfonso, together with a campaign of slander, all ably exploited by Republicans and revolutionaries, had had their effect, though it is fair to add that popular manifestations against him had not been apparent.

The weak and inefficient governments that had followed the departure of Primo de Rivera had dislocated trade, industry, and prosperity; the king could not avoid incurring a share of responsibility and blame. And it must be remembered that it was not an oppressed peasantry that made the Spanish revolution, as ignorant propagandists stated, but the population of the industrial towns after a period of prosperity, increased wages, and improved standard of living. It was in the towns that the revolutionaries carried on their work, and the first step towards a popular front had of necessity to be the discrediting and destruction of the monarchy.

VI

KING ALFONSO XIII, 1886–1931

The part played by the king before and through the revolutionary period is worthy of study by itself.

It is a far cry from the Spain of such great statesmen as Canovas and Sagasta, which on May 17th, 1886, witnessed the arrival in this world of the baby Alfonso XIII, to the Spain of proletarian or bourgeois revolutionaries such as Alcalá-Zamora and Alejandro Lerroux, which on April 14th, 1931, saw him leave his kingdom and step on board a Spanish man-of-war in the port of Cartagena.

His father, Alfonso XII, had died a few months before his birth, and so Alfonso was born a king. His advent followed closely upon nearly 100 years of great calamities and political unrest, including two long and bloody civil wars. The first sixteen out of this forty-five years of his reign were passed under the regency of his wise and able mother Queen Maria Cristina, and on May 2nd, 1902, he took his oath according to the constitution and assumed full kingship. His reign covered, as regards foreign affairs, the Spanish-American War with the loss of Spain's colonies, the Great War and the conclusion of the Spanish-Moroccan War, while internally it covered a series of kaleidoscopic political and administrative changes, with an astonishing amount of spiritual, material, cultural and social progress; this was especially noticeable in the years 1923–30.

Apart from choosing an English princess for his consort, that regal personality Queen Victoria Eugenia, the king had many close connections with this country; his generosity in maintaining at his own expense, throughout the first Great War, an organization for finding missing and captured people relieved much misery among all classes in Britain, and will long be remembered.

His personal courage was typified on the occasion of the king and queen's wedding procession in Madrid in 1906, when a bomb was thrown at his carriage, thirty-seven people killed, his horses killed or stampeded, while he and his bride only escaped by a miracle. The procession proceeded notwithstanding, and the king drew back the curtains of the carriage, which had been drawn, and showed himself in full view. In the afternoon he drove out unguarded to visit the wounded. He was renowned for his great personal courage—he carried his life in his hands continually, but yet moved freely and often unprotected among the crowds—his military knowledge, his sportsmanship, his patriotism, and statesmanship. As regards the last quality, he is often blamed for being too much of a politician. This criticism is perhaps true, though it is difficult to see how he could have been otherwise in a country where parliamentary government was often at an impasse. When the dictatorship came, he accepted it, though it must have been humiliating to him. He was criticized and accused of having broken his oath to the Constitution of 1876. It is a debatable point, but the alternative was civil war. Would it have been preferable to plunge his country into such a war on so doubtful an ethical question? He continued with self-effacement to work with the dictator and was apparently satisfied to see his country happy and prosperous until he quarreled with Primo de Rivera after the Sanchez Guerra revolt, as already described in the previous chapter. He then appeared to show some lack of judgment in his choice of men in the very difficult situation that arose, and this fact, with what appeared to many as his abandonment of Primo de Rivera, was perhaps the dominant factor in the loss of his crown and the sudden and unexpected success of the Republicans. A second time he saved his country from civil war by consenting to leave Spain at once, but he refused to abdicate and maintained for himself and his family their claim to the throne. The Republicans instituted a system of persecution against him as they did against the nobles and attempted to confiscate even the private fortune he had invested abroad. They went so far as to take and auction his polo ponies and sporting guns. These actions must have wounded him the more deeply as he had been highly popular among the people of all classes.

There can be little doubt that, when he left Spain, both he and his ministers believed that the majority of the country was in favor of a republic as against monarchy. There can be no doubt that he left Spain sooner than plunge his country into civil war, which the incomplete election figures seemed to foreshadow.

The plot or panic of the king's ministers, whichever it was, was illustrated by a telegram sent by General Berenguer to all the Captains General of Spain, announcing that the elections had been lost and to all intents and purposes giving an invitation not to resist the revolution. The inertia of the cabinet, the result of cowardice or treason, was in strong contrast to the courage and patriotism of their monarch. His parting message is so fine that no history, however short, should omit it:

> Sunday's elections have shown me clearly that I have no longer the love of my people. My conscience tells me that this alienation will not be permanent, because I have always tried to serve Spain, and the public weal has always been my only anxiety even on the most critical occasions. A king may make mistakes, and doubtless I have made them sometimes, but I know well that it has always been the habit of our motherland to be kind to genuine mistakes. I am the king of all the Spaniards, and I am also a Spaniard. I could find means more than sufficient to support my royal prerogatives against all comers, but, of fixed purpose, I will have nothing to do with setting one compatriot against another in a fratricidal civil war. I do not renounce any of my rights, because as well as being mine, they are rights accumulated throughout history, for which I shall one day be called upon to give an account. I wish to know the true and faithful expression of the will of the people, and until the nation speaks, I shall deliberately suspend the use of my royal power, and I shall leave Spain, thus recognizing that she must be the only mistress of her own destiny. I also wish to fulfill the duty to which my love of my country inspires me, and I pray God that all other Spaniards will recognize their duty as earnestly as I do mine and will fulfil it.

When King Alfonso landed in France he made the statement:

> I am not a conspirator; I will not move my little finger to assist in any way to make difficulty for the present government of Spain. If my people want me to return now, or on any future occasion, I will return and serve my country in the same way as I have done since I was sixteen years old. But my people's wishes for my return must be expressed in the same constitutional manner, free from all pressure, in which I allowed the expression of Republican opinion on the eve of my departure. If the present government are successful in making my people happier than they were before, I will be the first to rejoice heartily, and to congratulate them.

After his departure King Alfonso remained quietly in exile without any attempt to interfere in the politics of his country. Twice only did he break silence to address proclamations to his people and say that he would only return if the bulk of his people asked him to do so.

Monarchy, like Christianity, seems to be deeply rooted in the Spanish character. General Franco said in a speech in July, 1937, that Spain would return to monarchy, but under a different monarch, and a return to the traditional Catholic monarchy of Spain is implicit in the new policies and the new arms of Spain (see Chapter XXI).

The two elder sons of Alfonso XIII, whose physical defects militated against their succession, resigned their claims to the throne in favor of Prince Juan, who had been an officer in the British Navy.

When writing on the question of the Spanish monarchy, it is necessary to mention the Carlist claims to the throne, which produced two long civil wars during the last century. Though, during the reign of Alfonso XIII, no attempt was made to establish the pretenders, yet they never relinquished their claim, and had the support of the Traditionalist party, which was especially strong in Navarre and the Basque Provinces; the members of this party were the Requetés, who were the most ardent supporters in the civil war of General Franco and of Christianity, and the party was amalgamated, in May 1936, with the Falange party in order to form the one great national party into which it was attempted to fuse all parties of nationalist Spain. When the octogenarian pretender, Don Alfonso Carlos de Bourbon, died in 1937, the hereditary claim and leadership of the party devolved on King Alfonso as direct surviving heir of the pretender's branch of the family. The pretender, however, on his deathbed nominated another successor, the Prince Xavier of Bourbon-Parma, as leader of the party; this succession, which for a time caused a split in the Carlist party, was purely testamentary and lacked the claim of legitimacy on which Carlism was based.[2]

The death of Alfonso XIII, the succession as sole claimant to the throne of Prince Juan and the subsequent attitude towards the monarchy of General Franco are described in Chapters XXI and XXVII.

---

[2] In 1943 most of the Carlists accepted King Alphonso XIII's son as the legitimate heir to the throne.

VII

REPUBLIC TO CIVIL WAR, 1931–36

As has been stated in a previous chapter (V) the first government of the Second Spanish Republic consisted of Alcalá-Zamora as president with Indalecio Prieto, Alejandro Lerroux, Miguel Maura, Fernando de los Ríos, Manuel Azaña, Santiago Casares, Álvaro de Albornoz, Martínez Barrio, Nicolau d'Olwer and Largo Caballero as his ministers.

The first four years of the Republic witnessed the growth of socialist power to its apex in the first Socialist-Republican government, and then its gradual discredit and waning influence until it was resoundingly defeated at the polls. Its attempt to seize by force the power it was unable to conquer by democratic or constitutional (its own idea of constitutional) means, by an unholy alliance with all the most extreme and subversive elements, such as the F.A.I. or Iberian Anarchist Federation, the *Sindicato Único* or Anarchist Trade Union and the extreme separatists of Catalonia, was defeated. The revolutionary caucus, whose names have been given above, which became the first Republican government, was composed of politicians, intellectuals, demagogues, and orators, most of whom had been obliged to leave the country during the dictatorship because they were nuisances to the country. All of these were either socialists or radicals, with the exception of that aristocrat gone wrong: Don Miguel Maura. The first government was presided over by Manuel Azaña, and lasted until October 1931, when Azaña was succeeded by Alcalá-Zamora.

It has been already pointed out how oriental Freemasonry and a section of Jewry had, with the Comintern, been the principal causes of the fall of Primo de Rivera, and of the Spanish revolution. Interesting points, which are inexplicable except by this theory, are the facts that out of eleven members of the original Republican caucus eight were oriental Freemasons, and that almost the first decree of the Republic was one which cancelled the fifteenth century decree of Ferdinand and Isabella expelling the Jews, and invited them to return to Spain. This last decree was curious because it appeared unnecessary, for no legal prohibition against Jews in Spain was in force at the time of its promulgation, and consequently it gave the impression of an open acknowledgement of Jewish help in bringing about the revolution.

Another item of evidence was the consistent attempt to masonify the officers of the army and navy, which was strenuously carried out from the day that the Republic was set up.

It was not until July 1931, that the *Cortes Constituyentes* (Parliament to make a constitution) was elected, and it was of pronounced socialist and left color. In December 1931, it drew up and promulgated the new Spanish constitution, under which Niceto Alcalá-Zamora became president of the Republic, and Manuel Azaña replaced him as prime minister. Meanwhile, the Republican government had not waited to put in practice their socialist doctrines, but, acting more dictatorially than the dictator they decried, they legislated by decree on many of the fundamental elements of the Spanish national fabric, such as the relations between church and state, the army, education, and many other matters. The *Cortes Constituyentes*, only elected with the special object of making a constitution, continued to function and legislate until December 1933, when the socialist government at last were obliged to follow their own constitution and hold the general elections, at which they in their turn received a smashing defeat, after which their rule was at an end for the time being. They had, however, by the means they employed, saddled Spain with a complete set of legislation of the purest doctrinaire type, which it was the subsequent work of their radical successors to undo or modify. Some of the chief directions in which they had legislated were:

(1)   The complete secularization of education, the confiscation of all religious and church properties, the expulsion of the Jesuits, and the cutting off of the salaries of the parish priests. This meant serious offence to the Christians of Spain and without providing any substitute deprived parents and children for the moment of the only good education in the country. These measures, together with the burning of churches and convents, while the government troops and police stood by, gave the actions of the socialist government the aspect of a persecution of Christianity.

(2)   An agrarian law, based on the Marxist doctrine, that the land belongs to the peasant and not to its owner. It comprised the confiscation of many estates; not because they were maladministered, but because the owners had the misfortune to

be nobles. What happened in practice was that these estates ceased to be worked at all, as the peasant had neither the means, ability, nor capital with which to work them, and in his anger he often killed the cattle and burnt the crops.

(3) The Statute of Autonomy to Catalonia was the price paid by the socialist government for the support of the Catalan deputies in passing their legislation. Owing to the share of the Catalan government in the October 1934 revolution, a great part of the autonomy was gradually withdrawn by the governments of 1934–35, only to be regranted with additional features when the turn of the wheel brought back the lefts to power in February, 1936.

At last, in June 1933, when they had passed all the more important part of the legislation that they desired, the socialist government consented to hold the long-promised general elections for the first regular Cortes of the Republic. The result was a complete defeat of the socialists, who came back with only 58 seats against the 120 they had had in the previous Cortes. Out of the 480 deputies who formed the new Cortes, the grouping was approximately 210 right, 170 center, and 100 left, though these groups were subdivided into many separate parties. In view of this result the socialist ministers resigned and a new government under the old radical, Alejandro Lerroux, was formed. A professional politician of great experience and ability, he was looked upon before the revolution as an extremist agitator, and he was one of the members of the revolutionary committee of 1931. Up to this moment he had been on very intimate terms with the socialists, but he now began to separate himself more and more from them; he continued to preside over several subsequent governments until October 1934. In the Cortes of December 1933 the most powerful party was the CEDA party (*Confederación Española de Derechas Autonómas*), a conservative agrarian party of which the leader was a young politician, Señor Gil-Robles, who continued to be a dominating figure in the political arena until the events and elections of February 1936, returned the extreme left to power. At the time of the 1933 elections this party was monarchist but, whether from change of heart or political expediency, became later Republican and co-operated with Lerroux in giving his radical government a majority.

The successive radical or radical-cum-CEDA governments proceeded to revise or undo a great part of the socialist legislation of their predecessors, to the ever-growing discontent of the socialists, who thereupon resolved to abandon the constitutional and democratic practices to which they had given lip service, and to capture by force the control of government, of which the votes at the polls had deprived them. Led by Manuel Azaña, the former premier, they proceeded to ally themselves, first with the ultra-left party (*Esquerra*), which was in power in the now almost autonomous province of Catalonia, and with all the subversive labor and political parties, such as the Anarchist *Sindicato Único* and the Iberian Anarchist Federation, which already on two occasions had attempted revolutions to establish the dictatorship of the proletariat. Gun-running with a view to arming their followers took place on a large scale, and was indulged in by socialist ex-ministers and deputies, who not only bought arms from abroad, but also in various tortuous ways obtained them from the arsenals of the government. And so the socialists, together with the *Esquerra* of Catalonia, prepared for the attempted revolution of October 1934, which wrecked the chances of a socialist return to power, temporarily lost Catalonia her autonomy, and brought about a civil war in Asturias costing Spain some 2,000 lives, much money, and the destruction by the Asturian miners of the public buildings, library, and convents of Oviedo, the capital of Asturias.

Fortunately for the forces of law and order, the army was fully prepared, and able to suffocate the revolution within a comparatively short time. As a result, martial law was declared all over Spain and was only taken off in the following April; numerous arrests were made, among them those of the members of the Catalan government, with Companys, the president of Catalonia, Manuel Azaña, the ex-premier, and the leaders in Asturias. Searches, resulting in the confiscation of stores of arms and munitions, were made all over Spain. Among the more important caches of arms were those found in the Casa del Pueblo, the socialist headquarters in Madrid. It was expected that the revolutionaries would be treated with severity and that law and order would be reestablished in Spain, but the expectations were falsified. To the dissatisfaction of the army, which had cleaned up the mess, acting constitutionally under the orders of the Ministry of War. Though a few unfortunate subordinates were shot, the leaders and instigators were imprisoned, and their trials allowed to drag on. Some were condemned to death and the penalty commuted; while Manuel Azaña, who was, perhaps, the prime mover, was set free. Public opinion and political expediency would not allow severe punishment so long after the event, and the prisoners stayed in jail until the amnesty of March 1936 restored them not only to freedom but to power.

Attempts, partially successful, were made by international socialism to whitewash the socialist politicians of Spain, by alleging that the attempted revolution was the result of oppression of the socialists, and that the damage done and deaths caused in Asturias were the work of a brutal soldiery. They also stated that the revolutionaries in Asturias and Catalonia were not armed. There was no evidence in the Spanish press or from impartial observers on the spot to support these allegations; in fact, the contrary is the case. However, the attempt to influence opinion was so successful that the Labour Party of Great Britain had the effrontery to send a telegram to Spain, a friendly foreign power, asking for leniency to be shown to the revolutionaries, and an incident even more amazing—because of its lack of proportion and its self-complacence—took place when a self-appointed commission of inquiry, composed of two British socialists (the late Miss Ellen Wilkinson and Lord Listowel) and some socialists of other nationalities, arrived in Spain with the avowed object of interrogating the deputies in the Cortes itself and of conducting a tour of inspection in Asturias and Oviedo. The commission was treated with traditional Spanish courtesy, though the press clamored for their expulsion from the country; the president of the Chamber, with dignity and politeness, denied that any foreigner could have permission to interrogate deputies in the precincts of the Cortes. The prime minister, however, gave them permission to go to Oviedo and see for themselves, while the governor of that place put automobiles at their disposal to enable them to do so. The crowds of Oviedo were, however, so hostile that the Civil Guards had to protect the commission to save their lives, and conduct them out of the town, for which the commission must indeed have been grateful.

The incident is not in itself important, but there was so much misrepresentation around it that it is worthwhile to quote the note that Señor Alba, himself a radical and president of the Chamber, issued to the press:

Lord Listowel announced to Señor Alba in the name of all of them (the commission) his intention to carry out an investigation in Spain on the happenings in Asturias in all their phases in view of the contradictory reports which had appeared in the foreign press. The president of the Chamber declared to his visitors that neither as president nor as a Spanish citizen could he acquiesce in the idea of a collective investigation carried out by foreigners. Within the Chamber itself all political parties, even the most extreme ones, have free exercise of all privileges which the constitution and procedure allow them. Anything further would not be allowed by any Chamber in the world and is not allowed by the Spanish Chamber. Contradictory reports, such as those to which Lord Listowel has called attention, happen daily in England between the *Daily Herald* and the *Times*, for example, and it would not occur there to anyone to admit a foreign organization to examine the problem of India or other problems in which British subjects are concerned. The president of the chamber also recalls bloody political struggles which have taken place in Europe during recent months, in regard to which neither England nor France had considered it necessary to authorize their citizens, either directly or indirectly, to make an investigation such as is now being attempted in Spain.

While not failing to show all the courtesy necessary, the president of Congress refuses categorically to answer the questions put to him by the commission or to allow them to make any inquiries from the deputies within the Chamber.

The failure of the October revolution and the subsequent revelations of the gun-running activities of some of their leaders, added to the serious accusation of misappropriation of public moneys brought against some of the Catalan ministers, dealt such a blow to the prestige of the socialist party in Spain that they had to hide their heads for a while.

Subsequent to the revolution of October 1934, there were five successive governments composed of a combination of radicals and parties of the right under the premiership of Lerroux. They showed an ever-progressive tendency towards the right, as was proved by Lerroux's last cabinet of May, 1935, which contained five *cedistas*, five radicals, two agrarians and one liberal-democrat—to such an extent had the old revolutionary Lerroux abandoned his former colleagues and turned to the right. This period was chiefly marked by the inability of the members of the right to take advantage of the situation, owing in great part to the temporizing policy of Gil-Robles. Parliamentary democratic government again proved itself to be unsuitable to Spanish ways, under which political parties owed allegiance not so much to programs as to individuals, who intrigued and maneuvered for power and places, leaving no time for carrying on the legislation and business of the country, which, therefore, was conducted by means of governmental decrees. In fact, government in Spain under the king, under the Socialists, under the Radicals, and under the Popular Front, was always in practice partly dictatorial, though theoretically parliamentary, and democratic. Legislation by parliament alone simply did not work and, under the Popular Front, government was more autocratic than it was under any of the previous systems.

In October 1935 came the Straperlo scandal, which shook the Radical Party to its foundations and indirectly caused the fall of Lerroux. "Straperlo" was the name of a special form of roulette table, brought to Spain by an international financier called Daniel Strauss, for which he nearly obtained a special concession, contrary to the legal restrictions on gambling, owing to the intervention of various influential radical politicians and officials. In the months of November and December there followed three inefficient, short, and colorless governments under the premiership first of Señor Chapaprieta and then of Señor Portela Valladares, both of whom called themselves independents. They were miniature Kerenskys and completed the picture of Spain as a rudderless ship drifting on to the rocks.

For some considerable time there had been a clamor among those of the left for a dissolution of the Cortes and, after much vacillation, the President, Señor Alcalá-Zamora, surrendered to their demand. General elections were held in February 1936, and one of those surprises for which Spanish politics are famous took place and power passed back completely into the hands of the left, now united under the name of *Frente Popular*. Thus, things were back again in the same place and practically under the identical men who had fallen from power in June, 1933, and had attempted the abortive red revolution of October, 1934.

The figures and facts of this general election are important because, after the civil war broke out, and the world was divided into two camps of the sympathizers with the different sides, the argument that brought the greatest contingent of supporters to the Republican government was that the government put into power by these elections was the legal, democratic constitutional government of Spain, and consequently must be supported by all true democrats.

The official figures of votes, as given at the time by the Spanish Government itself, were: Popular Front 4,356,000, Parties of the Right 4,570,000, Center 240,000, or a majority of Right and Center over Popular Front of 454,000. This was the result, notwithstanding the fact that election irregularities in favor of Popular Front candidates, such as the destruction of the urns and voting papers by the mob, and the falsification of election figures took place in many centers. When the Cortes first assembled, the figures for the deputies were: Popular Front 256 and Right and Center 217, or a majority of 39 for the Popular Front.

This did not in itself prove that the elections were irregular, owing to the peculiar electoral system, but the proved irregularities at the polls should have made them invalid. The Popular Front were not content with this majority and adopted an entirely new parliamentary procedure in annulling by a mere majority vote in parliament the mandates of many of their prominent opponents, and expelling them from the Cortes. In this highly unconstitutional and undemocratic way, the Popular Front raised their majority to 118.

From his retirement in Paris in 1937, this is how Alcalá-Zamora, the very father of the revolution and of the constitution and president of Spain at the time of the elections, qualified the electoral proceedings, and gave his estimate of the figures of the elections:

> In spite of the syndicalist reinforcements, the Popular Front obtained only a few, a very few, more than 200 seats out of a total of 473. Thus, it became the largest minority group, but did not secure a majority in parliament. It managed, however, to obtain this majority, by hurrying through two stages of procedure, in defiance of all legality, and with utter disregard to scruple.

Though the evidence of an elected leader of the revolution should be accepted with caution, it must be placed on record, and it does in this case receive confirmation from the undeniable facts of the electoral procedure witnessed by all observers on the spot at that time.

The first act of the new Cortes was summarily to dismiss the president, on the plea that he had no right to dissolve the previous Cortes. This was contrary to the constitution, but legality did not appear to concern the majority, who desired vengeance on a former leader and colleague, who had tolerated the swing to the right in the legislation of the previous two years.

As in April 1931, the elections were won by the support and votes of the F.A.I., the workmen's syndicates U.G.T. and C.N.T., and the Communist Party. All these groups, and the socialists also, refused to take part in the new government and were prepared to continue as the tail that wags the dog. The new government was formed almost completely of left Republicans under the premiership of Manuel Azaña, only recently acquitted at the trial for complicity in the 1934 revolution. He was, however, subsequently elected president of the Republic, while his place as premier was taken by Casares Quiroga. Immediately, by legislation in the Cortes and by decrees, the government put back the clock to 1933 and reestablished all the confiscatory and persecutory measures against the Church and the landowners, which have already been described. Also immediately, the greater part of Spain was given over to the mob violence of the Reds, and within three months some three hundred churches and numerous public and private buildings were burnt or destroyed. Strikes, many of them of the communist "stay-in" type, became universal. Perhaps the most serious feature was that the police and civil guards, apparently under orders from the government, in many cases stood by while the sabotage and burning took place, and refused to interfere, while the government was continuously on the side of strikers to such an extent that strikes were always "settled" by giving all that the strikers demanded. Meanwhile the employer was not allowed to close his works, and when rising wages, shorter hours, and other demands exhausted his resources, he was obliged either to hand over his works to the strikers or go to prison, for he was forbidden by law to close down.

In July 1936, the situation was this: socialists, C.N.T., Communists, all had arms and in some cases semi-military formations; so also had *Falange Española*, or Spanish Phalanx, but the dice were loaded against the latter, for the government was against them and the jails, emptied by the amnesty of the previous March, soon were filled to overflowing with members of the Falange. This organization was national and patriotic and its leader (July 1936) was the courageous young Jose Primo de Rivera, son of the great dictator, who had been for some months in prison; its numbers were small at this time but its ranks were being augmented by seceders from the CEDA Party, whose hopes in their leader, Gil-Robles, were frustrated. Victims of shootings and assassinations were many on both sides and also among the civil guards, who with the army were the great target for the revolutionaries, as the only visible support of law and order. This culminated on July 15th, in the assassination by the government shock police of Señor Calvo Sotelo, an outstanding Conservative parliamentarian of great intelligence and integrity, who was arrested at night in his house and brutally murdered by the police in the van that took him away. He might have been the savior for whom all those who loved Spain were sighing—perhaps that was the reason for his removal. It was short-sighted on the part of those who instigated the deed. Nothing strengthens a cause so much as a first-class martyrdom. That the Spanish government and the Popular Front appreciated this was evident from the wholesale arrests of members of the Falange, Traditionalist, and other right-wing parties.

Throughout the Republican period there seemed to be no directing hand over Spain unless it were a hand directing the country through further disorder towards the destruction of the edifice of civilization and society. The work of the Comintern and of the Freemasons (Orient and Grand Lodge of Spain) was evident throughout the revolution, working by and with the doctrines laid down by Karl Marx, which permeated first the professional intellectuals and then a section of the proletariat. Who could doubt this when they saw the symbols of the red flag, the sickle, and the hammer, the Internationale and the vocabulary of red revolution everywhere in Spain? At the core of the conflict was the struggle between those who held the doctrines of Karl Marx and those who held the doctrines of Christ; the latter based on universal brotherhood and obedience to authority and the other on class warfare and revolution. There could be no reconciliation between these two ideologies, either in Spain or elsewhere, and the murder of Calvo Sotelo set the light to the civil war between them, which broke out on July 18th with the revolt of the Spanish army in Morocco.

VIII

Outbreak of Civil War

Just as there can be no further doubt that in May–June, 1936, a proletarian rising against the already extreme Left government (Popular Front) of Spain and the establishment of soviets under the dictatorship of Largo Caballero were fully prepared, so there can be no doubt that a counter-revolution was preparing to fight against communism and restore law and order to Spain under the leadership of the Army. The immediate sparks that set light to the conflagration and fixed the date of the rising of the army officers were the murder of the leader of the opposition in the Cortes, Señor Calvo Sotelo, under the most savage conditions by uniformed government police and the discovery of the secret document containing the complete details for the proletarian communist rising with the establishment of a Soviet Spain under the dictatorship of Largo Caballero.

As regards the secret document detailing the instructions and outlining the procedure for the proletarian rising timed to start on some date in June or July, 1936, its authenticity was doubted by some people, and the apologists of the Republican government attempted to discredit it, saying it was invented subsequently as an excuse for the civil war. But there need no longer be any doubt about it in the minds of students of history. It was stolen from the anarchist headquarters; a copy was received in England by the writer of this history in June 1936, a month before the civil war broke out and handed to the British Foreign Office, who curiously enough rejected it. Subsequently, during the course of the war, copies of it were found at communist-socialist headquarters in Majorca, Seville and Badajoz, after their capture by General Franco's army and its authenticity was proved and accepted generally (see de Madariaga's "Spain").

The internal evidence of the document's authenticity is so great as to be overwhelming, for, not only were many of the plans and policies laid down in it actually fulfilled, but some of the very people indicated by name for various positions, actually and subsequently filled them (cf. Largo Caballero, Belarmino Tomás, Margarita Nelken, etc.).

The document (see also Chapter XV) is so important, as conclusive evidence of the Communist causes of the civil war, that it is published as an appendix (II).

When General Francisco Franco raised the standard of revolt against the Madrid government in Morocco on July 18th, risings of the cadres of the military garrisons took place all over Spain simultaneously or on the following day, but were only successful over about one-quarter of Spain, comprising roughly Galicia, part of Asturias, part of León, two out of four of the Basque provinces (Navarre and Álava), parts of Castile and Aragón and in Cádiz and Algeciras. In the rest of Spain, and notably in Madrid, Barcelona and Valencia, the risings failed and after some fighting the garrison cadres surrendered; the officers, except the small number who threw in their lot with the government, were imprisoned and gradually exterminated after condemnation before the popular tribunals, set up in imitation of the French Revolution.

It is important to notice that in the barracks at the time of the outbreak of the civil war, there only existed, except in Morocco and in the Foreign Legion, the cadres of the regiments, because the 1935 conscripts had already been dismissed and the 1936 conscripts had not yet been called up; this was done probably of set purpose by the Popular Front and their Communist allies. The fact that General Mola in Pamplona had only 400 soldiers and General Queipo de Llano in Seville had only 185 soldiers when the revolt started is adequate proof of the situation, and proves conclusively that the movement behind General Franco and his fellow-officers was popular and not military, because their forces were composed of the volunteers that at once flocked to their standards. The mendacious international propaganda, which captured and held the bulk of the press of the world throughout the war, completely obscured this very important fact.

At the moment that the counterrevolution broke out, a government of the extreme Left, without representatives of the Anarchists and Communists, but put into power by their votes and influences, was in existence under Señor Casares Quiroga, who was immediately succeeded by Señor Giral on July 19th, and he in his turn soon gave place to Señor Largo Caballero, the man openly and publicly predestined by the Comintern to be the Stalin of Spain. The state of the country, of which the writer of this history had been an eyewitness over a lengthy tour of Spain during the previous month, was one of complete disorder in business, industry and the civil life of the nation; in large tracts of the country neither life nor property was safe and travelers on the roads were constantly held up and robbed by men with red shirts and rifles; in the big towns churches and other buildings had been destroyed; strikes were universal; the red flag, sickle and hammer, Internationale, pictures of Lenin, Stalin and Dimitrov protruded themselves on all sides. The bookstalls of Madrid, Barcelona, Valencia, Bilbao and of various other towns visited were irrefutable witness to the efforts and influence of the Comintern and Soviet; they were full of communist literature of all sorts, together with the pornographic and anti-Christian literature that always accompanies it.

This is not a surprising feature but indeed natural, because the destruction of religion and family and the establishment of unbridled sexual license are part of the published Marxist program. But perhaps more significant and important were the red militia to be found drilling in many parts of Spain in preparation for the coming communist rising of the proletariat, and as laid down in the secret document; these militia were called red because they professed to follow Soviet Russia and wore red shirts; they were the military organizations of the anarchists and syndicalists, who had been armed, if not by the government itself, at all events with their connivance, for no attempt was made to disarm them or keep them in control by the government police or military. On the other hand, the army officers were constantly subject to hostility and insults on the part of the mobs, who always appeared to have the support of the government when any incident took place.

Such was the state of Spain in June 1936, and it made inevitable the civil war which broke out m the following month.

As soon as the rising of the army officers took place, the government proceeded openly to arm further red militias and also to distribute arms and munitions not only to the masses in the industrial centers but also to the criminals of all sorts, after throwing open the prisons. All these people were formed or formed themselves into brigades under self-elected commanders, acting more or less independently of each other, and gradually began to learn to shoot and act as soldiers until they reached a considerable state of proficiency first as fighters in streets and behind barricades, and subsequently as soldiers in the field. One of the great characteristics of the Spaniard is personal courage, and doubtless many of the young men believed that they were fighting for a great cause, for a new world where everything would be free and easy and to their liking; so to courage was added enthusiasm and faith to fight against an undefined but evil enemy called "fascism," against which they were constantly instigated by a tireless and clever propaganda.

This outline of the faith of anti-fascism, if it is a correct one, will show how bitter and irreconcilable such a struggle must be when on the other side the people are inspired to a man with the belief that they are fighting a crusade for their Christian faith and for all the decencies that make life worth living.

Volunteers flocked to both camps and on both sides. The 1936 conscripts were called to the barracks.

In Republican Spain the enthusiasm was confined to the proletariat, and restricted to the recruiting for the militias of the various Anarchist, Communist, and Socialist unions, which had been already formed, and were drilling in preparation for the ordained communist rising; these various militia acted at first completely independently of one another and of the government, which for some time militated against any military efficiency. Strangely enough the Catalans, throughout history renowned for revolution and as the center of strength of the anarchist organizations (F.A.I. and C.N.T.), were notably backward in joining the fighting forces in comparison to the other people of Republican Spain.

In Nationalist Spain, the enthusiasm among all classes was enormous, but it was especially noticeable among the Basques of Navarre, renowned throughout history for their Christian and monarchical fervor. It was calculated that 30,000 of these, most of them with sporting or antiquated firearms and wearing their famous red berets, flocked to General Mola's standard in Pamplona within a fortnight. These Navarrese Basques, under their old traditionalist name of Requeté, became one of the two great political parties under General Franco, and formed some of his most famous regiments.

The naval situation of the two sides will be dealt with in a later chapter, but it is well to state here that, throughout the months of July and August, 1936, the Republicans had command of the sea, which in September began to pass to the Nationalist side until, by the end of the first year of warfare, it had been completely captured by the latter. This was a further proof that the rising was a popular one and not, as was often represented, purely one of the professional Army.

IX

SEVILLE—TOLEDO—MADRID, 1936

The situation after the first days of the counterrevolution was that General Franco, the hero of the Moors and the foreign legion, which he and General Millán-Astray had created in the 1920's, was in full control in Morocco, General Mola in command in Pamplona, General Cabanellas in Zaragoza, and General Queipo de Llano had captured Seville with his 185 men. How he did this by pure bluff is now a matter of history. He first captured the radio station, and constantly sent out news about his imaginary army of 40,000 men that was advancing on Seville; he then put his few men into lorries, and sent them out again and again to various quarters of the town, to give a false impression of their numbers. This so impressed the garrison and their commander, the civil guards and the populace, that they first evacuated the town, and the others flocked to General Queipo at the rendezvous he had announced by radio.

Less known to the world, because there were no correspondents with him, is what is known in Spain as "La Marcha de Castejón." Captain Castejón of the foreign legion flew across the straits with thirty-five men, landed at Algeciras on July 19th, and proceeded with the help of those who flocked to his standard, and a liberal use of bluff over the telephone wires, to capture Andalusia in conjunction with General Queipo de Llano. His thirty-five men became a column which, joining the forces under Generals Franco and Varela, continued a triumphal march of 700 miles, till they were held up in November before Madrid by the unexpected International Brigades formed of foreigners recruited by communist centers all over the world.

The stories of the capture of Seville and Castejón's march, and many others, such as the defense by Col. Moscardo and the relief of the Alcázar, which provided an epic that has caught the imagination of the world, the less known but equally glorious nine months' siege and fall of the Sanctuary of the Virgin de la Cabeza, and the sieges of Oviedo and Huesca, make one believe that after all there is little difference between the true Spaniard of today and the conquistadors of America, or the famous infantry of the sixteenth century, or the crusaders who broke the power of the crescent at Lepanto in 1571.

The tenacity and heroism of the seventy-day defense of the Alcázar cannot be better described than by the following words of Mr. Geoffrey Moss in "The Epic of the Alcázar":

> The Alcázar was held by a thousand men and boys, always short of rest and sleep, and starving for the greater part of the time. It was held in spite of artillery bombardments, air attacks, the explosion of three enormous mines and eight separate general assaults delivered by overwhelming numbers.

How was this possible?

> It was possible in part because of the qualities and faith of its defenders; in part because of the cool yet sometimes reckless skill by which all they did was directed.

The "qualities of faith" of the defenders were illustrated by the story of how Col. Moscardo was called to the telephone at the beginning of the siege and told by the chief of the besieging militias that he had his son in his power, and would shoot him unless the Alcázar were surrendered in ten minutes. A conversation took place between father and son, which is said by the same authority to have been:

> FATHER: All you can do is to pray for us and to die for Spain.
> SON: That is quite simple. Both I will do.

A few minutes later the father was called to the telephone, and informed that his son had been shot.

Throughout July, August, and September, the Nationalist Southern Army under General Varela continued its rapid advance towards Madrid. Badajoz, considered a strongly held town, which Wellington's army experienced great difficulty and months of delay in reducing, was captured on the 15th after a few days' siege. The victorious advance continued along the Madrid road with short struggles at every town and village, which were defended by the Republican forces. Mérida, Trujillo, Navalmoral, Oropesa, Talavera de la Reina, were all successively captured, and the advance continued to Maqueda, the junction of the Madrid and Toledo roads, and twenty-five miles away from the latter town. Here the armies turned aside to relieve the garrison of the Alcázar in Toledo, which they successfully carried out on September 29th, 1936, when the Nationalist troops entered the town.

To this delay is often attributed the failure of General Franco's armies to capture Madrid, in whose suburbs they first arrived on November 5th and were unexpectedly held up. Simultaneously the advance by General Mola's army across the Guadarrama Mountains was also held up. The advance so far had been so rapid and continuous that this first setback came as a surprise, but it was soon realized that it was caused by the fighting efficiency in men and tanks of the International Brigades, composed of men of many nationalities recruited by communist centers all over the world, but consisting chiefly of Russians and Frenchmen, whose preparation had been carried on secretly. It was this Russian and French assistance that was the start of the employment in Spain of foreign volunteers and caused the sending of Italian and German volunteers to help the Nationalists, for these two countries could not afford in their own safety to allow a Soviet state to be established in Western Europe and at the gate of the Mediterranean.

Controversy and propaganda were very active on one side and the other as regards which side first received help from foreign volunteers, but this controversy was practically settled by the celebrations in Republican Spain on October 17th, 1937, of the anniversary of the International Brigades. This proved that they were constituted and present in Spain on October 17th, 1936, by which date there was no evidence or even suggestion that Italian and German volunteers had begun to arrive.

At this period, the line between the opposing sides became stabilized for a time as shown in the map elsewhere. The total line amounted to over 1,000 miles, but, though everywhere it was more or less clearly defined, it was not in any sense a continuous line of trenches and defenses as in the First World War.

Spain is a country of vast and precipitous mountain ranges, and, though mountain peaks were often strongly defended and stormed by one side or the other, the course of fighting generally followed, especially in the early days of the war, the lines of valleys, roads and railways across which defenses of trenches, barbed wire, etc., were flung. Such a situation and the configuration of the country made rapid advances appear very dangerous, and it requires some explanation and analysis to understand how the small armies of Queipo and Varela could advance 400 miles in 3½ months along the main road to Madrid, without leaving large garrisons behind them in the captured towns and on the bridges, to protect them from at tacks in rear and flank.

The explanation is that the populace of the country through which they advanced was entirely on their side; the advance could not have been made under any other circumstances. That this was so, was further borne out by every visitor who went to Spain during the subsequent months and witnessed to the fact that General Franco did not have to guard his lines of communication. They also witnessed the traces of the reign of terror and destruction, which had been left in the towns and villages of Andalusia and Estremadura by the retreating government forces; the inhabitants related to visitors how the communist and socialist elements, a minority but an armed one, had massacred the civil guards, priests, and often all members of right party organizations and destroyed and pillaged the churches, the condition of which for a long time continued to be a standing proof of the truth of their statements.

When the revolutionary minority fled before the advancing armies of General Franco, they left behind the recently terrorized majority, who hailed the Nationalist forces as saviors, and obviated any necessity of guarding the lines of communication.

X

THE CONDITIONS AND GOVERNMENTS ON BOTH SIDES, 1936–37

FROM NORTHERN CAMPAIGN TO TERUEL

The Madrid government, which at the outbreak of war was under the leadership of Señor Giral, resigned on September 4th, 1936, after the fall of Irun, and a new government was formed under Señor Largo Caballero; this cabinet for the first time included two Communists. The Cortes, reduced by the flight, death or imprisonment of many of its members from its full membership of some 450 to a rump of some 100 of the extreme left, entirely ceased to function except for a few short sessions of a day's duration and from the outbreak of civil war had no further control over the destinies of Spain. It is an interesting commentary on the power of propaganda that, notwithstanding this fact and the continual infringements of the constitution, the government was still hailed by the greater part of the press and by the B.B.C. as the legal constitutional and democratic government of Spain.

On October 16th, 1936, Señor Largo Caballero was appointed supreme head of the Republican forces; on November 5th the government was reconstructed with four Syndicalist members and on November 7th the new government accompanied by the Soviet Ambassador, who was usually present at cabinet meetings, left Madrid for Valencia in view of the Nationalist attack.

This government was succeeded in May, 1937, as the result of the revolt of the anarchists (C.N.T.) in Barcelona, by a new government, without any representative of the C.N.T., under Doctor Negrín, with Indalecio Prieto as Minister of Defense. This was a victory for the Communist-Socialist syndicate U.G.T., which had throughout its history carried on an internecine strife with the Anarchist C.N.T.

Señor Prieto was now the power behind the new ministry, and practically dictator of Republican Spain with the full support of the Soviet, which increasingly dominated and controlled affairs and the war in Republican Spain. Thus ended a long personal struggle for power between Caballero and Prieto.

The following was the constitution of the new Government:

- ~ Prime Minister and Finance, Señor Juan Negrín (Socialist).
- ~ Foreign Affairs, Señor Jose Giral (Republican Left).
- ~ Defense, Señor Indalecio Prieto (Socialist).
- ~ Justice, Señor M. Irujo (Basque Nationalist).
- ~ Home Affairs, Señor J. Zugazagoitia (Socialist).
- ~ Education and Health, Señor Jesus Hernandez (Communist).
- ~ Agriculture, Señor V. Uribe (Communist).
- ~ Public Works, Señor B. Giner de los Ríos (Republican Union).
- ~ Labor, Señor Jaime Aguade (Esquerra).

On October 30th, 1937, the government migrated again, this time to Barcelona, where it dominated the existing Catalan government under President Companys without much apparent difficulty. Señor Azana had continued to be President of the Spanish Republic throughout the war, but appeared to be a complete cypher and seldom showed any evidence of his existence.

The headquarters of the Nationalists was established in the early days of the counterrevolution at Burgos; the leading figures of the Nationalist Junta were Generals Franco, Mola, Varela, Cabanellas and Queipo de Llano. On October 1st, 1936, General Franco was installed at Burgos as Generalissimo and head of the Spanish State and established a government under a series of departments which continued to administer the country as he conquered it. He issued a decree stating the basis on which he intended to organize the government, which was to be that of a corporative system and seemed to be similar to that of Portugal, and without the state-worship inherent in the German system.

His various posterior declarations have in no ways departed from his original scheme, and full particulars of them will be found in subsequent chapters.

Such is the outline of political events up to the autumn of 1937, and we will now return to the military history where we left it, in the last chapter, at the end of 1936.

While the armies under Generals Varela and Queipo de Llano were advancing on Madrid, the armies of Generals Mola and Dávila had started from Pamplona for the campaign against Asturias and the Basque provinces. The first success was the capture of Tolosa, the capital of the province of Guipuzcoa, on August 15th, 1936. After rapid successes on the Bidassoa River, Irun, which had been partly reduced to ruins by the fleeing troops, fell on September 4th, San Sebastian on September 13th, and the line of battle then became almost stable for some nine months.

Meanwhile an interlude was provided by the relief of Oviedo, the capital of Asturias, of which the garrison was hard set to hold out, and the account of its defense by Colonel (afterwards General) Aranda rivals in some ways that of the Alcázar of Toledo. The relief columns set out from Coruña in Galicia 100 miles away and encountered very severe fighting as they neared their objective; their enemies decided to do their utmost to anticipate them and attempted to reduce Oviedo by fierce assaults. Only a part of the city was held by General Aranda and street fighting was constant during the last few days before the relief, which took place on October 17th with the entry of the relieving columns. However, although relieved, the city continued to be fiercely besieged, with a narrow corridor three to five miles wide and twenty miles long connecting it to the west with Nationalist territory, until the fall of Gijón on October 21st, 1937, relieved it permanently.

The more or less stabilized front in the north ran at first from Ondarroa, on the coast west of San Sebastian, southwards for some twenty miles to the Arlabán Pass, then westwards in an irregular line to the Leitariegos Pass in the Cantabrian mountains and then north to the coast some twenty miles west of Gijón with an excrescence to take in Oviedo and its corridor. The length of the territory still under the Republican government was at its greatest point no less than 200 miles. Though stabilized, this front was the scene of many attacks and counter-attacks by both sides until, on March 31st, 1937, the advance on Bilbao began under General Mola. On April 28th and 29th Durango and Guernica were occupied, after the latter had met the same fate as Irún, partial destruction at the hands of the retreating militia.

Bilbao had been protected with a powerful system of trenches and defenses called the Iron Belt; this was pierced for the first time after fierce fighting on June 11th, and on June 19th the victorious armies entered Bilbao. The Basque soldiers of Bilbao prevented their Anarchist and Communist allies from any wholesale destruction in Bilbao, though most of the bridges were destroyed and large quantities of loot, including the contents of bank strong rooms, were taken away, much of it to be embargoed by the legal authorities in the French ports at which it arrived and eventually returned to its owners.

After a pause to clean up and consolidate the captured country, which, like all the country through which this northern campaign took place, is a very difficult one with a series of high mountain ranges, a sudden and heavy offensive was begun on August 14th towards Santander, which fell to the nationalists on August 31st.

This was immediately followed by an attack on Asturias from the east by the columns that had captured Santander, from León in the south, and from Galicia in the west. The advance of General Franco's troops was well prepared and irresistible, though taking place over some of the most difficult and mountainous terrain in Europe, and his continual victories eventually so demoralized the Republican troops that both Gijón and Avilés were surrendered without fighting on October 21st, 1937, and the last inch of northern Spain passed into the hands of the Nationalists.

Though large numbers of troops had surrendered both on the fall of Bilbao and of Santander, the remainder of the Republican armies, and especially the brigades of Asturian miners and Anarchists, had retreated westwards before General Franco's armies and surrendered en masse in Oviedo. A considerable number of troops escaped by sea from Bilbao and Gijón to France, whence they were sent by train to Barcelona to swell the Republican forces. This procedure of the French government of helping Republican soldiers to escape their enemies and returning them to Barcelona instead of interning them continued throughout the war, and was one of the many examples of the assistance given by the French government to the Republican government, notwithstanding their professed support and signature of the nonintervention pact.

Great irritation was aroused in Nationalist Spain by the unfortunate though perfectly legal assistance given by the British flag and fleet to merchant ships, many of them the camouflaged property of the Republican government, to run the blockades of Bilbao, Santander and Gijón, which the Nationalists considered with reason as a measure prolonging the siege and the war. Once the British government had, however, adopted a new nonintervention policy instead of the traditional policy of the belligerent rights of peoples at war, such an assistance was inevitable and an obligation under the nonintervention pact.

The conclusion of the war in the north was an immediate sign for the revival of business and commercial activities. Business and commerce require law and order under which to function, and the lack of them had paralyzed the iron, coal, smelting and other industries in northern Spain. In the chapter on business it will be seen how production and export reacted immediately and enormously to the conditions of order and freedom given as the result of the Nationalist victories.

The rapid reconstruction of destroyed railways, bridges, roads and buildings as soon as the country was conquered both in the north and elsewhere, was a convincing tribute to General Franco's organization, and to the fact that the people of Spain were behind him. The facts that he never had to guard his many thousand miles of communications or increase the police were conclusive proofs of this.

Meanwhile, when the campaign in the north came to an end, the front of Madrid had not shown much alteration since we left it in November nine months previously. During the winter of 1936–7 no advances of importance were made but fighting of varying ferocity continued backwards and forwards in the western suburbs of Madrid throughout the succeeding months.

When the Nationalist armies, after fighting their way from the very south of Spain, had reached Madrid, their advance was held up on the steep banks of the Manzanares River and at the bridgeheads over that river. An attack was then made over the more open ground of the Royal Park (Casa de Campo) towards the University City. The construction of the University City was a scheme in which both Alfonso XIII and the dictator had taken the initiative and the greatest interest; it was begun in the last years of the monarchy and consisted of many enormous well-built edifices of good Spanish twentieth century style. Several of these were captured by the Nationalists, who then proceeded to attack and capture, after a long and bitter struggle, the great new hospital (Hospital Clínico). This hospital became the outmost redoubt of the Nationalists, and the most savage fighting continued around it and the part of the University City held by the Nationalists, but the Republican troops were never able to dislodge them throughout the next two years and warfare on this part of the long front became one of trenches, as in the first Great War. The buildings held by the Nationalists were converted into ruins by shelling and mining, whereas the buildings held by the Republican side, such as the enormous Medical School were left severely alone by General Franco, who always avoided useless destruction.

At the beginning of March, 1937, the Nationalists made an offensive with a view to the encirclement of Madrid; they made advances on the northwest and southwest but suffered a defeat at Guadalajara, where Italian mechanized units were defeated and put to flight. This seemed to paralyze any further offensive at Madrid on the part of the Nationalists and fighting was restricted in that front for several months, except in the air. Both in the case of Madrid and Bilbao, General Franco proved by his actions that his intentions were to destroy the towns as little as possible, for captured ruins were of no use to him or Spain.

In July 1937, came the battle of Brunete near Madrid; this was a Republican offensive which was defeated by the Nationalists with great loss of life on both sides. In October took place the battle of Belchite in Aragón, where the Nationalists were driven back to the line of the Huesca-Zaragoza road.

In Aragón, at Huesca in the north, Zaragoza in the center and Teruel in the southwest, all of which were outposts of the Nationalist forces, there was intermittent fighting, and accounts of their capture were constantly reported in the Republican war news, but nevertheless these places all continued in possession of the Nationalists and the war map showed little change on those fronts between October, 1936, and February, 1938.

Similarly, the fronts of Córdoba and Granada showed small changes after October 1936. At the beginning of February, the Nationalists started an offensive against Málaga, which they entered unopposed after a series of battles of which the last took place at Torremolinos, some miles to the east of Málaga and the front then became stabilized on the coast at the port of Motril. Málaga had suffered great destruction at the hands of the red mobs during the seven months of terror to which it was subjected and from a series of bombardments by the Nationalist airplanes. However, by the end of May 1937, life and business were reestablished on normal lines and some 35,000 people, consisting of the wives and children of the red elements and all destitute people, were receiving food and lodging from the voluntary welfare organizations, which were an outstanding feature of Nationalist Spain throughout the conquered territory.

The position, roughly, at the end of 1937 showed that the Nationalists had increased their hold on Spanish territory from the one-fourth that they held on the outbreak of the war to two-thirds of Spain.

The land forces at the disposal of the Nationalist in June 1937, were given as 602,000 men armed and trained with 800,000 called up, while the numbers of the forces at the disposal of the Republic were not published, but were reported to consist of an army of 500,000 men. Decrees of the opposing leaders showed that General Franco had at that date called up men between the ages of eighteen and twenty-eight, and that the Republican government had called up men up to the age of twenty-nine. Subsequently in the later phases of the war the Barcelona government mobilized the whole population from the ages of sixteen to fifty but were only able to compel them to comply by force and terrorism.

Strife was constant in Republican Spain between the various communist and anarchist organizations during the course of the war, though it appeared that, with the help and organization supplied by Moscow, at the end of 1937 the former dominated the latter and that unity had been achieved at the cost of a merciless system of terror, of which an account is to be found in another chapter. Up to this time the divided authority of the different military organizations had frustrated any efficiency, but this new unity undoubtedly strengthened the fighting efficiency of the Republican forces considerably. It appeared that first the leaders of the P.O.U.M. (United Marxist Party) were "liquidated" and then the C.N.T. (National Labor Confederation of the Anarchist party) were forced to accept the domination of their socialist-communist opponents, the U.G.T. (General Workers Union). In this way there was one command instead of three or four and the Commander- in-Chief, in name at any rate, was General Miaja; it was subsequently revealed (see Chapter XI) that military policy and operations were directed by the Soviet Union.

When the battle of Teruel began in December 1937, it is probable that the actual forces on both sides were approximately equal in numbers and armament, but morale and discipline were on the side of the Nationalists. When at this time British Labor M.P.s, under the leader of the opposition, Mr. Attlee, visited Republican Spain, they were so impressed by the armaments and efficiency of the army on that side that they announced publicly to the whole world that their victory was inevitable. When later on their friends began to be beaten, they forgot their previous declarations and cried out that they were being beaten by the superior armaments of the Nationalists.

Relations between Great Britain and Nationalist Spain were regularized by the appointment in July 1937, of Sir Robert Hodgson as British agent to the Government of Nationalist Spain, and by the appointment of the Duke of Berwick and Alba as Nationalist agent in Great Britain. It was stipulated at the time that this did not mean official recognition of General Franco's government, and so the situation between the two countries was more or less normalized under this politico-diplomatic quibble, to which the left wing politicians were unable to object. On the recognition of General Franco's government, the Duke became the Ambassador of Spain at the Court of St. James.

No one could have been more acceptable to England than the Duke on account of his name, his descent from the Royal Stuarts, his great culture, and last but not least, his sporting proclivities. He is descended from the first Duke of Berwick, one of the greatest generals in Europe in his day, who came to Spain and whose descendants inherited through marriage all the titles and possessions of the historical dukedom of Alba; his name is James Manuel Fitzjames Stuart. He had been for many years President of that greatest of picture galleries, the Museo del Prado, and was the possessor of vast private collections of pictures, manuscripts and treasures of all sorts, which suffered heavily at the hands of the mob and their leaders. The Duke was also Director of the Spanish Academy of History, among other important cultural institutions on which he had a seat, and he held an honorary degree at more than one of the British universities, and in 1943 he was received into the Real Academia Española, that treasured goal of all great Spaniards.

XI

THE CONDITIONS AND GOVERNMENTS ON BOTH SIDES, 1938

FROM TERUEL TO EBRO

The next phase of the war opened with the battle of Teruel, a sharp salient towards the Mediterranean coast, which had been in the hands of the Nationalists since the first days of the war. Though the world was expecting an offensive from General Franco, it came first from the Republican side, whose nominal Commander-in-Chief was General Miaja, and proved that they had a much larger and better equipped army than was generally believed. There seems little doubt that they took the Nationalists by surprise, when they attacked on December 21st; they drove them back some distance, capturing Teruel on January 9th. General Franco's counteroffensive was launched immediately; the terrible winter conditions in this mountainous country hampered his movements but he recaptured Teruel on February 22nd.

Then began General Franco's long-prepared offensive over a wide front, beginning between Huesca and the country south of the Ebro near Zaragoza and sweeping on with irresistible force on an expanding front, which soon stretched from the Pyrenees to the south of the mouth of the Ebro. Catalonia was entered, Lérida fell on April 4th, Tremp with the greater part of Barcelona's power and light supply a few days later. On Good Friday, April 15th, the Nationalist forces reached the Mediterranean and occupied the towns of Benicarló and Vinaroz, thus cutting Republican Spain in two and severing all land connections between Barcelona and Valencia and Madrid.

Having acquired the most important of the electric power stations of Catalonia, which had fortunately escaped destruction by the Republican forces on their retreat, General Franco proceeded to clean up and organize the enormous stretch of country he had captured on the Catalan and Aragonese fronts. The accompanying maps indicate the respective fronts at the time of the capture of Teruel and after the Nationalist armies reached the coast. The front in April 1938, started at the Pyrenees north-cast of Sort, ran down the valley of the Noguera Pallaresa river to the

Segre, followed the Segre valley to the Ebro and the Ebro valley to the sea. General Franco held almost all the slopes, valleys, and bridges on both sides of the two former rivers but only the southern bank of the Ebro. He called a standstill here, while he continued his advance southwards towards Valencia with the Ebro at his back.

The principal commanders on the Nationalist side in the Aragón battles were:

General Yagüe in command of the Moorish army corps. General García Valiño in command of the 1st Navarran division. General Monasterio, the great cavalry commander. General Moscardó, the defender of the Alcázar, leading the army corps of Aragón. General Aranda, the hero of Oviedo, at the head of the Galician army corps. General Sánchez in command of the 5th Navarran division, and General Solchaga. The General commanding the Nationalist air force was the Spanish General Kindelán, who had been in command of that branch since the beginning of the war.

The higher commands were entirely in the hands of Spanish generals, and British military observers on the spot calculated that there were 20,000 Italian troops under an Italian general engaged throughout the Teruel offensive out of a total army on that front of 250,000 men drawn from all parts of Nationalist Spain. The total nationalist army at this time was estimated by foreign military experts at 600,000-750,000 men.

The contrast between the Spanish Civil War and the First World War was signalized by the French General Duval in the "Journal des Devats," in which he showed how, on the basis of an army of 750,000 men, General Franco was fighting on a front of 1,100 miles, whereas the allied western front during the First World War was 400 miles and was held by an army of 2,500,000. In Spain there was no consecutive line of trench defenses as in France, for the mountainous character of the country forbade it, apart from the comparison of length to man force. Thus, large stretches of the lines were very sparsely defended, though the division between the opposing sides was everywhere clearly defined.

It was impossible to discover the names of the real military leaders on the Republican side; a veil appeared to be drawn over their names and over the numbers and nationality of the troops engaged, which was not allowed to be drawn aside even in the war bulletins published in the Barcelona newspapers. The only generals whose names appeared at this time were Generals Miaja, Rojo and Modesto, and it was subsequently established that these men, and especially the first, who succeeded the Russian General Kleber as Commander-in-Chief, were puppets whose real superior officers were foreigners mostly Russian, with headquarters first at Albacete and then at Barcelona. Of the veil of secrecy the evidence of the Republican press bulletins was sufficient, and the only evidence as to who were true commanders came from prisoners and from returned members of the International Brigades, who, on inquiry, produced some Russian or French names of generals but also stated that most of them took assumed names on arriving in Spain.

There was equal secrecy as to the numbers fighting and the corps engaged, but information gained by the Nationalists in the battles from prisoners, and from these same members of International Brigades showed that the cream of the Republican army was the International Brigades and the two Spanish Communist Brigades, called Campesino and Lister. On January 20th, 1938, General Franco issued a decree transforming his Junta or Council into a government of eleven ministers with himself as President with the supreme command of army, navy, and air force. The other ministers were:

~ Vice-President and Foreign Affairs, General Gómez-Jordana.
~ National Defense, General Dávila.
~ Interior, Señor Ramón Serrano Suñer.
~ Public Order, General Martínez Anido.
~ Justice, Conde de Rodezno.
~ Agriculture, Señor R. Fernández-Cuesta.
~ National Education, Señor Pedro Sainz Rodríguez.
~ Finance, Señor Andrés Amado.
~ Industry and Commerce, Señor Juan Antonio Suanzes.
~ Public Works, Señor Alfonso Peña.
~ Syndical and Social Affairs, Señor Pedro González-Bueno.

Most of these men were well known and with reputations based on past achievements. General Jordana was sixty-one, with a military reputation gained in Cuba and Morocco, of which he was High Commissioner after the pacification of that country by General Primo de Rivera. General Martínez Anido was older than the other ministers; he was a strong and fearless character and had for twenty years been the man that Spain had called upon in her hours of need and disorder; he was one of Primo de Rivera's right-hand men. General Dávila had also had a distinguished military career and succeeded General Mola, on the latter's death, as Commander-in-Chief of the northern armies.

All the other ministers were civilians from various walks in life. The

Conde de Rodezno was fifty-four, an old politician and for many years the head of the Traditionalist party; he was the chief representative of the Requetés in the ministry, while Señor Serrano Suñer, a brilliant young lawyer of thirty-six, was one of the chief friends of the founder of the Falange, Jose A. Primo de Rivera. Señor Amado was also a lawyer, Señor Suanzes an engineer, Señor Peña a road engineer, Señor Fernández-Cuesta a doctor of law and national secretary of the Falange since 1934, Señor González-Bueno a civil engineer, while Señor Sainz Rodríguez, who was only forty-one, was one of Spain's great intellectuals, a Professor of Madrid University and a prolific writer.

General Franco's government received the recognition of Germany and Italy on November 18th, 1936, and during 1937–38 of Japan and various other countries.

The new ministers, some of whom placed their ministries in Burgos, some in Valladolid and some in Bilbao, proceeded rapidly in the reconstruction and reorganization of the New Spain on the lines already laid down in General Franco's decrees and speeches, of which an outline is given in another chapter.

The Republican government of Dr. Negrín with Señor Prieto as Minister of War and Defense continued in power until April 5th, 1938, when a reconstruction was made without any reference to parliament or the people, thus further destroying the constitutional and democratic theory about the Republican government, which continued to form the central argument of international propaganda for their support by the so-called democracies of the world, among which Russia was curiously included. Señor Prieto, till then considered the virtual dictator, disappeared from the government, and Dr. Negrín assumed the portfolio of Minister of Defense. The disappearance of Señor Indalecio Prieto was the result of clashes in the cabinet between himself and the Communists, as he refused to be completely subservient to Moscow. His departure marked the final and complete domination by the Communists of the Republican government. A representative of the Anarchist syndicate C.N.T. was again admitted to the government, presumably to cement the much advertised but doubtful union between that syndicate and their immemorial enemies the U.G.T. or Socialist-Communist syndicate. The Minister of Foreign Affairs was once again Señor Álvarez del Vayo, who was said to have been the chief agent of the Comintern in Spain previous to the civil war.

The reconstructed government was as follows:

~ President and National Defense, Dr. Juan Negrín (Socialist).
~ Foreign Affairs, Señor Álvarez del Vayo (Socialist).
~ Home Affairs, Señor P. Gomez Saiz (Socialist).
~ Labor, Señor Jaime Aguade (Esquerra).
~ Instruction and Health, Señor S. Blanco González (Anarchist).
~ Agriculture, Señor Vicente Uribe (Communist).
~ Finance, Señor F. Méndez Aspe.
~ Public Works, Señor A. Velao Oñate (Republican Left).
~ Transport, Señor B. Giner de los Ríos (Republican Union).
~ No portfolio, Señor Manuel Irujo (Basque Nationalist).
~ No portfolio, Señor Jose Giral (Republican Left).
~ Justice, Señor Ramón González Peña (Socialist).

Manuel Azaña continued throughout as titular President of the Spanish Republic; he lived in a virtual retirement, only very occasionally appeared in public, and was seldom mentioned even in the press.

Catalonia did not at first cut a great figure, except as the chief industrial center, producer of munitions and the scene of constant conflicts between the revolutionary organizations of socialists, communists, anarchists, and Trotskyists, which stultified her war effort. In 1938, however, her military effort became increasingly important. Throughout the war her autonomous government under President Companys continued in office and also in power until the advent of the Republican government submerged their actual power, leaving only the semblance.

Living conditions in Barcelona, Valencia and Madrid at this time were miserable. The civil and military population were under an iron system of spying and terrorism superintended by a Russian Cheka, food and clothing were increasingly scarce and the price of both soaring, not only on account of scarceness but on account of the depreciation in the local currencies; those who had friends abroad had for more than a year been supplied with parcels to keep them from starving. Perusal of the contemporary Barcelona press prove that these conditions existed, and it published almost daily a list of those condemned to death and shot for offences ranging from desertion in the field to the holding of opinions contrary to the Republican government; on one day alone the Barcelona newspapers published a list of forty-one of these unfortunates.

After crossing the Ebro and reaching the coast, General Franco now attacked that region of difficult and mountainous country, highly fortified on the passes, bridgeheads and other points, which roughly composes a triangle with Teruel at its apex, and Tarragona and Sagunto at its other two angles. His bombardments of the Mediterranean ports, their harbors, manufactories, petrol tanks, etc., were intensified and great damage done to them.

The Nationalist advance continued east and south of Teruel and down the coast. Castellón was reached on June 13th and the advance continued southwards. The Republicans made some attacks on the Nationalist lines in the direction of Tremp, which were repulsed without difficulty, while on July 25th they crossed the Ebro at several points on a ninety-mile front between Mequinenza and Amposta, taking the Nationalists by surprise and threatening their rear.

Just at this time the southwestern front awoke, after eighteen months' comparative stagnation, and General Queipo de Llano made a stroke down the Guadiana valley from Mérida towards Almadén, where the famous quicksilver mines are. It appeared that his objectives were to capture these mines, which were one of the last productive assets of the Republic, and also to shorten his front by the reduction of the large existing salient.

If those were the objectives only the latter was gained, the bulge or salient was cut off to a depth of about thirty miles, but the advance was stopped with Almadén still another thirty miles to the east. On August 29th the Republicans launched a counterattack on this front without success and with heavy losses, and the line became stabilized.

The air arm became more and more important on both sides as the war progressed, both in the actual battles and in the bombing of towns, ports, railways, and ships.

When the civil war broke out the Spanish air force consisted of some 300 planes, of which about 250 were in the hands of the Republican government who also held all the principal airfields—Getafe, Cuatro Vientos, Barcelona and Cartagena, while the Nationalists had only the smaller airfields of Seville, León, Cádiz, Majorca and Granada. This superiority in the air was used by the Republican government to bomb freely Nationalist towns both open and military and some 2,000 raids took place in the first one and a half years of the war without any protest on the part of the foreign press or governments. When the superiority in the air passed to the Nationalists and continued in their hands and they used it to bomb Barcelona, the seat of their enemy's government and the center of their supplies, ports, railways and ships, which were bringing war supplies to the enemy, a strange and significant outcry against this inhumanity broke out throughout the world. No stronger proof of the power and direction of world press propaganda and of the control of the press would be possible.

Spain herself did not build airplanes and, after August 1936, Russia, France and Czechoslovakia supplied Republican Spain with them and pilots, while Germany and Italy did the same by Nationalist Spain. The latter rapidly built up an air force of Spaniards under the instruction of Italian and German technicians and directed by the Spanish General Kindelán; contrary to the belief fostered in foreign countries by propaganda there were soon far more Spaniards than foreigners in the service and they proved to be able and courageous airmen. Testimony of these facts are the published figures of Nationalist airmen killed, which had reached the figure of 88 by December 31st, 1937. The chief ace of the Nationalist air service was also a Spaniard called García-Morato, whose fame resounded throughout the Peninsula.

On the Republican side one encounters a veil of secrecy everywhere that made it impossible to ascertain either names or statistics, but it is probable that a bigger percentage of pilots were foreigners than was the case with their enemy, and it is notorious that Spanish Republican pilots were continuously trained in French military aviation schools, notwithstanding the French signature to the nonintervention pact. This matter is further dealt with in a later chapter, but it can be repeated here that, according to an official statement, General Franco's forces had brought down 948 planes by June 30th, 1938, of which 800 were Russian, and over 100 were French.

Some mention must be made of atrocities, though it is not the intention of the author to enter into the details of the atrocities and murders committed throughout all that part of Spain, that was not under the control of the Nationalists in July, 1936. Accounts of these atrocities, properly and adequately documented, have been published in book form ("Communist Atrocities," Messrs. Eyre & Spottiswoode, London). The perpetrators of and apologists for these crimes sought successfully to palliate their acts and avoid the detestation of all the world by the common method of accusing their opponents of having done the same as they had. This had the desired effect of making people either discredit the accounts altogether or believe that all Spaniards are excessively cruel, and that one side was as bad as the other, though the fact that the atrocities were not denied by the Republic but merely palliated by counteraccusation, should give to the unprejudiced onlooker credence of their having occurred.

Figures of those murdered in cold blood were given at anything between 200,000 and 400,000, but the controversy as to the figures is an unprofitable one. Such a controversy is of its nature unending. Suffice it to say that the horrifying numbers and quality of the atrocities were confirmed to the author, not only by personal English friends resident in Barcelona and Madrid for many months after July 1936, but also by Spanish peasants and people of all classes in the conquered regions through which he traveled in 1937. Nor did the murders or executions cease with the comparatively more orderly state of affairs existing in Republican Spain in 1938, for the popular tribunals, which usurped the legal systems, continued to send people to their death for such offences as "defeatism" or "being contrary to the regime." The evidence that this was the case is conclusive owing to the publication of the death sentences in the local press.

In Nationalist Spain, where the ordinary Spanish legal system of courts and judges continued, there was no evidence of cases of execution without proper trial according to law. This does not mean to say that all administration of justice and punishment was perfect on the side of the Nationalists; cases of injustice and victimization were inevitable at a time when the passions of warfare and of people, bereaved of their relations and friends by torture and assassination, ran high. But it is important to keep this point clear, that in one case (the Republican) the judges were self-constituted tribunals of ignorant men usually drawn from the mob, as in the French Reign of Terror, while in the other case (the Nationalist) the judges were usually professional men belonging to the upper and bourgeois classes.

To deny the existence of an acute reign of terror throughout Republican Spain, and especially in Madrid and Barcelona, during the whole period of civil war is to deny the evidence of the numberless Spaniards and several Englishmen, who witnessed it. Two items of evidence, which should be convincing to people in this country are:

1. The existence of the Cheka torture chambers found in Madrid and Barcelona at the end of the civil war. British friends of the author visited them and described them and photographs of them appeared in British illustrated papers.
2. The British population, with the exception of officials, had to be evacuated from Republican Spain; their lives were in danger and their business and properties were stolen. Nothing of this sort happened in Nationalist Spain, foreigners were not evacuated, for their lives and property were safe and respected.

In the years immediately following the civil war there is no doubt that the Spanish prisons and concentration camps were filled with criminals and political prisoners, augmented considerably from 1939 onwards by foreign refugees from German occupied countries. This was not surprising in view of the hundreds of thousands of people assassinated during the civil war and the number of their relatives clamoring for vengeance, and it presented Franco and his government with a most difficult problem. The numbers of prisoners and their sufferings were undoubtedly heavy and they existed in a country suffering for some time from starvation, but they were grossly exaggerated by the foreign press and then used by sympathizers of the defeated Republicans as propaganda with which to abuse General Franco and his regime and as a counter accusation to excuse the abominations of the reign of terror, which had been their primary cause. This was a confusion of two different subjects, which should be each treated separately on its merits—the reign of terror of 1936–1938 and the imprisonments and executions of 1939–1943. The latter subject is more fully treated in Chapters XXIII, XXV, XXVIII and XXXI.

It was easy for ill-informed English people to preach pardon before 1939 but in 1945 we could see the difference, when we ourselves were trying to find the mean between criminal and political offences.

XII

THE CONDITIONS AND GOVERNMENTS ON BOTH SIDES, 1938-9

EBRO TO THE FALL OF BARCELONA

The advance of the Republican forces south of the Ebro, which began with a surprise attack on the night of July 4th–25th, was eventually held on a line Mequinenza, Fayón, Gandesa, Cherta. Thus, began the long battle of the Ebro, which completely paralyzed the southward advance of the Nationalists towards Valencia.

There then ensued a long series of battles and counterattacks, with engagements in which both sides held strongly fortified positions, and the struggle developed into a trench warfare similar to that of the First World War. The Nationalists gradually and slowly reconquered the lost territory; the pocket between the line Mequinenza-Fayón and the Ebro was recaptured on August 6th and 7th, and the battle continued fiercely with comparatively small alterations in the line until the end of October when a frontal attack was made, which broke through the Republican line of defense, while a simultaneous enveloping movement took place on the right wing by the army under General García Valiño, which was completely successful, resulting in the capture of Móra del Ebro on November 7th. This favorite maneuver of General Franco turned the defenses of the Republicans, whose defeat was completed and their armies routed and completely driven back across the Ebro by November 16th.

The air arm was made full use of throughout the Ebro battle. Losses were heavy on both sides, though considerably higher on the Republican side on account of the air supremacy of the Nationalists, and the fact that General Franco was always more economical of lives than the Republicans. The Nationalist General Staff announced that in the course of the Ebro battle they had captured 19,779 prisoners, buried 13,275 bodies and had shot down 242 planes for certain and 94 probable.

The world in general, still guided by the biased press propaganda, talked throughout the last months of the year 1938 about the "stalemate of the war in Spain," but there can be little doubt that, though originally taken by surprise, General Franco of set purpose held the major part of his enemy's army to this ground with the strategic objects of exhaustion and attrition.

On August 16th the composition of the Republican cabinet was modified; two of its less extreme members Jaime Aguadé of the Esquerra party and Irujo of the Basque Nationalist party were replaced by two Socialists, Moix and Tomás Bilbao. It has been shown in a former chapter how socialists and communists became united under Caballero in 1936 and so the effect of this change was to strengthen further the control by Moscow and the Comintern and to unify the command both military and political.

On September 30th, the rump parliament held one of its rare and brief sessions in the church of San Cugat near Barcelona. This session of parliament and the speech of Dr. Negrín had little interest or object except for foreign consumption, as both parliament and executive were in reality mere puppets of the Comintern. The complete supersession of parliament as an instrument of control was evidenced by its vote suspending its own half-yearly sessions unless summoned by the government; it thus committed suicide.

On October 30th, the P.O.U.M. (Trotskyist) leaders, who had long been in prison, were at last sentenced publicly to long terms of imprisonment. In December, the government paper *La Vanguardia* announced the discovery of a pro-Franco plot and a purge took place in the Republican army with many arrests of officers and civilians. The reign of terror under the Russian-controlled Cheka police and prisons continued in Barcelona, Madrid and Valencia and in the army, and successfully suppressed the discontent of the civil population, which continued to suffer the extremes of misery and famine. A League of Nations commission reported that there was an acute food shortage and appeals were sent out to all the world for food supplies. Left-wing organizations and thoughtless but charitable people responded readily without considering that the only result of their action would be to break the siege-blockade of Republican Spain and prolong the war and the misery.

On December 9th, a Republican government decree declared the return to religious freedom and set up a Council of Public Worship and a few masses were said, but the measure appeared to be eyewash for foreign consumption for the churches were destroyed and the priests who remained alive dared not show themselves for fear of imprisonment and death.

On September 27th, when a European war was widely believed to be imminent, the Duke of Alba presented to the British Foreign Office a declaration from General Franco that National Spain would remain neutral in the Czechoslovak crisis. This was proof positive that National Spain was not, and did not intend to be, subordinated to Germany and Italy, and should have silenced the press propaganda, which had so powerfully influenced public opinion to believe the contrary. By the end of the year all European countries except the U.S.S.R., France, Latvia, and Lithuania were represented at Burgos.

On December 15th a decree was published in Burgos restoring to Alfonso XIII his rights as a Spanish citizen and his private possessions, of which he had been deprived by the law of the Republican government of November 26th, 1936. This was taken to be a further sign of a possible return of the monarchy.

From August to January the Nationalists continued their policy of constant bombings of coast towns, railway centers and other military objectives, with a view to preventing supplies reaching their enemies, which the refusal to grant belligerent rights hindered them from effecting on the high seas. Thus Barcelona, Valencia, Tarragona, Almería, Alicante, Cartagena and other towns were continually bombed. In view of the perpetual protests in the British parliament and press against the bombings, the Duke of Alba presented a note to the foreign office on December 13th showing that from July, 1936, to June, 1938, Republican planes had bombed 373 towns, most of them far from the battle zone, with a total of 2,091 air raids causing 18,985 deaths; the note pointed out that this had been forgotten and attention paid by the British press and government exclusively to Nationalist air raids. The note stated that the latter were carried out on objectives considered in the First World War as military and under the orders of the Spanish general staff and not of foreign aviation.

Throughout this period the Nationalist navy captured a number of ships carrying supplies and on November 2nd the gunboat Nadir sank in the English Channel the Cantabria, a Spanish-owned steamer, which had been confiscated from its owners by the Republican government. This was considered by the Nationalists to be a further proof that their naval power was such that belligerent rights should be accorded to them. On October 9th General Franco, on declaring that 10,000 Italian volunteers had been evacuated, insisted that there was now no further reason to deny him belligerent rights, but they were still withheld owing to the opposition of the French government and left-wing agitation in England.

The opinion of international lawyers was practically unanimous that, according to international law, belligerent rights could not be withheld and Professor H. A. Smith in the "British Year Book of International Law," (p. 13) stated:

> If we continue to withhold recognition of a state of war and to use our navy to restrain the insurgent warships from the exercise of their legal rights we shall, in my submission, have delivered a staggering blow at the whole edifice of the law of nations.

The invention of the entirely new policy of nonintervention had, however, already threatened that edifice.

During the last six months of 1938 the Nonintervention Committee's plan for the evacuation of foreign volunteers on both sides had not progressed in any way. The Barcelona government, having converted most of the members of the International Brigades into Spanish citizens, stated to the League of Nations assembly that all foreign volunteers would be withdrawn immediately and asked for the League to appoint a commission to supervise the evacuation. This was undoubtedly a measure intended to create friction and to escape the supervision of the Nonintervention Committee.

Farewell celebrations to the brigades on a large scale were staged in Barcelona and the press was flooded with news of their evacuation to such an extent that most of the world was led to believe that they had all left. However, the commission reported to the League of Nations council on January 16th that only 4,640 had left, and the Nationalist armies continued to capture soldiers of all nationalities, who could not even speak Spanish.

In November, the Nationalists published a note giving the names and nationalities of 100 foreign officers serving in the International Brigade and the Republican army, of which eight were generals and a large proportion were Russians.

On November 29th, Admiral van Dulm, the chairman of the Nonintervention Commission, resigned.

Intervention as regards supplies to both sides continued unabated throughout this period and neither side showed the smallest sign of shortage of weapons or military supplies of any sort. The extent of Republican supplies was evident from the enormous captures in the Ebro and Catalan battles by the Nationalists, though, whereas before the battles the cry of the Republicans and their English friends was "our army is perfectly equipped and we are invincible," the defeats were always attributed to the superior equipment of the Nationalists.

French and Russian material continued to pour into Spain by sea and across the frontier notwithstanding France's signature of the nonintervention pact with her additional assurance in June 1938, that the frontier was truly closed. French patriots had become uneasy about the transfer to the Republican government of arms possibly required for the defense of France and, during a debate in the French Chamber on March 22nd, the Minister of Defense had been challenged and refused to answer if this were so or not.[3]

Another illuminating proof of French intervention and the numerical strength of the International Brigades was given during the amnesty debate in the French Chamber in December 1938, when it was stated that "from 20,000 to 30,000 Frenchmen had gone to Spain."[4]

As the hopes of the Republicans receded, they made more and more strenuous efforts to get foreign nations to intervene and save them from defeat. One of their last efforts was to make the world believe that mediation was possible and to get some nation or nations to propose it, notwithstanding the repeated declarations of General Franco, his ministers and press, that no mediation was possible or desired, and notwithstanding the proof to the same effect that an elementary knowledge of Spanish character and the causes of the war provided. The instruments of this effort in this country were League of Nations enthusiasts, none of whom had the necessary prerequisite knowledge of Spain. They based their appeal for mediation on a meeting in Paris said to consist of representatives of all Spanish parties, when it was evident that neither the Falange, Requeté, nor Lliga, whose membership comprised 50-75 percent of the population of Spain could possibly have been officially represented.

There was a pause in military operations after the conclusion of the Ebro battle on November 16th. 1938. Rumors were rife of an approaching offensive and on December 23rd General Franco struck and opened his offensive on a 200-mile front which started from Sort, followed the valley of the Noguera Pallaresa river to its junction with the Segre, the valley of that river to the Ebro and the right bank of that river to the sea.

---

[3] See Official Report, French Chamber of Deputies, March 22nd, 1938.
[4] Lil Temps, December 31st, 1948.

The Nationalist army consisted of six exclusively Spanish army corps (the Urgel under General Muñoz Grandes, the Maestrazgo under General García Valinño, the Aragón under General Moscardó, the Navarre under General Solchaga, the Morocco under General Yagüe, and the Catalonia under General Badia), and an army corps of legionaries consisting of one completely Italian division and three other divisions of whom 94 percent were Spaniards and 6 percent Italians.

The veil of secrecy over the numbers and commands of the Republican army was still down and was not lifted even in the Republican press and communiques. General Hernández Saravia was said to command the Catalan army based on Barcelona and General Miaja the army of the Levante based on Valencia, but it is now proved that the real command was still in the hands of foreign generals.

The Nationalist advance began between Sort and Balaguer in the north towards Artesa and in the country south of Lérida towards Borjas Blancas and Falset. His now traditional method of outflanking his enemy was followed by General Franco; Artesa fell on January 3rd and Borjas Blancas on January 4th, giving the Nationalists control of important road junctions leading towards Barcelona and Tarragona. Strong defensive positions built by the Republicans were conquered and large quantities of arms and supplies fell into Nationalist hands, while the great number of prisoners taken (24,800 in the first thirteen days) could only be accounted for by large-scale desertion. The advance continued in the center along the roads towards Barcelona and Tarragona, and the second line of defense of the Republicans along the road Artesa-Tarrega-Montblanc was completely overrun with the capture of the last-named town on January 11th, 1939.

The advance of the Nationalist armies over the whole front continued steadily day by day and, though Barcelona and the foreign press spoke of vigorous counterattacks, their effect was not visible on the map. The resistance of the Republican armies appeared completely broken and the advance swept on towards Barcelona. In the south Falset fell on January 12th leaving the road from Gandesa to Tarragona open and almost immediately Tortosa, at the mouth of the Ebro, was captured, opening the coast road. The Nationalist troops converged by these two roads on Tarragona, which fell on January 15th.

The advance had been rapid and successful, enormous quantities of military supplies were captured and one to three thousand prisoners taken daily. The Nationalist front at the time of the capture of Tarragona was shortened by 50 percent from the 200 miles which it approximated on the opening of the offensive on December 23rd. In all the hundreds of towns and villages liberated, General Franco's troops were received with jubilation, for they brought food and freedom. The rapidity of this advance could only have been possible in a friendly country, where it was unnecessary to guard lines of communication—a repetition of the experience throughout Spain of the previous campaigns and for the same reason.

The advance continued steadily on an ever-narrowing front. In the south Vendrell, Villanueva and Vilafranca del Penadès all fell in succession and on January 24th General Franco's forces were at Prat de Llobregat and had captured Barcelona's airport five miles from Barcelona. On the main Lérida-Barcelona road in the center, first Cervera and then Igualada fell, the Bruch Pass, one of the historic gateways for the defense of Barcelona, was passed with ease, and on January 24th the army advancing by this route was also within a few miles of Barcelona. Simultaneously further north Solsona and Manresa fell, thus cutting off a large section of Pyrenean valleys.

This advance of General Franco, apart from his other successful campaigns, must assuredly send his name down to history as a great general. In one month he had led his armies 80–100 miles on a front beginning at 200 and diminishing to 50 miles, defeating his enemy as he went in a series of engagements and supplying not only his armies but the starving people of the vast country liberated.

After reaching the outskirts of Barcelona on January 24th, General Franco paused, probably with the intention of allowing as many as possible of his real enemies to escape. These enemies were the minority which had terrorized Barcelona for so long, and by leaving them a loophole, he saved the town from looting and street fighting and himself from filling his prisons. On January 24th the *Times* correspondent said: "to tighten the belt and to hold out are still the citizens' resolve," a view widely held, yet the truth was that for one-and-a-half years the vast majority of the citizens of Barcelona had been sighing to be liberated by General Franco and could only be made to fight by terrorism.

On January 25th, 1939, most of the members of the Republican government left for Gerona, forty miles northeast of Barcelona, and it was reported that refugees were pouring out of the town towards France by road and by sea.

On January 26th, the entry into Barcelona of General Franco's troops began from the southwest, west and northwest. The much-vaunted communist-anarchist resistance to the last (*no pasarán*) did not take place; the town was rapidly and peacefully occupied, the civil administration, already prepared beforehand by General Franco's government, took charge and the food supplies accumulated in anticipation by his commissariat poured into the city to feed the starving population, whose delirious rejoicings gave the world another proof of the extent to which the people in Republican Spain had been sighing for liberation from a reign of terror.

XIII

The Conditions and Governments on Both Sides,

Fall of Barcelona Until the End of the Civil War

Though Madrid, Valencia and much of Southern and Eastern Spain were still in the hands of the Republicans, the fall of Barcelona meant that the war had been won by the Nationalists and, if the Republican government had really had the interests of their country and people at heart, they would thereupon have declared the war at an end, but they decided to continue. They undoubtedly wished to save their own skins and enable as many as possible of their followers to escape from Spain and, by a delaying action, to obtain better terms on the basis of "no reprisals."

It is also true, as the Republican statesman and historian Señor Salvador de Madariaga describes in his history ("Spain," page 407):

> Dr. Negrín was not free. He was attached to Moscow by a chain of gold... One thing is certain: at that moment, none but Dr. Negrín and the communists were for fighting. It is obvious that the communists had instructions to carry on the war and to hold fast to Dr. Negrín.

So the war continued and the victorious Nationalist armies advanced northwards. Granollers, Caldetas and Vich fell within a few days and the Republican government fled from Gerona to Figueras, where on February 1st the rump of the Cortes, said to consist of 62 members, met in a vault in the fortress. There Dr. Negrín preached to them that resistance should continue and that they could still continue to fight in central and southern Spain and he carried the day. The Nationalists knowing that the Republican government was at Figueras bombed the fortress heavily and as a result it fled to the frontier village of La Jonquera.

The rapid advance of General Franco's armies continued. On February 4th they occupied Gerona, swept on and within a few days had reached the frontier by the Pyrenean (Puigcerdà) route and, by February

10th, the Nationalist flag was flying at Puigcerdà, Cerbère and the other frontier posts.

The agglomeration and sufferings of the refugees on the French side of the frontier during and after these last days were heartrending and terrible. It was a problem unprepared for by the French, for the refugees amounted to hundreds of thousands, who were eventually crowded into improvised concentration camps, in some of which the conditions were appalling. Most of these refugees were gradually allowed to filter back into Spain, but others, who had to their charge crimes against individuals or against the state or who feared reprisals, were wanted by no one and remained in French prisons and concentration camps for several years.

On February 4th, 1939, the day that Gerona was captured, three presidents crossed the frontier into France; they were Señor Azaña, President of the Spanish Republic, Señor Companys, President of Catalonia and Señor Aguirre, President of Euzkadi (Basconia). Of these, Azaña and Aguirre remained in asylum abroad but Companys was returned to Spain by the Vichy Government and was tried and executed in October 1940.

As the Nationalist armies were approaching the frontier, the strongly fortified naval base of Mahón on the island of Menorca, famous in English history, which had been in the hands of the Republicans since the beginning of the civil war, surrendered to the Nationalists without bloodshed. This was brought about by the mediation of the Captain of H.M.S. Devonshire, who brought a Nationalist representative to the island and presided over the negotiations, to which a dangerous element was added, for the island was the object of several air raids by Nationalist planes while the negotiations were taking place. It appeared to be a case of General Franco's left hand not knowing what his right hand was doing, which in this case fortunately failed to cause trouble.

On February 12th, 1939, Dr. Negrín, who had been to Paris, flew to Madrid with a decree signed by President Azaña declaring that Madrid was again to be considered as the capital of Spain. Dr. Negrín thereupon established his government in Madrid, though some of the government departments remained in Valencia and other places.

Señor Álvarez del Vayo, the Foreign Minister, and Señor Martínez Barrio, the President of the Cortes, went to Paris to persuade President Azaña to return to Spain, but he refused to do so and counseled unconditional surrender. On February 27th, 1939, the British and French governments officially recognized the Nationalist government and on the following day Señor Azaña announced publicly from France that he resigned the presidency of the Spanish Republic; he stated that before leaving Spain he had unsuccessfully recommended to his government the conclusion of peace and that, now that the Powers had recognized the Nationalist government, he could no longer retain office. He was never more than a mediocre political figure and he thus slid into oblivion from a position in which he had never been more than a puppet among more able and self-seeking colleagues.

The recognition of General Franco's government by France was followed by the nomination as French ambassador of Marshal Pétain, who was not only one of the most outstanding figures of France but also a personal friend of General Franco. This was an indication that the French government desired to erase as far as possible from Spanish memory the active assistance given to the Republicans throughout the civil war by the French government of M. Léon Blum and notably by M. Pierre Cot, the Minister for Air, as described in other chapters.

The British government followed later the French example and showed their appreciation of the importance of a return to Anglo-Spanish traditional friendship and of the overwhelming value to the English position in the Mediterranean of Spanish neutrality. On the 24th May 1940, the appointment of Sir Samuel Hoare as ambassador to Spain showed that a change of heart had taken place.

On its recognition by the British Government, the government of Burgos named the Duke of Berwick and Alba as Spanish ambassador in London, where he had been since November, 1937, acting as Nationalist agent. After the return to Madrid of Dr. Negrín and his government, affairs moved rapidly towards the disintegration of the falling regime. Intrigues and counter-intrigues were rife. Dr. Negrín, to whom courage and energy cannot be denied, attempted to reorganize the commands of the Republican armies, and accumulate all power into his own hands.

In the early days of March Dr. Negrín held a meeting of the army and navy commanders in which Admiral Buiza, the naval chief, Colonel Camacho, the air chief, and Colonel Casado, commander of the central army, were in favor of immediate negotiations for peace, while Dr. Negrín and General Miaja, who represented the Communist party, were for continued resistance.

Colonel Casado now appears as the principal figure on the tottering Republican stage. He proceeded to negotiate with his fellow generals and with all the Republican parties except the Communists to eliminate Dr. Negrín and Señor Álvarez del Vayo from the authority which they had usurped (for there was neither president nor parliament in existence from which a Prime Minister or a Foreign Secretary could draw their authority). On March 5th, the fleet mutinied in Cartagena and General Miaja abandoned the Communists and joined forces with Colonel Casado. They proceeded to set up a Council of Defense, representing all the parties except the Communist and consisting of Señor Julián Besteiro and Señor Wenceslao Carrillo (Socialists), Señor M. Gonzalez Marín (Anarcho-Syndicalist), Señor Eduardo Val (Anarchist), Señor Miguel San Andres (Republican Left), Colonel Casado and General Miaja. Colonel Casado was at first the President of the Council but he conceded the place to General Miaja, though he himself remained the controlling spirit.

Dr. Negrín and his ministers fled from Madrid, first for Yuste in Extremadura and then by air to Paris. They accused the Defense Council of rebellion against an established government, whereas in reality and legality they were usurpers of authority just as much as were their successors, who were however representative in that they reflected all opinion on the Republican side except that of the Communists. In his book "The Last Days of Madrid" Colonel Casado shows how Soviet-Communist influence had gradually permeated the Republican army until more than 70 percent of the commands of the people's army were given to the Communist party, which finally also had in its service both the minister of national defense and the sub-secretary of the army.

There then developed a civil war within a civil war, the army corps commanded by Communists against the Council of Defense; there was considerable fighting within Madrid and the neighboring villages with atrocities reminiscent of 1936. The fighting came to an end on March 12th with the defeat of the Communists and all Communist commanders and commissars were relieved of their posts.

Negotiations for peace with the Nationalists began at once, and we must now turn again to the activities of General Franco and his army since they had swept Catalonia clear of their enemies and arrived at the Pyrenean frontier on February 10th. No time was lost and, after a victorious parade of 70,000 troops before General Franco in Barcelona, the armies left Catalonia for the south in preparation for further campaigns, but the Nationalists then stood aside for more than a month and watched the internecine conflicts and the gradual disintegration of their enemies in Madrid without undertaking any military activity against them.

The negotiations of the Council of Defense for peace began through fifth columnists[5] in Madrid and through two officers, Colonel Garija and Lieut. Colonel Ortega, who were sent to General Franco's headquarters at Burgos on March 23rd. The details given in various accounts of the negotiations are conflicting, but there is no doubt that they broke down at the last moment and hostilities were renewed on March 26th by Nationalist offensives under General Queipo de Llano on the Cordoba and Toledo fronts, which were rapidly successful and ended in a few days with the capture of Almadén, the center of the famous mercury mines.

The next day General Franco broadcast his conditions of surrender to the people and army in Madrid; broadly speaking they consisted of complete surrender and the laying down of arms with promises of generosity and pardon to those not guilty of murders and to those who had been misled into the civil war. The resultant action of the people and army showed how ready they were to welcome the Nationalists, for, without any official surrender, the Republican army melted away and its members mostly returned to their homes. The Republican air force was handed over on March 27th and on the next day the Nationalist troops peacefully entered the city. The jubilations of the populace and the sense of release exhibited by them both in Barcelona, Madrid and throughout Spain as it was progressively conquered by the Nationalists, were speaking evidence of the wishes and sympathies of the great majority of the people. All eyewitnesses gave testimony to this at the time and it is only necessary to refer to it here on account of subsequent attempts of interested propagandists to show that the bulk of the people of Spain were against the Nationalists. A further proof of where the sentiments of the people lay was that, as the Nationalists advanced throughout their campaigns, it was never necessary for them to guard their lines of communication behind their armies. This important fact has already been mentioned; all foreign observers on the spot, and among them the author, had confirmed that it was so.

The Council of Defense fled to Valencia, whence they followed their predecessors into exile abroad with the exception of the courageous

---

[5] This expression has become so common and of such universal use that it is interesting here to give its origin. In November 1936, General Franco's Nationalist armies advanced on Madrid in four columns. There were in Madrid a number of Nationalist sympathizers ready to assist General Franco and these were referred to as the "fifth column." It has now come to be generally used to mean traitors within any country working in the interests of that country's foreign enemies.

Julián Besteiro who, though holding no office, had gained great prestige by remaining in Madrid throughout the civil war, instead of seeking safety abroad as did most of the Republican politicians.

The surrender of Madrid was followed on March 29th by the surrender of the remaining provincial capitals and that date thus marks the end of the civil war.

XIV

The Rival Navies During the Civil War

The Spanish navy at the outbreak of the war was chiefly concentrated at Cartagena, though some ships were at Ferrol, most of them without crews; the former became the Republican navy and the latter the navy of the Nationalists. The navy had, during the Republican period, become saturated with communism and on July 21st. 1936, the crews of the ships at Cartagena set up soviets from the lower deck and massacred all their officers. This crime and the undenied story of how it was done might in other days have caused some countries to break off relations with a government which continued to employ such men, and to treat their ships as pirates. It was recounted that many of the officers were imprisoned and shot by the crews, and how the rest of them were cast into the sea to drown tied in couples' arm to arm and leg to leg.

It is necessary to know of this massacre of officers, for it eventually resulted in the almost complete neutralization of the Republican navy, while the Nationalists were able gradually to man their ships with the officers they already possessed, and with volunteers. Thus, at the end of a year's warfare, they had gained almost complete control of the sea, as far as Spanish forces were concerned, and the Government ships remained bottled up in Cartagena harbor most of the time.

At the outbreak of the war the Republican government had, at Cartagena and other ports, the battleship Jaime Primero, the cruiser Libertad, 16 destroyers and 12 submarines; they also had the cruisers Miguel de Cervantes and Menéndez Núñez, which were at sea, and whose crews mutinied and massacred their officers.

The Nationalists, on the other hand, had at Ferrol the cruiser Almirante Cervera, and the cruiser España, which was refitting, both of which had to be captured by shore forces from their crews, who had massacred most of their officers; they also had the new cruisers Canarias and Baleares, which were under construction and not completed, and the destroyer Velasco. At Cádiz they had four gunboats, and soon after the outbreak of war, the old cruiser República, which mutinied but had to surrender to the shore batteries and was afterwards renamed the Navarra.

The gunboat Dato at Ceuta was on the Nationalist side and covered the transport of troops from Morocco in the face and presence of the powerful Republican fleet, which it put to flight. Without the officers they had murdered the Republican sailors could not effectively fight with their ships, which continued to be an almost negligible element in the civil war until the dead officers were replaced by Russians.

The construction of the Canarias and Baleares was hurried forward at Ferrol and was an astonishing example of what can be achieved by enthusiasm and discipline, for the former cruiser was in commission by September 1936, and her sister ship four months later.

Manning difficulties as regards officers were overcome by the return from a foreign cruise of the naval training ship with 100 cadets, which were supplemented as time went on by the volunteers who came forward and were rapidly trained for service.

In the first days and months of the war, the Republican navy was able to blockade the Straits of Gibraltar and hinder the passage of General Franco's legionaries and Moors, but within two months for all practical purposes it had ceased to appear in the Straits, and it made no further interference with the passage of troops.

In September 1936, the Nationalist destroyer Velasco sank the Republican submarine B.6. near Gijón, and a few days later in the Straits the Republican destroyer Gravina was sunk and the destroyer Almirante Ferrándiz seriously damaged in a fight with the Nationalist cruisers Canarias and Almirante Cervera. Though there were a few subsequent actions, which will be recalled later in their proper sequence, this engagement in the Straits of Gibraltar marks the passing of the command of the sea, as between the Spanish forces, into the hands of the Nationalist navy.

On November 22nd, the Republican cruiser Miguel de Cervantes was torpedoed, and it was reported that it was the work of submarine B.5. which deserted from the Republicans and surrendered at a Nationalist port on the following day. International propaganda at once launched the report that the damage was done by an Italian submarine, but no atom of evidence was ever produced to substantiate the accusation. It was an illuminating fact, visible to every observer throughout the war that this propaganda made constant efforts to exploit incidents of this sort, and also those of the attacks on H.M.S. Havoc and the German battleship Deutschland to irritate and acerbate feelings between the Mediterranean powers, possibly with a view to bringing about an international incident, which might provoke a world war.

In December 1936, the Republican submarine C.3 foundered at Málaga, where she was later salved and repaired by the Nationalists; this was the submarine that torpedoed Russian ships in the Aegean Sea. Two other submarines, C.5 and C.6 fell into the hands of the Nationalists during the year, and the Republican destroyers Churruca and Almirante Valdés were damaged.

On April 30th, 1937, the Nationalist cruiser España hit a mine off the coast of Biscay and sank, while in June 1937 the Republican battleship Jaime Primera suffered an explosion on board and sank at her moorings in Cartagena harbor, but was subsequently refloated.

At the end of the first year of the war, the position was that the Republican fleet was inoperative, while the Nationalists were able to blockade parts of the Spanish coast and intercept many of the merchantmen destined for their enemies. They were able to do this notwithstanding the new nonintervention policy carried out by foreign navies, which refused them the usual rights of belligerents, and convoyed their enemy's ships up to the three-mile limit, whence they were usually able to make a dash into port.

In September 1937, there was a naval engagement off the coast of Algiers between the Nationalist cruiser Baleares and the Republican cruisers Libertad and Menéndez Núñez with some destroyers and armed trawlers. The engagement was inconclusive, but the Libertad was seriously damaged, and sent to refit, while the Baleares had a hole through her funnel.

On March 6th, 1938, another engagement took place 70 miles off Cape Palos, when the Nationalist cruiser Baleares was torpedoed and sunk with the loss of some 300 lives and British destroyers picked up and saved 365 men. These engagements showed that the naval forces of the Republic, like their army, had somewhat improved in fighting qualities, though they did not further challenge the Nationalist superiority at sea.

The Commander-in-Chief of the Nationalist navy was throughout Admiral Cervera, the son of the gallant admiral who sailed his squadron of antiquated ships to meet certain defeat and destruction from the modern and powerful American squadron at Santiago de Cuba in the Spanish-American War; his chief of staff was Vice-Admiral Moreno. The Nationalist naval supremacy stood them in good stead, for it enabled them to capture a large number of ships carrying airplanes, arms, and all sorts of war supplies for the Republican ports. Indeed, a very large part of General Franco's arms and munitions came from this source and were thus provided at the expense of his enemies. By the end of the first year of the war, some fifty cargoes had been captured, and a further fifty by May 1938 these cargoes came mostly from Russia, France, Czechoslovakia and Mexico, and from some other countries on a lesser scale.

The enormous value of these captures can be gauged by quoting two examples. On the Sylvia, captured in the Straits of Gibraltar, were 250 machine-guns, 28,000,000 cartridges with many mortars, bombs, etc. On the Mar Cantábrico, captured on the high seas off Bilbao, 13,000,000 cartridges and thousands of rifles.

XV

COMMUNIST AND OTHER ORIGINS OF THE REVOLUTION AND CIVIL WAR, 1920–38

A curious situation had arisen owing to the fact that, notwithstanding their success, the Communists and the sympathizers with the Republican government in the civil war endeavored to prove by every means in their power that communism had little to do either with the revolution or the war. It is consequently necessary to present the evidence available on this subject, for it appears to the author to be overwhelming in proving that the Comintern of Russia was the chief instigator and the chief upholder of both.

Reasons for the desire to obscure the true situation and for the success in deceiving the greater part of the world were that communism found it convenient and successful to work under the surface, and that the Comintern, as was openly expressed in its publications, decided on the subtle and clever policy of the anti-Fascist and pro-democracy slogan, which sought to identify communism and socialism with democracy and to qualify as Fascist everyone who was opposed to it; its widespread propaganda was able to inculcate successfully this idea and gain extensive support, for it caused very many people to believe that in Spain the Spanish people were being attacked by Fascists and were struggling for their freedom against an invasion of Germans and Italians instead of, what was obviously the fact on the basis of all evidence, that the Spanish people had been attacked by communism and were struggling to free themselves.

It is best first to present the evidence to show that it was the openly expressed intention of the Comintern to bring about first a revolution in Spain, then a Popular Front Government, which is an express invention of communist theory, and then the civil war, as a prelude to the dictatorship of the proletariat.

It is not the intention here to quote verbatim from the various publications because this has already been done in various French and English books, and more especially in G. M. Godden's "Conflict in Spain"; it will suffice to quote a few of the authorities among the legion of publications: "The Communist International," the official organ of the Comintern. The reports of the 4th and subsequent Congress of the Communist International and especially of the 7th Congress held in Moscow in August 1935, and considered to be the masterpiece of Dimitrov, the Secretary-General of the Comintern. As well as the resolutions and decisions of the various World Congresses of the Red International of Labor Unions published by the R.I.L.U. in London and Moscow, and the reports of the 11th and 12th Plenum of the Executive Committee of the Communist International, London, 1931 and 1932, and the International Press Correspondence, of Imprecor, the Comintern propagandist agency, 1935.

The *Times* article, "Comintern," May 3rd, 1938. So much for the words of the Comintern, which is, as all know, inseparable from the Soviet government. We will now proceed to show how it carried out its declared policy by deeds.

Some knowledge of the planting of Continental Freemasonry (Grand Orient, which has nothing to do with British Freemasonry) in Spain after the Napoleonic wars, the planting there of organizations of both Marx and Bakunin breeds in the 70's of last century, and the influence of both in all the troubles and disorders of Spain in 1891, 1909, 1917, 1920–23 is necessary as a background.

During a residence in Barcelona from 1921 onwards the author was able to watch the traffic of agitators, propaganda and ideas between Moscow and Barcelona, at that time the headquarters in Spain of both the anarchists, the followers of Bakunin, and the communists, the followers of Marx. The very men who in the early 1920's were obscure agitators became the big men behind the scenes after the revolution in 1931 and the open leaders after the victory of the Popular Front and the beginning of the civil war. Throughout this period communists, anarchists, and socialists, though periodically quarrelling, followed the policy and dictates of Moscow.

Such men were Durutti, Maurin (both of them later assassinated or killed in the fighting), Peiró, Pestana, Prieto, Álvarez del Vayo and García Oliver, all of them members of or closely connected with the Anarchist syndicate C.N.T. or the Socialist U.G.T., which was later captured by the Communists. There was also Andreu Nin, the leader of that section of communism called P.O.U.M., the followers of Trotsky, which in 1937, suffered persecution and suppression, as shown by the British communist Mr. McGovern of the I.L.P. in his pamphlet "Terror in Spain." All these names were well known in Spain during the 1920's as those of men going backwards and forwards between Barcelona and Moscow.

From small beginnings, but through patient and subtle work underground in the labor movements, they possessed themselves first of the syndicates and then, by the votes of the latter, they gained control of the government of Spain. Álvarez del Vayo, for years recognized as the agent of the Comintern in Spain, finally became Foreign Minister and Prieto the Minister of Defense.

The writer of this history lived at the time in Barcelona and was so much impressed with the meagerness and misrepresentation of Spanish affairs in the British press, even in its most reputable organs, that he sought a London newspaper that would publish his Spanish information and found hospitality for his news in the columns of the *Morning Post*. As contemporary writings about what actually took place should be acceptable as valuable evidence, a series of extracts from his dispatches are here given from the files of the *Morning Post*:

> June 30th, 1930: Communist professional agitators, who recently engineered strikes in Andalusia, are trying to foment strikes in Barcelona.

> Barcelona, November 10th, 1930: The general strike continues here... There is no doubt that the strike here and in Madrid is brought about by the communist Sindicato Único.

> Perpignan, May 12th, 1931: Statements such as 'the number of communists is small' or 'the Spanish people are not communists at heart' are true, but cannot be considered as conclusive with the examples of Russia and Mexico before one, for in Russia, a handful of communists succeeded in establishing bolshevism over 150 million people. By far the most militant and strongest element in labor in Spain today is the Confederación Nacional de Trabajadores (C.N.T.), which is affiliated with the Sindicato Único of Barcelona; this syndicate is the tail which wags the dog and is purely communistic in its doctrines, publications, and methods.

> Barcelona, Oct. 20th 1931 (Article reproduced in Appendix I).
> Barcelona, Jan. 21th, 1932: A revolutionary movement has broken out over the whole district lying between the Pyrenees and Barcelona. A communist Republic has been proclaimed by the revolutionaries in the towns to the North of Barcelona, where the Town Halls have been seized.

Perpignan, March 31st, 1932: RED ORGANIZATIONS IN SPAIN, OPPOSING BODIES WITH ONE AIM. MOSCOW THE HUB. Complicating the already confused political situation, and continually disturbing labor and industry, are a network of organizations professing creeds with different names and apparently in conflict with each other. They are all inspired by the doctrines of Karl Marx and Engels with variations, and all employ the same weapons of the strike, picketing, terrorism, pistolmen, and revolutionary newspapers and literature, using a common vocabulary and phraseology. The names of these different organizations are:

1. F.A.I. or Federación Anarquista Ibérica (Iberian Anarchist Federation), which appears to be affiliated with the International Anarchist Federation.
2. C.N.T. or Confederación Nacional de Trabajadores (National Federation of Workers), which appears to be affiliated with the organizations of the same name existing in France and other countries. This organization is commonly called the Sindicato Único, and names its creed Syndicalist-Anarchist.
3. U.G.T. or Unión General de Trabajadores (General Workers' Union), which is the official Socialist workmen's syndicate in Spain, supported by the Socialist Parliamentary Party. This organization professes to be violently opposed to Moscow and to depend on the Amsterdam International.
4. Partido Communista Español (Spanish Communist Party) which owns open allegiance to the Comintern of Moscow.
5. The Bloque Obrero y Campesino (Workers and Peasants Block) which is also openly connected with Moscow, and use the Red Flag with the hammer and sickle at its meetings.
6. The Sindicato Libre (Free Syndicate) of obscure affiliation, originally supported by the pre-dictatorship governments as a counter to the Sindicato Único, but since the revolution, persecuted by the Republican government.

All these organizations are definitely anti-capitalistic, disruptive of government. and destructive of law and order, and though in minor directions they profess different creeds and publish pamphlets to propagate them, and are professedly at enmity with each other, yet the result of their activities is so identical that it is a convincing probability that their origin and inspiration are also identical.

Where does the money come from to pay for all these activities? A reasonable analysis of the situation would appear to be that all the above organizations, or most of them, radiate like the spokes of a wheel from Moscow, which is the hub.

Perpignan, Nov. 1st, 1932: The question of Monarchy and Republic is no longer the dividing line between the parties... The issue now is the quarrel between Capitalism and Socialism, between bourgeois rule and mob rule, between God and Karl Marx.

Barcelona, Jan. 3rd and 4th, 1933: An attempt to burn the airfield of Barcelona was discovered and frustrated yesterday... The police search of the premises resulted in the discovery of documents which reveal an extensive plot to bring about an anarchist revolution in Spain. It would appear that the most militant forces of disorder in Spain have changed their description from communist to anarchist, though the people, their methods and objects, are the same as formerly.

Barcelona, March 13th, 1934: At any moment, but most certainly within the next few months, the world may witness the conflict taking place in Spain between Marxism and Christianity take on a new and perhaps a very violent phase. In many countries the fight for domination between the Marxist forces, call these what you will, and the rest of the community has been waged with rather confused motives and issues, but in no country is the issue such a simple and a clear-cut one as it is in Spain.

These reports, coming from a British businessman on the spot, were soon forgotten, but they are accurate historical evidence proved by subsequent events, and the conflict, foretold in the *Morning Post* alone of all British newspapers, broke out with the attempt in October, 1934, to set up a Soviet in Asturias and with the simultaneous revolt against the government in Barcelona. Both were suppressed, as related in another chapter, without any punishment being meted out to the instigators. Comintern activities continued until they were successful in the next step of orthodox communist action, the establishment and capture of parliamentary power through the Popular Front which took place in February 1936.

As already indicated, it was part of the technique of communism to work behind the scenes (this was called by Dimitrov the policy of the "Trojan horse,"), to support socialist and more moderate left-wing candidates to parliament with their votes, instead of presenting candidates of their own, until the time comes when as the "Popular Front" they can seize power. Then there was to come the next and last step in communist action, the dictatorship of the proletariat. Thus, Señor Azaña, the president of the Spanish Republic, who until he sided with the communists appeared to be the counterpart of Kerensky, stated in a speech in July 1938, that the danger of communism had never existed because in February 1936, the communists had only sixteen deputies. This is exactly the argument insinuated by communist strategy and publications, but it can be met and vanquished by this question:

"If the smallness of the number of communist deputies proved that the movement was not communist, did not the complete absence of any Fascist deputy or candidate also prove that there was no Fascist menace such as Señor Azaña and his friends sought to prove to the world?" What is sauce for the goose is sauce for the gander!

Again, when the government of Señor Largo Caballero was followed in May, 1937, by the government of Dr. Negrín, with Señor Prieto as Minister of Defense, it was made to look as if a more moderate regime had come into power; but on that occasion there is the evidence of one of the closely censored and controlled newspapers of Republican Spain. *La Vanguardia*, May 20th, 1937, says distinctly: "The trick by which they (the Communist party) do not appear in the new government with any greater preponderance than before is too naive to deceive anyone." Furthermore, it says that the change represents a complete success for the Communists.

The Communists and Socialists represented by the U.G.T. in 1938, gained more and more the upper hand in the situation by establishing an iron reign of terror and a complete system of informers throughout the army and the civil population. The leaders of the P.O.U.M. (United Marxist Party) had long since been "liquidated" on the plea that they were Trotskyists, to the great indignation of the British Independent Labour Party, with whom they were affiliated. The communist McGovern of the I.L.P. made a visit to Barcelona on behalf of his Spanish friends and returned to England to publish an account stating that republican Spain, in return for assistance in arms, had allowed the Comintern and the Soviet government to establish a bloodthirsty tyranny under an international Cheka, which proceeded with "arrests, abductions, tortures and assassinations."

In the same way the anarchist C.N.T., up to that time the most powerful of the revolutionary organizations, was obliged to unite with and succumb to its immemorial enemy the U.G.T., which was the Socialist-Communist syndicate. Thus the divided authority and duplicate organizations which had existed since the beginning of the war, were replaced by a unity of command, which controlled all things civil and military, while the puppets, the president of the Republic, Azaña, the president of Catalonia, Companys, and their governments continued to function superficially as a facade for the reign of terror, which they doubtless feared as much as the humblest citizen.

The popular tribunals, which are also described in another chapter, gave terrible testimony to the evidence and functioning of this reign of terror. *La Vanguardia* day by day published columns headed "Republican Justice", recounting the names of people condemned to death by the Tribunals and sent out to be shot for all sorts of offences ranging from desertion to non-approval of the Republican government (*desafectos al régimen*); as many as forty condemnations to death were reported in this newspaper on one day and other death sentences were reported almost daily. Also daily there were published the lists of people in business who were fined enormous sums or sent to prison for thirty years by the same popular tribunals for such offences as hoarding food stocks or selling goods at prices above the official ones. This was the state of affairs in the last half of the year 1938; it is necessary to emphasize this in view of the propagandist attempt to show that the earlier excesses had ceased and that a more moderate and orderly policy was pursued in the later stages of the conflict. Señor de Madariaga, himself a Republican holding portfolios in pre-civil war governments of the Republic, shows conclusively in his history ("Spain," p. 402) how the Communists progressively acquired possession of power by a series of steps. The first had been the formation of Señor Caballero's cabinet, with their own henchman, Señor Álvarez del Vayo, at the foreign office. The second, the expulsion of the same Señor Largo Caballero, found too impervious to Communist suggestions. The third was the expulsion of Don Indalecio Prieto, who so far had walked along with them for his own ends but would not consent to walk behind them for their own ends.

Thereafter, Dr. Negrín formed a government in which he and Álvarez del Vayo exercised their control to the satisfaction of Moscow, which thereupon showed its satisfaction by a renewal of the provision of supplies, which it had begun to cut off.

In previous chapters it has been related how, even in the earlier period of the war, the Russian ambassador took part in cabinet meetings and how progressively Russian generals and Communist commissars permeated both the military and the civil controls. Up to the very last days of the civil war, Dr. Negrín and the Communists demonstrated their loyalty to each other, until both were ejected by the defection of General Miaja and Colonel Casado's formation of the Council of Defense, which fought and defeated them in the bloody internecine battles in Madrid in

March, 1939.

Further convincing evidence of the Russian Communist control of the Republican army and war effort from the earliest days of the civil war is to be found in the book "Men and Politics" by Louis Fischer. He was a prominent American newspaper correspondent, who had lived for many years in Russia, went to Spain in 1936, served for a time in the International Brigade, acted as an intermediary between Madrid and Moscow and was in the confidence of and on intimate terms with leading Republican politicians and especially with Dr. Negrín. As he was an ardent supporter of the Republican cause and an equally bitter opponent of General Franco and the Nationalists, his evidence has all the greater value.

He shows in his book that as early as October, 1936, the Russian O.G.P.U. was functioning in Spain; that before General Franco's unsuccessful attack on Madrid in November, 1936, military affairs were in the hands of the Russian General Goriev; that Russian tanks manned by Russians were in action in Spain in October, 1936; and that the International Brigade under Russian officers was operating in Spain before any Italians or Germans had arrived to assist General Franco. To add to all this overwhelming mass of evidence of Comintern Soviet instigation and control of the civil war, there was the evidence of returned International Brigadiers, the evidence of Mr. Stalin's letter to Señor Largo Caballero published in Señor de Madariaga's history, and the evidence of the published correspondence of Señor Prieto, Dr. Negrín and others of the fallen Republican politicians after they had begun to squabble in exile.

XVI

GENERAL FRANCO

The name of General Francisco Franco Bahamonde was unknown to the public outside Spain until 1936. His fame, as far as the world in general was concerned, only began with his leadership of the revolt of Spain against the Republican government in July of that year, but he had long been known in Spain itself and to prominent French staff officers as a most brilliant and successful soldier.

To look at, he was at that time handsome, dark eyed and dark haired, of medium height, with a small military moustache and somewhat bald on his forehead. His eyes were bright, clear, and smiling and he appeared to possess tranquility, imperturbability and that outward sign of efficiency—time at his disposal to receive and discuss matters with a foreign visitor, as he did with the author of this history, even during the time that his armies were fighting on 1,000 miles of battlefront.

His history and career bear witness to his personal courage, mercy and industry, his military and administrative ability and to his qualities of leadership and judgment of character. In the early days of his access to power these qualities were accompanied by a modesty, which is not usually a characteristic of dictators, and he showed no tendency towards self-advertisement and stage play such as was the stock-in-trade of Hitler and Mussolini. He was a devout and practicing Christian, and the historian is at a loss to discover evidence for the picture of him that international propaganda and the left-wing press painted, portraying him as a baby-killer, a coward and a puppet of German and Italian soldiers. As the years went by, however, the effect of an almost absolute power became increasingly evident and he seemed to adopt some of the minor characteristics common to dictators.

General Franco inherited a fighting tradition, for his father was a sailor and commandant of the naval port and dockyard of Ferrol in Galicia. There were three sons in the Franco family, all destined to hold prominent places in the history of their country. First, there was Nicolás, the eldest, who went into the navy, and had attained the rank of captain when the civil war began, when he became for the first year of war the confidential assistant of his younger brother Francisco, the Generalissimo, at his headquarters in Salamanca. The third brother Ramón went into the air force and in 1926 attained world fame by being the first airman to fly across the Atlantic; during the dictatorship of Primo de Rivera, Ramón Franco engaged in revolutionary activities: he and General Queipo de Llano were the leaders in an attempted and abortive rising in December, 1930, at the airfield of Cuatro Vientos, from which he and the General escaped to Portugal by airplane and were exiles until the end of the dictatorship. He subsequently became his brother's chief commander of the air force in Mallorca during the war; both he and General Queipo are examples of how some of the left-wing elements in the army joined with their brother officers in 1936 in their revolt against communism and anarchy.

Francisco Franco joined the infantry academy at the Alcázar of Toledo in 1907 at the age of fourteen; at the age of seventeen he obtained his commission and in 1912 went to Morocco, where the war against the Sultan was in progress and where General Berenguer was reorganizing the "Regulars," as the Moorish troops of the Spanish army are called. In this campaign Franco gained great distinction on the field of battle and was made a captain at the age of twenty, when he took command of a company of "Regulars."

During this period of his career, as in fact throughout his life, he was noted as a constant and untiring student of strategy and military history; after receiving serious wounds in the battle at Buit, he was promoted to the rank of commandant (the equivalent of major) at the age of twenty-three. Then, as the youngest major in the army, he spent two years with the Principe regiment at Oviedo in Asturias, where in 1920. he became engaged to Señorita Carmen Polo, to whom he was married in 1923, after an absence of two years of strenuous work and fighting in Morocco.

In 1920, he left Oviedo for Morocco, where he became the chief assistant of the gallant General Millán-Astray in his formation of the Spanish foreign legion, which comprised the only long-term soldiers in the Spanish army; the tradition of the legionaries for bravery, discipline and endurance in the Moroccan war, and subsequently in the civil war, is an outstanding testimony to the legion's founders. When General Franco headed the counterrevolution in 1936, the war-scarred Millán-Astray immediately put himself under the orders of his former subordinate, a tribute to the characters of both men.

The following is a translation of a part of the "Legionary's creed," which inspires the Foreign Legion, and gives a sidelight on the characters of its founders:

> The spirit of the legion is unique and unsurpassable; it consists of attacking blindly and fiercely and getting as near to the enemy as possible.
>
> The spirit of comradeship consists in never abandoning a man in the field of battle until all are killed.
>
> The spirit of friendship must be sealed by an oath between every two men.
>
> The spirit of mutual assistance. At the cry of 'To me the Legion' wherever it may be uttered, everyone must rush to the help of the legionary who has called and help him, whatever the reason may be.
>
> The marching spirit. A legionary must never say that he is tired until he falls exhausted.
>
> The spirit of suffering and endurance. A legionary must never complain of fatigue, pain, hunger, thirst or sleepiness; he must do every sort of work, dig trenches, pull guns and wagons, be detached from his regiment, take part in convoys, and, in fact, work in anything he is ordered to.
>
> The spirit of discipline consists in fulfilling duty and obeying unto death.
>
> The spirit of dying. To die in battle is the greatest honor.

In 1922 Franco was decorated with the military medal for service in Morocco; in 1923, at the age of thirty-one, he became Lieut. Colonel of the Legion, and as Colonel he commanded the Legion under General Primo de Rivera in the landing and capture of Alhucemas, at which he acted with great bravery. The Moroccan war, which had for so long drained the resources of Spain, was brought to a successful end in 1926 by General Primo de Rivera, acting in connection with, the French against the Moorish leader Abd el-Krim, and Franco found himself Brigadier General at the age of thirty-three, with a great reputation in the eyes of his general, the dictator, and of the Spanish nation. He was given the second military medal and made Knight Commander of the Legion of Honor and granted the badge of Military and Naval Merit of France.

He was then chosen by Primo de Rivera to direct the new military academy at Zaragoza, for which he was so well fitted that the academy gained the reputation of being one of the best in Europe. He remained at the academy until 1931, with an interval during which he took a course for higher officers at Versailles, where he also gained a great reputation.

In 1931 came the revolution and the establishment of the Republic with, subsequently, Azaña's purge of the army of monarchists, right-wing supporters, and non-masons (Orient). Franco always refused to take part in politics, saying that "soldiers should stand aside from politics and think of the nation," but he was nevertheless removed by the government from the academy and relegated to an unimportant post in Coruña, where he stayed until 1933; he was then made Military Governor of the Balearic Islands.

In 1934 came the communist revolt in Asturias and Barcelona, and Franco was called to Madrid, whence he directed the operations which led to the suppression of the revolt. After a year as General-in-Command in Morocco he became Chief of the General Staff under Gil-Robles, who was Minister of War. The discipline and organizations of the army had greatly deteriorated during the three years of republican government, but, as a result of much hard work on the part of General Franco, they had been in part reestablished when the Popular Front seized power in February, 1936. He was then virtually exiled, owing to a fresh army purge, and sent to the Canary Islands, to reappear in Morocco on July 19th, 1937, in the airplane provided by an English sportsman, to head the revolt against communism and the Popular Front government.

He had already, a month previously, sent a reasoned warning to the Minister of War, pointing out the dangers to his country caused by the failure to maintain law and order and by the indignities at the hands of the mob to which the army and army officers were being submitted, but no notice was taken of his warning, and, as stated in an earlier chapter, the army officers were preparing to save themselves and their country, which was visibly and rapidly sliding into anarchy and communism, in the only way that seemed possible—namely by revolt. This warning was contained in a letter dated June 23rd, which is so illuminating regarding the condition of the army after Azaña's attempts to purge it and destroy its tradition, that it is necessary to reproduce it. The letter is also important evidence in the destruction of the false theory that the civil war was caused, not by the complete failure of the government to govern, but by a rising of Fascist generals under General Franco greedy for power and dictatorship. The word fascism advanced greatly in use and misuse during subsequent years, but at that time it had no meaning or use as applied to Spain. The letter reads as follows:

HONORABLE MINISTER:

So serious is the state of uneasiness which the recent military decrees seem to have produced among the officers of the army, that I would incur a grave responsibility and disloyalty were I not to inform you of my impressions of the state of the army at the present moment, and of the dangers to its discipline brought about by the absence of inner satisfaction and the moral and material uneasiness which can be well discerned without detailed investigation among both officers and petty officers. The recent decrees reinstating in the army the generals and officers sentenced in Catalonia (for their participation in the revolution of October 1934), and the more recent decree transferring officers by ministerial appointment to positions formally allotted by the rule of seniority, a rule which had not been broken since the reorganization of the army in June, 1917, have awakened a spirit of uneasiness among the great majority of the army. The news of the incidents which took place in Alcalá de Henares, and the disturbances and provocations on the part of extremist elements which preceded them, together with the reassortment of the garrisons, have undoubtedly produced a feeling of dissatisfaction. This feeling, unfortunately and crudely manifested in moments of confused thinking, has been interpreted as a collective transgression of army discipline producing serious consequences among the generals and officers who participated in those acts, and occasioning sorrow and regret among the ranks of the army.

All this, your Excellency, apparently reveals either that the information which may possibly be reaching you in this respect is incomplete, or the ignorance which those elements of the military, who are collaborating with you, may have with respect to the internal morale of the army. I should not wish this letter to detract from the good names of those who inform you and advise you in the military field, for they may sin through ignorance, but I do feel that I can say, with all the responsibility of my position and of my vocation, that the decrees so far published show obviously that the information which prompted their promulgation is contrary to reality and at times even contrary to the interests of the nation, presenting the army to you in a vicious light far removed from reality.

Those who have been recently removed from their commands and thus thwarted in their careers, are for the most part generals of brilliant record and highly respected in the army. These, as well as others of great trustworthiness and distinction, have been replaced by men who are considered by fully 90 percent of their comrades-in-arms to be of inferior qualifications. Those who approach our present rulers to flatter them and to demand the reward for their collaboration are not necessarily more loyal to them, for those removed distinguished themselves in former years both under the dictatorship and under the monarchy. Those who paint the army as hostile to the Republic are not telling the truth; those who are accusing the army of conspiracies in their confused passions are deceiving you; those who are misrepresenting the uneasiness, the dignity, and the patriotism of the army, making it appear as the symbol of conspiracy and dissatisfaction, are rendering a miserable service to their country.

Out of the absence of fairness and justice in the public service in the administration of the army in 1917, there arose the Juntas of Military Defense. It could be virtually said that today, in spirit at least, the military juntas still exist. The writings which are clandestinely appearing with the initials U.M.E. and U.MR. are convincing symptoms of their existence and heralds of future civil strife if steps are not taken to prevent it. I consider it easy to prevent it by measures of consideration, impartiality, and justice. That movement of collective insubordination of 1917, provoked in large part by favoritism and arbitrary caprice in the matter of promotions, was produced under circumstances similar to, though perhaps worse than, those which exist today in the ranks of the army. I will not hide from your Excellency the dangers inherent in this state of collective opinion at the present moment, when it is accompanied by professional uneasiness, an uneasiness felt by all good Spaniards confronted by the grave problems facing their country.

Though many miles removed from the Peninsula[6], reports do not fail to reach me, through various channels, which affirm that the state of mind which can be noticed here exists equally, if not to a greater extent, not only in the peninsular garrisons, but also among all the military forces charged with maintaining public order. As one who knows the meaning of discipline, to the study of which I have devoted many years, I can assure you that such is the spirit of justice that reigns in the ranks of the military, that any harsh measure which is unjustified produces self-defeating consequences in the rank and file of the garrisons and slanderous accusations. I feel it my duty to bring to your attention something that I consider of grave significance to the discipline of the army, which your Excellency can easily verify if you obtain your information from those generals and commanding officers who, free from political passions, live in close contact with their subordinates and are always mindful of their intimate problems and feelings.

Your devoted subordinate greets you most respectfully,

FRANCISCO FRANCO.

---

[6] General Franco was in the Canary Islands.

General Franco conducted with success the rising of the army in Morocco, the crossing of the Straits in the face of the Spanish fleet, which had murdered its officers and joined the Republican government, and the march northwards of the Army of the South until it was held at Madrid. It is probable that he would in any case have been the unchallenged Commander-in-Chief, but the deaths first of General Sanjurjo and then of General Mola left him the undisputed leader and on October 1st, 1936, in Burgos he was invested by the Junta of National Defense with the title of Head of the Government and of the Spanish State.

General Franco's history throughout the civil war and throughout the difficult years that followed is the history of Spain itself, which, with his policies and speeches, is outlined in other chapters of this book.

Suffice it to say that, after the conclusion of the civil war, General Franco became increasingly the national hero and leader and adopted the name "El Caudillo" (Leader), probably in imitation of his Axis friends. As time went on, though taking a leading part in all public functions, he appeared to become more and more difficult of access, even to the foreign diplomats, and it were strange indeed if so much power and popularity had not affected his character, though external signs of swollen pride, such as were exhibited by his contemporary dictators of Germany and Italy, were not evident.

In Spanish internal affairs he maintained his hold and control over the various elements that composed the body politic of Spain, the army, the church, the Falange, the monarchists and the traditionalists, though the two latter became increasingly restless as he appeared to forget that they were his chief supporters during the civil war, and to look more and more to extreme Falange as the main pillar of the regime. On the other hand, the dismissal of his brother-in-law, Señor Serrano Suñer, and shuffles among the higher Falange posts showed that he sought to balance the conflicting elements.

As time went on, it was increasingly evident that he had been unsuccessful in uniting his fellow Spaniards and that his policies had failed in his great task of creating a Spain "One, Great and Free." A student of history and the Spanish character cannot be surprised at this failure and must agree that General Franco had attempted the impossible and failed as General Primo de Rivera had done before him; they were both inspired by sound and logical ideals, which broke down owing to the weaknesses of human nature. To the student and observer, complete Spanish unity appears as a mirage, the Spaniard, with all his very noble characteristics, is so intensely individualistic that complete unity of action is seldom attained, and he is also restless and often ungrateful. Whether or not that analysis is accurate, General Franco's regime became increasingly unpopular, especially in respect of the Falange, which became riddled with corruption and used gestapo methods. As described in their chronological position in subsequent chapters, in proportion to the growth of the unpopularity of the Franco/Falange regime was the growth of the desire for a restoration of the monarchy; as seen in General Franco's early speeches, he stated his desire that Spain should return to the monarchy at some future date but in his 1942–44 speeches such references were notably absent; the growing momentum of monarchial opinion was illustrated by the three manifestos or petitions to General Franco on the subject in 1943, first by a prominent group of Spaniards headed by the Duke of Alba, secondly by five of the most famous generals and thirdly by over 100 university professors.

In November, 1944, in an interview with *United Press* he stated that the return of the monarchy was not a question of the moment but that, when the existing difficult European situation had changed and if it appeared necessary for the greatness of Spain, then would be the time to install a monarch. He added that it would be a different type of monarchy from that which had existed before. He confirmed this attitude in a speech in July 1945. In foreign affairs it must be acknowledged that during the early days of the Second World War General Franco proved himself as astute and able a statesman as he had proved himself a soldier. Judging from his speeches and actions, he was very well disposed towards the Axis powers and wished them to be victorious, disliked intensely anything to do with communism and Marxist socialism and mistrusted liberalism and the English and French parliamentary systems. But he was first and all the time a patriot and intent on keeping Spain out of the war. He was successful, though it required great subtlety and at times meant the offending of both sides. His neutrality, though inspired purely by the interests of Spain and by nothing else, was incidentally of immeasurable advantage to the cause of the United Nations.

His regime became more and more unpopular abroad, through misrepresentation, and brought serious repercussions on his country; both the incidents of the San Francisco conference and the manifesto of the Infante Don Juan, which are described on other pages, were adequate proofs of that unpopularity.

Justice must be done to General Franco for the merciful manner in which he conducted affairs in two notable directions, and this is especially necessary because both were used unjustly as weapons by foreign critics with which to belabor his regime.

The first of these was his use of airplanes in the civil war in the bombing of his enemy's towns. The condition of Barcelona, Madrid, and Valencia at the end of the war proved how restrained had been his action in refusing to destroy those cities except as far as was essential for the success of his military objectives. In Madrid small damage was done by bombing except to the University City, which was in the front line of battle. In Barcelona and Valencia little except the ports and oil installations suffered serious damage. This restraint was only appreciated later by contrast with the destruction of cities in Europe and Japan during the world war. The exaggeration of the case of Guernica has been exposed on another page.

The other matter was the number and treatment of prisoners in Spanish prisons and concentration camps. It must be remembered that during the terror in the Republican territory at least 300,000 people were assassinated; this meant a large number of criminals and the survivors clamored for punishment of the murderers. Naturally in such a situation the prisons were full, though the figures of millions given by propagandists were fantastic and unsupported by any evidence: the Minister of Justice declared officially in 1945 that there had never been more than 270,000 prisoners everywhere at one. There is no evidence that those condemned and executed were tried otherwise than in properly constituted courts in contrast to the spectacle of the self-elected popular tribunals, which condemned and shot their thousands under the Republican regime and in happy contrast to the mass purges, assassinations and internments in Germany and Russia.

In 1940 a system of substitution of labor for penal sentences in prisons was instituted for those condemned for less serious offences and as time went on ever-increasing numbers of sentences were remitted under a ticket-of-leave system. Doubtless injustices were committed, and it would be strange if it were not so; they occur also in all countries. In subsequent years there were progressive remittances of sentences and liberations of prisoners condemned for political and minor criminal offences until in May 1945, there was a general amnesty for purely political offences.

The treatment of prisoners and the conditions of Spanish prisons were also the objects of much denunciation and abuse, but escaped or discharged foreign prisoners, who published their experiences, such as the Belgian journalist, d'Ildewalle in "An Interlude in Spain" and a Jew refugee Eli Rubin, who with his wife sampled many of them during a long period, did not give an unfavorable account of the prisons; though the conditions they described were often harsh and uncomfortable, that would be expected in the prisons of all countries, but there was no evidence of the persecution and starvation that was prevalent in the camps of Germany and Russia to which Spanish prisons were unfairly likened. Imprisonment and internments in Spain saved the lives of tens of thousands of refugees and, thanks to the complacence of the Spanish authorities, tens of thousands of British, French, Belgian, Canadian and Polish soldiers or escapees made their way to England to fight against Germany. As to the unfounded rumor of Jewish persecution, M. Eli Rubin after nearly three years in various prisons told the writer that there was none and that the interrogatory of a foreign prisoner on entering the prison did not even include a declaration of either his religion or his political tenets.

XVII

THE RELIGIOUS PERSECUTION AND THE CHURCH

It has been set forth in previous chapters with all the weight of the evidence of proved facts that the revolution in Spain was initiated and fostered by communism. One of the chief items in the communist and Marxist-socialist programs is the extirpation of all religion, and especially of the Christian religion, and the establishment of an anti-God regime; all communist textbooks say so openly, and they are at the disposal of all the world, so it is quite useless to deny it. Far, then, from it being surprising that religious persecution of the vilest type was evident in Spain, it would have been astonishing if it had not been so.

The first manifestations of this religious persecution took place at the advent of the Republic in April 1931, when some 100 churches and convents in various towns of Spain were burnt, and for some weeks in many places it was dangerous for people to show themselves in clerical garb in the streets. The author resided in Spain at the time and personally witnessed that this was so.

That this was not merely the uncontrolled action of irresponsible mobs seems to be proved by the anti-religious legislation that was immediately begun and continued by the Republican government. Laws were passed, promulgated, and put into practice (*vide* the Spanish equivalent of Hansard, the *"Diario de las Sesiones de las Cortes"*):

1. Secularizing all education and forbidding any priests to teach in the schools.
2. Nationalizing the churches and depriving the secular clergy of their already exiguous stipends.
3. Confiscating the properties of the religious orders and closing their schools.
4. Expelling the Jesuits.

Some of this legislation was modified by subsequent less extreme Republican governments, but in general it remained unaltered and most of the modifications were canceled on the advent to power of the Popular

Front.

The following quotations from a dispatch from the author to the *Morning Post*, on June 2nd, 1931, is illuminating. After detailing the events it says:

> One is compelled to draw the conclusion that the Republican revolution in Spain has so far had a definite anti-Christian bias. This does not mean that because it is Republican therefore the movement is anti-Christian, but that the elements raised to power by the recent revolution are those of the extreme Left, who in Roman Catholic countries are generally anticlerical and anti-Christian. The Pope has recently incontestably defined this irreconcilability between Marxism (communism and socialism), and Christianity.

Again, in the *Morning Post* of October 20th, 1931, the author published an article headed "Church issue in Spain. Cross v. Hammer and Sickle," in which he gave details of the attack on Christianity as it appeared at that time and he concluded his article:

> It would appear that a counterrevolution has been brought appreciably nearer and, should it occur, there is reason to believe that it will be a fight led by the cross on one side and by the hammer and sickle on the other.

In 1933 the author in a descriptive article showing the progress in Spain under the Republic, said in the *Morning Post* of July 26th:

> A student of history cannot but be astonished at the many analogies between the Spain of today and France of 1792 and to speculate as to whether Azaña is to be the Robespierre of Spain. In its denial of God and in its persecution of Christianity... the Spanish revolution has shown how closely it follows its French prototype.

When the Popular Front captured power in February 1936, a veritable orgy of arson and destruction took place and continued for some months. On June 16th, the following statistics were read out in the Cortes and no one attempted to deny them:

> Churches totally destroyed, 160. Churches attacked, set on fire, and partially destroyed and attempts at such attacks, 251.

A fortnight before this statement was made, the author visited many of the most important towns in Spain and many unimportant ones and in almost all of them saw the burnt or desecrated churches; the evidence of independent foreign residents as well as Spaniards in these places was that the government police and soldiers stood by, made no attempt to stop or arrest the incendiaries, and in some cases prevented people from attempting to put out the flames. Even were this not true, and the evidence for it is overwhelming, the failure of any and every government to punish acts of crime and arson must inculpate them, and there is no record of any arrests or prosecutions in the courts resulting from these acts. The orgy of crime and sabotage against the church that took place during the first months of government by the Popular Front was mild in comparison with what was to follow. It will always be impossible to know the exact statistics of the murders and martyrdoms of priests, nuns and laymen, who suffered for their faith alone and not for their politics, but it can be confidently laid down that they took place in their thousands, as this is proved by the evidence of many eyewitnesses, and has never been denied. The most authoritative statement of figures is that given in the pastoral letter of July 1st, 1937, signed by eight Spanish archbishops and thirty-five bishops—that is to say practically the whole hierarchy of the Spanish church—with the authority of the Vatican. This pastoral says:

> Although the figures are premature, we calculate that about 2,000 churches and chapels have been destroyed or totally plundered. The murdered priests, counting on an average 40 percent, in the devastated dioceses—in some they reach 80 percent—amount to about 6,000 of the secular clergy alone. They were hunted with dogs, they were pursued across the mountains, they were searched for with eagerness in every hiding place. They were killed without trial most times, on the spot, for no other reason than that of their function in society.

The pastoral also says towards its conclusion:

> Remember our murdered bishops and so many thousands of priests, religious and chosen laymen, who perished only because they were the chosen armies of Christ and beg the Lord that He may make fruitful their generous blood.

It is of course possible to dispute the figures given, but it is impossible to set aside a carefully prepared statement backed by such signatories. It has been said that these crimes were committed by irresponsible mobs, but it must be remembered that the government opened the prisons, armed the mobs, and never brought the culprits to trial; they cannot escape responsibility.

The *Manchester Guardian,* a consistent supporter of the Spanish Republican government, said in June, 1937:

> The attack on religion has been more radical in loyalist (i.e., Republican) Spain than anywhere else in the world, including even Mexico and Russia. All Roman Catholic churches have been closed down as places of worship, and nearly all have been completely destroyed... Nor have the Protestant churches escaped... The two nonconformist places of worship at Clot and Puebla have been burnt... In loyalist Spain there is nothing left to persecute.

Notwithstanding the published program and the teaching of communism, it has sometimes been made to appear that the persecution was not directed against Christianity, but only against the Roman Church, on account of abuses said to exist. There is no available evidence to support this theory; it is possible that the Roman Church in Spain was sometimes obscurantist, has had at times a defective policy and needs reform, like all human organizations, but the whole tendency of this persecution has been, not to reform, but to destroy everything connected with the worship of God and Christ.

Protestantism simply does not come into the picture, for Protestants in Spain amount to quite an insignificant percentage of the Christians. It is an interesting, if unimportant fact, that all the Church of England chaplaincies in Republican Spain were closed at the beginning of the civil war and continued closed. The deans of Rochester and Chichester who visited Barcelona in 1937 in search of knowledge did not dare to appear in the streets in their clerical garb.

The sufferings of an intensely religious people, as the majority of Spaniards are and have always been, were very great at being deprived of religious ministrations. Throughout the war in Republican Spain there were no christenings, no Christian marriage, and no Christian burial. This is capable of proof by reading the contemporary Spanish press of Republican Spain, and by the evidence of residents who continued in Republican Spain throughout the war. Nor was mass said or services held; for there were no altars standing and anyone appearing as a priest was in danger of his life. All newspapers in Republican Spain were controlled, and consequently their statements cannot be considered as contradicting the government policy. One of them (*Solidaridad Obrera*) said in May, 1937:

> What is meant by the restoration of the freedom of worship? Does it mean that mass will be said again? As far as Madrid and Barcelona are concerned, we do not know in what spot this clownery could be performed again. There is not a single church left standing, not one altar on which to place a chalice.

Another extract taken from *La Vanguardia* some months later said:

> Yesterday verbal evidence was taken in the suit against Vicente Torrens, Juan Forcadas, and others accused of having heard mass in a private house.

That this was a true picture was vouched for by every resident and most British visitors to Spain, except that small number of deans and other visitors whose evidence must be discarded because it runs counter to the weightier evidence, the greater numbers and wider experience of the former. But not even these minority and apologist witnesses declared that the churches were not destroyed or in a state of desecration and often of defilement throughout the war; all that they could say in attempted palliation of what happened was that they knew of some one house or church among a population of several millions where a mass had been said or that they saw a Bible sold in the streets.

Against that is the evidence of the others, who saw with their own eyes the burning of the churches, the sacred things brought out and burnt in heaps in the streets, figures of Christ decapitated or riddled with bullets, infant Christs dressed up and exposed publicly in the streets for ridicule, priests pursued and shot in the streets.

The author himself in 1937 travelled hundreds of miles through the country that had been conquered by the Nationalist armies, and every church in every town and village had been desecrated or destroyed, many churches turned into receptacles for filth so that they literally stank to heaven. Thank God they were being as rapidly cleaned and restored as was possible and reconverted to worship.

That this was still the treatment meted out to churches and things revered or holy until the last phases of the war was proved by the witness of all British observers who visited the fronts during the Nationalist advance on Valencia.

The historian must balance his evidence and he cannot set aside his own observations and that of a multitude of experienced and qualified witnesses in deference to the opinions of the few inexperienced visitors of a few days to a country which and whose language were strange to them, especially as those visitors exhibited by words or occupation that they had political axes to grind.

It is necessary to analyze the statement that the Church was rich and oppressed the poor, because it had great vogue in England. As regards oppression, visitors to and residents in Spain before the war give evidence that, although there were undoubtedly some bad priests, as there are some in all countries, the relations between the parish priest and his people were in general exceedingly friendly and the priest was the father of his flock. In the country parishes he usually lived no better than the peasants of his flock.

As regards riches, a division must be made between the secular clergy or the Church of Spain and the religious orders, Jesuits, Dominicans, Capuchins, etc.

The Church of Spain had all its properties and possessions taken away in the year 1835, and at the time the 1936 Revolution took place the clergy were probably as badly paid as any in the world. In the year 1851 an arrangement was come to between church and state which was embodied in a concordat, which regulated relations from that date until 1931. According to this arrangement a value was set on the confiscated property and it was agreed that the state should pay 3 percent on this value to the Church. Originally the yield was Ps. 135,000,000 (£5,400,000 at par), but by the year 1916, owing to continual whittling down by the state, the figure had fallen to Ps. 42,000,000 (£1,680,000 at par). The annual state grants to the hierarchy and to priests were as follows:

	Ps.	£ (at par).
Archbishops	40,000–32,000	1,600–1,280
Bishops	27,000–10,000	1,080–400
Canons	5,000–2,000	200–80
1,711 parish priests	2,500–1,000	100–40
14,726 parish priests	900–500	36–20

Some parish priests received even less than Ps. 500—or £20 per annum at par. If the 1938 rate of exchange for Republican pesetas were taken, the sterling equivalents given must be divided by 10 to 20.

It is interesting to compare these figures with the stipends of the hierarchy and incumbents of the Church of England. According to 1937 "Whitaker's Almanack" these were:

P	£
Archbishop of Canterbury	15,000
Bishops average about	4,000
Cathedral dignitaries	900-850
12,698 Incumbents average	517

This disposes of the myth of the riches of the Church of Spain.

As regards the religious orders, their rural estates and farms were confiscated in the year 1837, but they had accumulated considerable riches in house properties and some investments during the subsequent 90 years. These, however, were confiscated by legislation in 1931, and so their misuse, where it existed, cannot be considered to have caused the war in 1936, any more than the riches of the Church of Spain which ceased to exist 100 years before. It is also fair to give honor where honor is due and to state that the religious orders, as long as they had riches, employed them in educating the people of all classes in their schools. State education was always insufficient and the only period in recent years, during which there was any adequate improvement in the number and efficiency of schools, was during the dictatorship of Primo de Rivera and probably 50 percent of the education, and certainly all the best education, was provided by the religious orders previous to the revolution of 1931. The confiscation of the religious schools in that year deprived thousands of children of a proper education, for the religious orders who provided the trained professors and teachers were forbidden to teach, and professors and teachers are not among the things that can be improvised. The Republicans paid great lip service to the cause of education and, as is customary during revolutions, they had at first the bulk of the lay intelligentsia behind them, but the results of their words and actions were not only negative but definitely harmful to education.

This chapter on the religious persecution in Spain cannot be complete without a tribute to the intense religious revival manifested throughout Nationalist Spain during the civil war. It is of course a repetition of the old, old story "*sanguis martyrorum semen Ecclesiae.*" Every visitor or resident in Nationalist Spain recounted that all the churches were full; that the regimental chaplain sat at the head of his mess at the front and that mass was customary before going into action; that there was great observance of Christianity officially, unofficially, and among all classes; most of the Nationalists believed they were fighting for Christ.

A small illustration is often worth many arguments and it is this: since November, 1936, when the advance on Madrid was held up, there stood before the high altar in the parish church of Ávila the portable wooden altar, which was ready at all times to be carried into Madrid with General Franco's troops so as to celebrate immediately an open-air mass in the capital to signify the return of Christianity, and it was so used in March, 1939.

It is related, in its proper sequence, how General Franco both before and after his victory endeavored to restore the Church fully to her position held in pre-Republican days and to strengthen the Christian bases on which he hoped to build the New Spain. The Jesuits were restored to their previous position and their properties and schools returned to them by a law of May 3rd, 1938, but this law only came into operation in Republican Spain as and when it was conquered by General Franco. In 1938 diplomatic relations were reopened between the Nationalist Government and the Vatican, the clergy's minute stipends were returned to them and the Republican divorce law was canceled. In 1942 a provisional agreement was signed with the Vatican, by which certain clauses of the broken concordat of 1851 were again made operative and by which the long outstanding dispute over the appointments of Spanish archbishops and bishops was settled. As in other ages the persecution of Christianity in Spain brought forth its natural and perennial fruit in a great religious revival.

XVIII

BUSINESS (BRITISH) DURING THE CIVIL WAR

Spain and Great Britain have for centuries been important to each other in trade and commerce. Total imports into Spain in 1935 amounted to roughly £35,000,000, of which £6,000,000 corresponded to Great Britain. Total exports from Spain were £23,000,000, of which £11,000,000 corresponded to Great Britain.

Thus, Great Britain took almost 50 percent of Spain's exports and provided 17 percent of her imports in the year 1935.

Spain is a country of great natural riches and resources, of which the principals are agricultural and mineral. In the region of the Cantabrian Mountains there is a large region of iron ore deposits, which are extensively worked and were originally developed and largely owned by British capital. This has been to a great extent superseded by Spanish capital, but British interests are considerable in the consumption and carrying of this ore. When this region of Spain was under the rule of the Republican government, disorder had reduced the export of iron ore to 5,000 tons a month, but this rose rapidly, after the capture of the region by General Franco and the reestablishment of industrial tranquility, to nearly 100,000 tons per month in 1938; a bigger percentage of this ore went to Great Britain than to any other country.

West of the iron ore region comes the coal mining area of Asturias, which provides a coal very much inferior to British coal, and in which Great Britain has no interest except as a competitor. Other important mineral riches are: the almost immeasurable potash deposits of Northern Catalonia, which have only begun to be developed within the last ten years, and in which British capital is interested; the copper and pyrites deposits of Río Tinto, Tharsis and Peñarroya, of which the first two are British companies; the quicksilver mines of Almadén in the Sierra Morena, which provide more than half of the world's supply of mercury, and which belong to the Spanish nation.

As regards agriculture, Spain is a great producer of wheat, wine, sugar, potatoes, oranges, olives, olive oil, nuts, and almonds, of most of which Great Britain is a great consumer, and in oranges and fine wines the principal one. The greater part of the agriculture of Spain is carried on under the system of irrigation introduced by the Moors during their 700 years' domination of a large part of Spain; the mountainous character of the country facilitates this, and the establishment of reservoirs for irrigation and hydroelectric uses. There are still vast regions which can be brought under irrigation, as was recognized by General Primo de Rivera as well as by General Franco. Large new schemes and works are being developed and the potential increase of production and wealth in Spain is very great in this direction.

The two chief industrial regions of Spain are Barcelona, with its neighboring towns, where there are all sorts of manufacturing industries, especially textiles, and Bilbao with its district where foundries and shipbuilding predominate. British interests were at this time considerable in hydroelectric plants, shipping, banking, insurance, various factories and imports of coal, machinery, raw materials, and all sorts of manufactured goods. Figures given merely comprise trade with Great Britain, but it must be remembered that there was also a considerable trade between other parts of the Empire and Spain, which is not included in the figures given in this chapter. Such trade comprised cotton and jute from India, wool from Australia, rubber from Malaya, motorcars from Canada, etc.

As will be seen by the statistics, the civil war caused an increase in British imports from Spain, and a still greater decrease in British exports to Spain, and thus the 1937 figures showed a heavy adverse trade balance with Spain. U.K. Imports from Spain and the Canaries rose from £7,035,000 to £7,310,000, and the exports fell from £3,430,000 to £1,179,000. Thus, the adverse trade balance from £3,605,000 to £6,131,000.

During this period, the British imports of oranges increased by 26 percent, wine by 45 percent tomatoes by 22 percent, iron ore by 7 percent, pyrites by 47 percent, while the imports of potatoes fell by 46 percent, and of nuts and almonds by 30 percent. The reasons for these sensational increases and decreases was that produce from Nationalist Spain, where conditions were normal and orderly, increased and that produce from Republican Spain decreased as the result of disorder and disorganization. Potatoes, for instance, which came exclusively from Republican Spain, showed a decrease of £500,000.

During this same period, the export to Spain from Great Britain of coal decreased by 37 percent, machinery by 90 percent, motorcars by 95 percent, cutlery and hardware by 90 percent, and electrical goods by 75 percent.

The chief reasons for this almost annihilation of British export trade to Spain were undoubtedly the civil war, the exchange difficulties, and the necessity for Spain's economy for her to import nothing but war materials, and some few raw materials. Up to the time of the signature of the nonintervention pact towards the end of 1936, all countries, England included, poured war material into Spain, but, after the signature of that pact, Great Britain was the only big manufacturing country that did not supply war materials to Spain; the Republican side received vast quantities of munitions, arms, airplanes, etc., from France, Russia and Czechoslovakia, while the Nationalists received similar supplies from Germany and Italy. Another cause of the cessation of British imports into Republican Spain was the elimination by confiscation of all British business in that zone and the evacuation by our navy of most British subjects, so that the agencies of British manufacturers ceased to exist, and there was no one to sell the goods. Madrid and Barcelona were, almost exclusively, the residences of these agents and both these places were in Republican Spain.

Previous to the outbreak of war, business conditions had become more and more difficult in Spain owing to the perpetually increasing power of the labor syndicates, who for some time past had been openly dominated by the Moscow Comintern, the reduction of hours and increase of wages to an uneconomic figure and an advanced socialistic legislation, which made it illegal for an employer either to dismiss his workmen or close down his business when it ceased to be profitable. These policies had been carried to such an extreme that some manufacturers had to choose between going to prison or handing over their factories to their workmen.

After the outbreak of war, all business of any importance in the territory under the Republican government, whether national or foreign was, with a few exceptions, confiscated by government decree and put under the control of committees of workmen, who were not only authorized to manage the business but also to draw on the banking accounts. Thus, all British businessmen found themselves deprived of their possessions and, as their lives were not considered safe, they were with a few exceptions evacuated by our navy.

This was not, however, the case of British business and Britons in Nationalist territory. No one had to be evacuated, while business and property continued to be possessed by its owners, though they had to experience the inconvenience, natural in wartime, of exchange control, which obliged exporters to hand over their foreign exchange to the government in return for pesetas at the controlled rate. These exchange regulations prejudiced the profits of the business concerned, but, in contrast to the fate of business located in Republican Spain, the owners still possessed their properties and enjoyed the advantages of law and order without the destructive hindrances imposed by Marxist legislation and Moscow-controlled trades unions. A telling illustration of these advantages was set forth in the 1937 report of the Río Tinto Co., which stated:

> It is interesting to note that with 6,000 men employed in December, 1936, we were able to export 143,000 tons of ore, 30,000 tons more than we were able to export in the month of May with 8,500 men employed.

In May they were under the Republic and in December under the Nationalists.

The other side of the picture was painted in the report of the Barcelona Traction Co., a company representing many millions of British capital and supplying light and power to an enormous tract of country in republican Spain. In this report it was stated that: "The seizure effected by the Workers Committee covers all the properties, funds, and banking accounts of the enterprise."

It was a curious and illuminating fact that no protest of any sort was made by the British government, nor any outcry in the press of England at this sequestration of and damage to British interests, but, when the Nationalists some two years later damaged (within Spanish territorial waters) ships and property of very doubtful British pedigree but flying the British flag, there were immediate protests to General Franco's government on the part of the British government, and protests resounded throughout all but a small section of the British press.

This was a further example of the ability of an interested propaganda to influence and obfuscate official and public opinion.

The war caused most of the long-established British steamship services trading in Spain to be suspended, but there arose a number of mushroom steamship companies with hastily purchased steamers of many categories, registered as British and legitimately flying the British flag under the British merchant shipping acts, which carried supplies of all sorts to the ports of Republican Spain. There could be no doubt that many of them were purchased with money supplied by the Republican government, and that others traded in order to gain the enormous profits consequent on their dangerous trade. They could not in any sense be considered as part of normal Anglo-Spanish trade, but the hindrance of their activities by one party in the war called forth much more protest than all the damage done to true British trade interests by the other party.

The Spanish exchange situation, which concerned British trade intimately, was a peculiar one. For some years previous to the outbreak of war, the exchange regulations and restrictions of successive Spanish governments, made with the object of maintaining the value of the peseta against foreign exchanges, had been an ever-increasing handicap to all foreign trade.

In 1928 the Spanish government set up a central exchange control office, through which all foreign exchange transactions were obliged to pass and to which the sterling or other foreign currency value of exports had to be delivered. In this way a stable, but fictitious, rate of exchange was maintained, but there was an ever-increasing shortage of sterling until, in 1935, British importers were having to wait any time up to nine months for payment of their goods and debenture bondholders were receiving no payment at all against interest. This position, which lasted for some years, appeared quite incongruous in view of the fact that Great Britain was buying more than she sold to Spain, and can only be accounted for by the evasion of the regulations and by the fact that money which should have come to Great Britain was being used to pay for goods from U.S.A., Germany, etc., and that freights and charges accounted for a big percentage of the value of exports.

The situation became more and more serious, until, in January 1936, there were arrears of payments for lack of sterling exchange amounting to 6½ million pounds. Then there came into existence the Anglo-Spanish Clearing Office in London, which took possession of all moneys paid for Spanish imports into England, in the hope that they would then liquidate the Spanish debt to England; in six months they had reduced the balance by 1½ million to £5,000,000 when the clearing office came to an end owing to the civil war.

Though the clearing office came to an end, the control system continued in Spain in both zones. In November 1936, General Franco set up his own currency and from that time there were two distinct Spanish pesetas quoted, bought and sold in foreign countries. Both these currencies had their controlled or official price and both their unofficial prices, at which transactions took place on what were known as black Bourses.

It was significant of the estimation of commercial and financial circles of the respective credits of Franco Spain and Republican Spain that the external value of Franco pesetas was always higher than that of Republican pesetas, notwithstanding the fact that the latter had illegally appropriated all the gold and silver reserves of the Bank of Spain to the tune of about £150,000,000 and that the former had no gold reserve. The official external value of the Republican peseta fell steadily throughout the war from Ps. 35 = £1 to Ps. 100 = £1 at the beginning of 1935, while the unofficial price at which they could be bought in London at that date was over Ps. 500 = £1. On the other hand, the official rate of the Franco peseta had started at Ps. 42.50 = £1, and had remained at that figure, while the unofficial price during the same period depreciated to Ps. 90 = £1. These figures show the respective credits of the two sides in the financial markets of the world—Nationalist credit five times as good as Republican credit.

The decline in the internal value of the Republican peseta was also assisted by continual issues of government and local currencies throughout Republican Spain, which decreased the internal purchasing power of the peseta just as much as it did its external value. On the other hand, in Nationalist Spain the internal purchasing power of the Franco peseta remained constant.

As already indicated, a most notable example of the comparative effects of government under the Republican regime and government under the Nationalist regime was given by the increased production of iron ore from Biscay and of pyrites from the Huelva province, when those regions passed from the control of one government to that of the other. Not only did the export immediately recover from the low levels which it had reached during the war period but soon surpassed the figure of the previous prewar years. Thus, adding to the proofs of the destructive effects on commerce of the Republican legislation and labor situation, exhibited by the figures already given for the Río Tinto Co.'s production. It was also satisfactory to note that an increasing percentage of the iron and pyrites production was exported to the United Kingdom, which showed that trade tended to return to its normal and natural channels, and contradicted the unfounded declarations of interested propagandists that these products were all going to Germany and Italy.

At the time the civil war broke out in 1936 the national debt of Spain was estimated at £888 million, but only about £3 million of this was held abroad; this was one of the lowest external debts in Europe. No doubt this external debt was very considerably increased directly by the foreign purchases of both sides throughout the war and indirectly by the accumulation of unconverted pesetas owed to exporters. Owing to their lack of credit abroad, as witnessed by the depreciation of their peseta, it is probable that the Republican government was obliged to pay cash for all their purchases, and this money was provided by the gold reserves of the Bank of Spain, to which reference has already been made.

This chapter is written with the object of showing how British business was affected by the civil war and what was its importance and extent in normal prewar times. Soon after the end of the civil war and before Spain had time to recover, the Second World War started, and Anglo-Spanish trade almost came to an end. At the end of the civil war the financial and economic condition of Spain was acute because all her gold reserves had gone to Russia and France and she had no foreign credits or gold with which to buy the essential foodstuffs, raw materials and fuel. In other chapters will be found related how Spain received assistance from both the U.S.A. and Great Britain to help her to weather the storm and how they gave her credits and facilities enabling her to pass her most urgent requirements through the blockade; without this assistance, her situation would have been still more desperate.

Notwithstanding the apparently insuperable difficulties in the way of recovery visible in 1939, the great natural resources and recuperative powers of Spain had enabled her by the end of 1943 to reestablish in great part the prosperity of her industries, to achieve a great amount of reconstruction and to improve enormously her exchange position.

XIX

FOREIGN INTERVENTION AND NONINTERVENTION DURING THE CIVIL WAR, BOMBING AND PROPOGANDA

As regards the vexed question of foreigners fighting on either side, there was little difficulty in ascertaining the approximate figures on the Nationalist side on account of the number of expert English soldiers who investigated on the spot and the fact that General Franco's staff were always open about the matter. These experts coincided in stating that there were never more than 46,000 Italians or more than 7,000 Germans, the latter being entirely airmen and technicians; these forces were openly kept up to strength by their respective countries until April 1938.

The numbers of the foreign forces on the Republican side in the form of International Brigades were impossible to estimate and will probably never be completely discovered, on account of the heavy mortality, secrecy, and lack of statistics. General Franco's staff put them at 100,000 men and other experts at from 50,000 to 150,000. In February 1938, General Franco's headquarters stated that the figures of foreign prisoners in the Nationalist prison camps were 5,475 French, 3,200 Russians, 2,763 Czechs, 882 Belgians, 275 Americans, and 236 British prisoners. This fact, together with the thousands who were captured, or who flocked over the Pyrenees after the Aragón offensive in March 1938, seems to prove that they were certainly as numerous, and probably much more numerous, than foreigners fighting for General Franco.

It is illustrative of the power of propaganda to spread misinformation that a large part of the press and the B.B.C. broadcasts made most people believe throughout the war that Franco's army consisted chiefly of foreigners and Moors, whereas English military experts, who visited the fronts, put the proportion of foreigners, including Moors, in his army at the end of 1937 at a minimum of 10 percent and a maximum of 12 percent. Sensational reports of mass landings of Italian or German troops in Spain on various occasions in 1938, of Italian invasion and occupation of Mallorca in 1937 and of German invasion and occupation of Morocco in 1936 were launched from time to time from the same source and were in every case proved to be false, and denied by the foreign secretary or the prime minister in the House of Commons.

The policy of the British government was honestly framed to keep the war within the boundaries of Spain, though the fairness of protecting ships running the blockade while outside territorial waters and of refusing to grant belligerent rights are open to discussion. The British government's object of avoiding an extension of the war was gained to their lasting credit.

The origins of foreign intervention in Spain are too little known; they started in the early 1920's with the activities of the Comintern, the inseparable twin of the Soviet Union, working underground within the workmen's syndicates, which were eventually completely dominated by Moscow, who supplied them with arms and munitions before the communist rising in 1934 and from 1936 onwards in ever-increasing volume. French intervention only began with the civil war and was probably more powerful than that of any other country; there were probably more Frenchmen than any other foreigners fighting in Spain throughout the war, and until July, 1938, the Pyrenean frontier was never closed to the passage of arms and volunteers, who continued to pour into Spain from France by land and sea. It was just as much a government intervention as that of Italy and Germany; the only difference was that no secret was made of the latter while France continued to pose as the protagonist of nonintervention. Italian intervention as regards airplanes and pilots began in August 1936, but the sending of Italian troops and German technicians began after the check at Madrid in November 1936, by the International Brigades to General Franco's advance. Judging from the numbers of airplanes and war material existing on both sides, nonintervention was generally flouted except by Great Britain.

While Russia, France, and Czechoslovakia supplied the Republicans, Italy and Germany supplied the Nationalists with war supplies, but a very great part of the Nationalist supplies came from the captures at sea (given as 100 ships loaded with war supplies), and on land from their enemies. Dispute of these facts is useless, because the capture of airplanes, arms, tanks and munitions on both sides revealed without any doubt the country of origin. As Spain produced no airplanes, it was obvious that those used on both sides came from their friends or were captured from their enemies and were of foreign manufacture. Both sides produced locally arms and munitions in their own factories in ever-increasing quantities as the war progressed; the center of the Republican production was Barcelona, which adequately accounted for the bombings of that town.

A very curious feature, which gave evidence of the efficacy of propaganda, was the silence in official circles, the press and the B.B.C., as to French intervention, while Italian and German intervention was emphasized in the attempt to show that Franco's battles were being won entirely by foreign troops.

Constant reports were put about that General Franco intended to barter Spanish territory in exchange for the help of the Germans and Italians, which was consistently denied both by the General himself and by the foreign governments concerned. To anyone with a knowledge of Spanish character and history, or a realization that any such attempt would strike at the nationalist basis of General Franco's support, such an idea refuted itself, though propaganda used it successfully to alienate British sympathy from the Nationalists. Great Britain's attempt to prevent the Spanish war from spreading were crystallized in the formation of the Nonintervention Committee under Lord Plymouth as chairman. It passed through the troublous incidents of the attacks on the German men-of-war Deutschland and Leipzig and the bombing of H.M.S. Havoc, and in September, 1937, the Noyon agreement was signed between England and France, and subsequently joined by Italy; under this agreement the seas were patrolled by the navies of the various signatory powers.

Constant attempts were made to close the land frontiers to volunteers and war material and to arrange for the evacuation of all foreign volunteers, but agreement appeared to be unattainable. On November 16th, 1937, at long last and after many months' delay the scheme for the withdrawal of foreigners was agreed to by the nonintervention sub-committee; the scheme was presented to the two Spanish governments and accepted in principle with some reservations and the committee decided to go ahead. After perpetual obstruction on the part of the Soviet representative, a scheme was finally agreed on June 21st, 1938, comprising a substantial and proportional withdrawal of volunteers on both sides, the recognition of limited belligerent rights as soon as 10,000 combatants had left the side found to have the smallest number and the reestablishment of control on the land frontiers. Commissions were to go out to Spain to count the volunteers. This scheme was submitted to the two parties in Spain, while France stated that her frontier was now to be closed to arms traffic—a confession indeed that nonintervention had not until that moment been observed in France.

On July 28th the Republican government accepted the plan with some small reservations, but the Nationalists did not reply until August

22nd, when they offered to withdraw 10,000 volunteers and establish two safety ports for shipping, one in Catalonia and one in Valencia, in return for immediate recognition of belligerent rights. They also pointed out the self-evident fact that proportional withdrawal was impossible because the numbers of foreigners in the Republican army was unascertainable owing to their having Spanish papers and being mixed up in Spanish units. The Nationalist note ended by reiterating former declarations that "National Spain does not consent, and will never consent, to the slightest mortgage on its soil or on its economic life and that it will defend at all times to the last every handful of its territory, its protectorate and its colonies, if anyone dares to make an attempt against them."

This last part was aimed against the constant and insidious propaganda to the effect that General Franco was mortgaging Spanish territory and economy to Germany and Italy.

This was the position when the Czechoslovak crisis became acute, and, in the middle of October 1938, General Franco returned 10,000 volunteers to Italy under the inspection of the nonintervention committee.

The Republican government, meanwhile, apparently with a view to making further international complications and to put on one side the nonintervention committee, had persuaded the League of Nations to appoint a committee to superintend the evacuation of volunteers from their side.

There were thus at this time (October 1938) no less than four foreign commissions concerning themselves with the Spanish war. They were:

1. The nonintervention committee.
2. The League of Nations committee mentioned above.
3. British commission for the exchange of prisoners under Field Marshal Sir Philip Chetwode.
4. British Commission on the bombing of open towns.

Many criticisms of the work of the nonintervention committee can be made, but it did achieve its principal object, which was to prevent the spreading of the war.

The sinking of merchant vessels by bomb and torpedo by one side or the other led to constant incidents and protests. Though some of these sinkings were doubtless due to Nationalist attempts to prevent supplies reaching the Republicans, yet there can be little doubt that a number of them, and probably the attacks on foreign warships also, were undertaken as a definite part of the program of the Republican government, who as their hopes of a victory receded, strained every nerve to provoke an international war in the hope that it would save them from defeat.

To a certain extent the bombing controversy which arose during 1938 was connected with intervention because, as regards bombing of ships, the question would hardly have arisen if declarations of neutrality had been made and the belligerent rights of the combatants had been recognized, instead of the new policy called nonintervention.

The bombing controversy can be divided into two parts, that concerning bombing of towns and that concerning ships. Throughout the first year of the war superiority in the air was with the Republicans and bombing of most of the important and many unimportant Nationalist towns was constant, some 2,000 air raids being reported. In May–June, 1937, the author visited Burgos, Salamanca, Ávila, Cáceres, Toledo, Seville, Granada, Córdoba, Málaga and other towns; in all of them air raids were of common occurrence; refuges with signposts directing the people to them were in existence in all of them; the windows were stuck with strips of paper to prevent splintering; and he experienced several blackouts and alarms, during which the people took to the refuges. Subsequently, when the air superiority passed to the Nationalists, these raids ceased and in late 1937 and the beginning of 1938 began the air raids on the ports and towns of the Mediterranean coast by the airplanes of the Nationalists.

Here again there was evident a strange influence at work in press and propaganda throughout the world. The bombings of Nationalist towns had never been heard of by the British public and no protest had been uttered against their inhumanity, but immediately the roles were changed and the bombers became the bombed, the humanitarians in the press and in parliament became vociferous in denouncing the bombings on the grounds that the towns were open towns; judging from the press and B.B.C. accounts it almost appeared as if the bombs only hit civilians, women, children, or hospitals, as only rarely was mention made of the military objectives damaged. Thus, when the bombings in March of Barcelona, the very nerve center of the Republican government, containing port, railways, power stations, stores, munition dumps and factories took place, the outcry was overwhelming; only the mortality among civilians was advertised and it was only later that it was discovered that the port, power stations and railway lines had been damaged, the petrol tanks set on fire, and munition dumps exploded, while only small damage was done to the living and business quarters of the city. A similar story could be told about most of the ports bombed.

Too much blame must not be placed on the press and foreign correspondents as, with the strict press censorship existing in Spain, a correspondent was obliged to send only what was pleasing to the censor or submit to expulsion. There were, however, unscrupulous correspondents who consistently propagated false and tendentious news.

Accusations and counteraccusations about bombings resulted in August, 1938, after lengthy negotiations at the instigation of the British government, in the appointment of a committee of investigators, who might be called in at any moment to investigate and report on any alleged bombing of open towns and civilians.

The other part of the bombing controversy, which concerned ships bombed in Republican ports by Nationalist airplanes, was even more troublesome than the bombing of towns, because these ships for the most part flew the red ensign. Left-wing parliamentarians and organizations became jingoistic in their demands that the British flag must be protected even to the extent of armed intervention by Great Britain on the side of Republican Spain. The legalistic position was obscure because, as Mr. Chamberlain pointed out in parliament, nonintervention and the bombing of merchant ships in ports were entirely new precedents; generally speaking the legalists were divided into two groups, one which said that the bombing of British ships in Spanish harbors was an infraction of international law and the other which said that territorial waters were as much national property as the land, and that ships and citizens that went into a war zone did so at their own risk. The nonintervention policy of Great Britain was throughout clearly defined and carried out on the lines that ships flying the British flag were protected up to the three-mile limit, but that, when they entered territorial waters, they did so at their own risk.

The British ships concerned, it must be said, were legally and technically within their rights in flying the red ensign, having been duly registered in some port in accordance with our merchant shipping acts. They were all carrying foodstuffs or supplies to Republican Spain and they consisted of three categories. First there were the ships purchased with money of the Republican government but technically owned by some British merchant or company as a cloak; second there came the ships in reality owned by Greeks and others, but possessing a legal right to appear as British, though dirty, ill found, and constituting (as Admiral

Sir Roger Keyes pointed out) a prostitution of the red ensign. Third came the ships genuinely British in ownership, whose owners and sailors were trading for the high profits obtainable in the business with complete knowledge of the risks they were taking; the wages and profits were as much as 300 percent of those normally ruling.

These were the ships that, by means of the clever propaganda that one cannot help stumbling across throughout the Spanish war, excited British patriotic indignation against the Nationalists and enjoyed the protection of the British navy at the cost of the British taxpayer. The Spanish Nationalists naturally did not look on these ships in the same light as did the British. They saw these ships, usually the same ones, assisting their enemies by running their blockade first on the northern coast and then in the Mediterranean; powerful foreign navies prevented them from searching the ships on the high seas and, when they reached their enemy's ports with the supplies he so much required, foreign powers protected them and protested when they were bombed. It is not surprising that long-tried friendship was strained.

This is even less surprising when it is remembered that in the First World War H.M. King Alfonso attempted to get some check placed on the bombings of undefended towns as between Germany and ourselves. A published memorandum of January 17th, 1918, on bombing operations setting forth the policy of Great Britain in the First World War said as follows:

> The policy intended to be followed is to attack the German towns systematically... It is intended to concentrate on one town for successive days, and then to press on to several other towns, returning to the first town until the target is thoroughly destroyed, or at any rate until the morale of the workmen is so shaken that output is seriously interfered with. Long distance bombing will produce its maximum moral effect only if the visits are constantly repeated at short intervals, so as to produce in each area a sustained anxiety.

It is not meant to suggest that this was General Franco's policy, unless it be proved, which it is not, that he had made deliberate attacks on civilians where no military objective existed; it is merely intended to show what was Great Britain's policy when she was at war, as a commentary to the criticism and condemnation levelled at the Spanish Nationalists.

A few more words may be said here about the manner in which the British public were misled throughout the war by the foreign news service of the press and the B.B.C. To such an extreme had the suppression or distortion of news been carried that many people believed almost to the end that General Franco's victory was doubtful, that his army consisted chiefly of Italians and Germans and that the war might end in a stalemate—all of them proved by events to be baseless suppositions.

Merely as examples of unscrupulous propaganda and in the interests of historical accuracy two of the many canards, which received wide publicity and belief, may be referred to here. One was the story of a massacre at Badajoz on the capture of that city by the Nationalists; it was the fruit of a forged press telegram over the signature of a *United Press* correspondent Mr. Reynolds Packard, who publicly denounced it as a forgery.

The other case was that of the supposed complete and deliberate destruction by bombing of the town of Guernica by General Franco's German airplanes on a market day when the streets were crowded. The originator of the story was a special correspondent of The *Times*, whose subsequent messages made it clear that he had not in fact been within some miles of Guernica at the time. An official investigation took place, which was translated and published in English with an introduction by Sir Arnold Wilson, K.C.I.E., C.M.G., M.P. From this it was clear that Guernica was a town containing an arms factory at an important road junction on the Republican lines of communication and in the front line of battle for two to three weeks, during which time it was undeniably bombed, and that by far the greater part of the destruction was the deliberate work of the retreating Republican forces just before its capture by the Nationalists. Subsequent investigation by prominent and reliable Englishmen showed that only about a third of the town had been destroyed.

Unfortunately, belief in the Guernica legend became an article of faith to all left-wing people, and it is interesting to compare the attitude of the British public and press to the Guernica story and their subsequent attitude to bombing in 1943–45.

XX

Social Conditions—Past and Present

One of the commonest and most plausible of the arguments of the protagonists of the Republic and of Republican Spain is that the civil war was primarily the result of bad social conditions, illiteracy, and the oppression and miserable conditions of the peasantry, that Republican Spain stood for progress and improvement in these respects and Nationalist Spain for oppression and the status quo.

Before accepting or rejecting this thesis it would be well to glance shortly at the conditions existing at the end of the last century, the conditions before and after the Primo de Rivera regime, the conditions immediately before the civil war, the conditions in Republican Spain during the war and the social plans and work already achieved in Nationalist Spain by the end of the war.

There can be no denial of the fact that social conditions were far from satisfactory, but, though they provided a fertile field for revolution, they were neither the primary nor the principal cause of the Spanish revolution. That revolution came, not from the peasantry but from the industrial cities and followed almost immediately on a period when social conditions, wages and standards of living had improved more in Spain than they had done for 150 years.

Spanish statistics are difficult to obtain, and, when come by, usually unreliable and consequently will be avoided here as much as possible.

Until the last quarter of last century there can be little doubt in the mind of any student of Spain that the conditions of the peasant, the industrial worker, and of public education were frankly bad, and that mendicancy and vagabondage were rampant. The reasons were political ineptitude, constant changes of government, and political and industrial strife, which not only paralyzed national productivity and prosperity, but also prevented social legislation and attendance to the welfare of the people. Hume, in 1908, stated that:

It cannot be too forcibly insisted upon that one of the chief reasons for the incurable extravagance of Spanish finance is the wasteful and unproductive expenditure on the public services. Each successive revolution or change of government means an entire change of the administrative staff from the prime minister to the doorkeeper through all departments of the state service and the payment of pensions to the outgoing staff, who thereupon become active intriguers all over the country for the return of their friends to power and themselves to full pay. This vicious system dooms thousands to idleness or worse, crushes enterprise, and paralyzes effort. To this must be added the need for finding places and wholesale promotion for the supporters of each successive military revolt. No government in Spain has ever dared to tackle this curse of bureaucracy.

This statement illustrates the central cause of the undoubtedly bad social conditions in Spain, which were chiefly the consequence of saddling Spain at the beginning of the nineteenth century with an Anglo-French parliamentary system quite unsuitable to her character and needs, which gave her a century and more of the worst government by ever-changing professional politicians. It was this evil and this system that General Franco destroyed, but which it was the desire of the protagonists of the government of Dr. Negrín in Barcelona to perpetuate. Dr. Negrín was the direct descendant of the politicians who misruled Spain for 150 years, to which had been added the effect of the virus of his Moscow training and his Russian wife.

Though still bad, the conditions of the people in Spain improved very considerably in the last quarter of last century, as the result of a more stable and orderly government subsequent to the Republican failure of 1873. In 1885, the population had risen to 17 million souls of whom 28 percent could read and write, as against 20 percent twenty years before, notwithstanding the wretched school system, compulsory only name.

Though undoubtedly some improvement took place during the next forty years it was relatively small, owing to the inability of the parliamentary system to function efficiently. The years of the first Great War brought great wealth and prosperity to Spain with the consequent increase in wages and raising of the standard of living, but again and again the industrial and political disorders set back the clock. However, when the extreme of chaos and disorder had been reached in 1923 and Primo de Rivera took charge of the state, it was said that the proportion of illiterates had fallen to 40 percent in a population of 23 million from the 72 percent in a population of 17 million in 1885. Here, as always, Spanish statistics must be mistrusted, but that is the generally accepted figure. At that time industry and the life of the nation were disorganized, wages were low, and unemployment at a high figure with all the inevitable and unhappy effects on the life of the masses.

The general effects on the nation of the six years of Primo de Rivera's dictatorship as a result of the elimination of the professional party politicians, have been described in an earlier chapter, and here it is only necessary to emphasize a few points as affecting social conditions. Industry and agriculture were prosperous; wages had increased as much as 50 percent; some 2,000 new primary state schools were in operation; mendicancy had been banished from the streets, and asylums provided for the beggars.

The industrial, commercial and agricultural unrest and disorganization consequent on the advent of the Republic in 1931, which have also already been described, had their natural repercussions on social conditions, which continued to deteriorate throughout the period culminating in the civil war, The gradual paralysis of industry increased unemployment, the beggars again appeared in the streets and the number of schools, already insufficient, was enormously decreased by the confiscation of the schools of the religious orders, which provided both schools and instructors for a large percentage of the education of all classes. The schools still remained, but it was impossible to improvise schoolteachers quickly, after losing a large proportion of the teaching profession by making it illegal for the religious orders to teach. Again, the same political ineptitude of the Spanish parliamentary system was evident and, together with the disrupting efforts of socialists, communists and anarchists, frustrated the intentions of reformers. Much legislation was passed, some of it excellent, but it did not get put into practice. It was a perpetual case of words without deeds.

The civil war dislocated all social conditions and in Republican Spain the state of disorder and chaos, resulting from the workers' control and their rival organizations, disorganized the life of the people and eventually reduced them in 1938 to a state of starvation in which a study of the social conditions and education was useless and impossible.

In Nationalist Spain, however, law and order prevailed, and almost immediately a social policy was formulated and put into practice. Nationalist Spain, free from the trammels of the professional politicians, attempted to tackle the problem of social conditions, and we shall now see the lines on which the attempt was made.

General Franco repudiated the idea that the workers were struggling to retain their privileges against a military and clerical caste, who were striving to bring them back to a state of oppression. He stated that:

"The conquests of the workers have nothing to fear from us; on the contrary we shall make all possible efforts to quicken the pace of social progress." As will be seen from the Falange program (Appendix III), which was supported by General Franco.

The policy of the New Spanish State was to be governed by a respect for social justice and the rights of individual ownership. Work was also to be the basis of the social order and it was recognized both as a right and as a duty, and the public authorities were to support those who were in enforced idleness.

Wartime social measures were various and excellent, but, as in other countries, it was found that it was easier to make plans than to realize them. These measures, many of which were put into practice comprised:

1. Support of the families of service men, financed by the proceeds of a "single dish day" per week and by a 10 percent tax on luxuries.
2. An Association for "Help at the front and in the hospitals" to provide extra comforts and clothes, and an Association of Friends of Combatants to provide homes for the wounded were set up, supported by voluntary subscriptions.
3. An organization to care for the disabled was formed under the gallant and disabled General Millán-Astray. Through it the Government provided pensions, and the completely disabled man received 3,000 to 12,000 pesetas a year.
4. A "Refugees' Aid" was established in August 1937. Its work started at the frontier, where it provided food and succor to the hundreds of refugees, and then cared for them in concentration camps at the expense of the State.
5. Prisoners-of-War received wages for their work and allowances for their families from the State.
6. Public Assistance throughout the country was carried on voluntarily, almost entirely by women, and supported by voluntary subscriptions supplemented by the State. Under this heading come the children's homes and dining halls and the maternity centers which existed in all important towns.
7. Orphaned and abandoned children were adopted into families under a careful legislation.

Housing reform, a problem in every country, was seriously undertaken under an Inspector-General of Housing. Although it was wartime, slums had already, by 1938, been cleared and substituted by new houses and blocks of flats in several towns. Visitors to Seville and Bilbao, and photographs of the buildings, bore witness to this, and the municipality of Seville had already constructed houses for 6,000 people previously living in bad conditions.

As regards education, courses for elementary teachers and university cultural courses were instituted to augment the number of teachers. Library commissions were set up. Access to free education for all was given and special attention was paid to bringing together the different social classes into the same schools. It was laid down that one in four of the pupils in the private schools must be from the poorer classes. The right to free instruction had to be made known through the press. All education was to have a definite religious basis.

Agriculture and the peasants were helped by subsidies and agricultural credits, which resulted in a considerable increase in production. The Bank of Spain and the agricultural societies were obliged to give loans to farmers at a rate of interest varying from 4 to 5 percent against their crops. In this way the small farmers were to be able to escape from the usury of which they were the victims and small holdings and peasant proprietorship increased.

Unemployment was not at that moment a serious problem in Nationalist Spain, but a register was formed and, for the first time in Spain, a government recognized that it is an obligation of the State to meet the needs of unemployment. The decree covering this obligation laid it down that Civil Governors in the territory under their jurisdiction must see that "there should not exist a single Spaniard in involuntary unemployment who should not receive in some form help proportionate to his family needs."

Further decrees give the unemployed facilities as regards house rent, light, and water, but no work-shy laborer or convicted criminal was to receive unemployment benefit.

A decree of September 1936, obliged employers to contribute to old age, maternity, and accident insurance.

The further conditions governing labor will be found in the Labor Charter, which is contained in Appendix IV.

Such was the situation and the program in Nationalist Spain, when the civil war came to its end and the program had to be stretched to cover all Republican Spain as well with its shortage of food and its disorganized agriculture and industry. In some parts the food situation was already serious and, when the Second World War broke out with the consequent blockade and polarization of trade and shipping, the condition of Spain and her food shortage became desperate. As the war progressed conditions became worse and reached their lowest state in the winter of 1941, when there was scarcity everywhere, soaring prices and acute starvation in many parts of Spain, as has been described in the historical chapters of this book. After that date, in great part owing to the assistance of Great Britain and the U.S.A. conditions improved greatly and continually.

These conditions during the years 1939–43 made even more difficult than it would have been otherwise the working of the social program of the New Spain. As usual in Spain intention marched far ahead of practice and the Spanish love of procrastination and hatred of discipline hindered it, but the new program was in great part put into practice. The consequent load put on industry was too heavy to bear both administratively and economically, while increased wages and social protection were more than set off by scarcity and high prices.

Attempts were made to control prices and supplies, but the measures were more honored in the breach than in the observance and supplies often found their way into the black market instead of into the rations of the poor.

Thus, in great measure the good intentions and the high ideals of the social structure of General Franco's regime disappointed almost everybody concerned, chiefly on account of economic conditions resulting from war and impossibility of producing the wherewithal to carry them out. The common defect of socialist planning, that of concentrating on methods of expenditure and forgetting about the production of the wealth necessary for carrying them out, came home to roost and will doubtless provide a useful lesson to other countries.

XXI

THE NEW SPAIN—GENERAL FRANCO'S POLICIES

"We do not want a Spain dominated by any one class whichever it may be, whether of capitalists or of workers." This sentence, taken from the speech of General Franco made in Zaragoza on April 19th, 1938, gives a central thought which runs through all his declarations of policy, and, as will be seen further on in this chapter, saturates the political creed of the one great party into which all political parties were officially fused in 1937. This was the Nationalist-Syndicalist party or, to give it its verbose and full Spanish name, *Falange Española Tradicionalista y de las Juntas Ofensivas Nacional-Sindicalistas* (Spanish traditionalist phalanx and the offensive committees of the national-syndicalists).

All the foreign opponents of the Spanish Nationalists wished to depreciate and discredit in the eyes of the public the projects and policy of General Franco by giving them the name of fascism, which was at the moment a name so unpopular as to gain a great measure of condemnation for them. It is difficult to arrive at a comprehensive analysis of the word fascism, which means different things to different people, but in the case of Spain, it was used inaccurately to describe a movement and a policy which was based on patriotism, service, duty, individualism and Christianity. This will be fully seen by a study of General Franco's declarations, and by the creeds of the party which are about to be quoted.

Just as social justice was one of the great principles running through General Franco's policy, so two other great principles are seen: that the New Spain was to be one and indivisible, and that her people were to be faithful to the Catholic faith.

With the advent of the civil war, all political parties except the Communist and Socialists were obliterated in Republican Spain, while in Nationalist Spain all parties ceased to exist officially except the Falange party and the Requeté or Traditionalist party, which were combined in F.E.T. (Falange Española Tradicionalista).

The man who, more than any other individual, with the exception of General Franco, had influenced the ideas and policies behind New Spain, was José Antonio Primo de Rivera, Marqués de Estella, who composed the twenty-six points of the Falange creed, and whose speeches were the party's initial inspiration.

He was the eldest son of the great dictator of 1923–30, General Primo de Rivera, Marqués de Estella, and was a barrister of great promise and eloquence. Shortly after the advent of the Republic, he formed the Falange, of which the central policy was the restoration of a national and patriotic spirit to Spain and the institution of social justice. The ideals of the Falange were undoubtedly influenced by the success of Mussolini in Italy, but so far from following the Italian Fascist program, Primo de Rivera refused to attend the International Fascist Congress in 1935 because he denied that the Falange was a Fascist movement.

In 1931, when his father's policies and actions were being criticized under the Republic and when the ministers of the dictatorship were being tried, he made a great and eloquent defense at the trial which resounded all over Spain. In 1933 he was elected by the town of Cádiz as the first Falange deputy to the Cortes.

In the February 1936 elections, when the Popular Front came into power, he was elected deputy for Cuenca by a large majority; he, like many other deputies of the right, was then illegally deprived of his seat by the majority vote of the left-wing parties in the Cortes. He was subsequently arrested and imprisoned some months before the rising under General Franco took place, and so could not have been implicated in the rising. His fate was in doubt for some time and he was referred to by the Falangists as "El Ausente" (the absent one), until the time came when there was no further doubt that he was condemned to death by a popular tribunal and shot in Alicante prison on November 19th, 1936. At the time of his death he was only thirty-three years old and his last will and testament, which was published in Nationalist Spain in November 1938, was a noble and moving document worthy of his life's work and of his family tradition.

Its first paragraph reads:

> Condemned yesterday to death, I pray God, should He not save me from it, that He will help me to maintain until the end that dignity and resignation with which I now look on it and that, when He judges my soul, He will judge according to His infinite pity and not according to my deserts.

Continuing throughout on a high note of Christian faith and forgiveness, he reiterates the central features of the Falangist creed, emphasizes his regrets at the shedding of blood that has taken place in Spain, and expresses his forgiveness of those who have done him harm "without any exception."

The last half of the will contains the testamentary dispositions of his documents and personal possessions.

As will be seen the inspiration of the Falange creed is patriotism and social justice, and its originator will go down to posterity as one of the chief spirits contributing to the construction of the New Spain.

Though he disappeared, the national-syndicalist creed of his twenty-six points, which he drew up, was one of the chief bases on which General Franco erected the edifice of the new Spanish state. Some of the most important of these points are:

~ Spain is one indivisible country, against which all separation is a crime. Individual and class interests must be used in the national interests.

~ Spain intends to play an important and independent role in Europe.

~ The army, navy and air force must be powerful and adequate.

~ The state will be based on municipal, syndical, and family representation without political parties as formerly existing, but with a parliament.

~ Formation of vertical syndicates representing the different branches of production.

~ Repudiation of the capitalist system and of Marxism for a system of fairness and cooperation called national-syndicalism.

~ The chief use of riches is to be the improvement of the standard of living of the Spanish people.

~ Recognition of private property.

~ Nationalization of banks and public utility companies through corporations.

~ Obligation to maintain the unemployed. Recognition of the right and obligation to work.

~ The standard of living of the agricultural laborer to be raised. Rationalization of land tenure. Return to the land from towns.

~ A rigorous reform of education. Compulsory education and military service.

~ Recognition of the Roman Catholic religion and regulation of the respective functions of church and state.

The other existing party, Requeté, was of no new foundation, having been in existence for more than 100 years, and it accepted the twenty-six-point creed. As has been explained, members of this party were originally Carlists, or supporters of the pretenders to the Spanish throne, for whom they had fought two long and bloody wars in the last century. They were conservative, ardent defenders of faith and Church and comprised the majority of the Basque race, their holy place being the town of Guernica.

Requetés and Falangistas on the outbreak of hostilities immediately became the chief supporters of General Franco and the Nationalists; volunteers of all classes and both sexes flocked to enroll themselves in the parties and their militias, until very soon almost every inhabitant of Nationalist Spain was enrolled in their membership. As a general but by no means a universal rule, it can be said that, though the Falange was looked upon as the Spanish substitute for Fascist, converted left-wingers usually became Falangists, and right-wingers became Requetés.

In May 1937 (Decree No. 255), probably as a result of some friction between the councils of the two parties, General Franco negotiated and announced to the world the unification of the two movements or parties. In his speech making the announcement, he said that there was to be unification of all parties and especially of their youth, in the interests of the Spanish nation, and under the sole leadership of himself.

- ~ That the greatest enemy of Spain and of all civilization was Russian communism, and that the world in general failed to realize this.
- ~ That the new Spanish state would follow Spanish tradition and respect the liberties of regions and communities.
- ~ That Spain sought an effective democracy based on the true interests of the people, on economic and social justice and on patriotism.
- ~ That the Catholic religion would be supported.
- ~ That the militias of Falangists and Requetés would be amalgamated under regular army officers.
- ~ That a political committee of control of the new organization would be established to assist him in constructing the new Spain.

In addition to these declarations, General Franco said that he accepted the twenty-six points of the Falange creed, but reserved the right to modify them in the national interest. The combined party of Falangists and Requetés under the new name already given adopted the twenty-six points as their creed.

In his subsequent speeches and declarations, the general never controverted or altered these original statements of policy, and the legislation and acts, first of the committee and afterwards of his ministry, were confirmatory of the social and constructive policy laid down. The labor charter was a very advanced one and fully bore out his promises. Spanish official translations into English of both the Labor charter and the twenty-six Falange points are appendices to this book. Students of the Falange having a knowledge of Spanish history and character will find that, though there is a similarity between the Falange and Italian fascism, they are by no means identical. Much of the Falange creed is rooted in Spanish tradition dating from centuries before the invention of fascism. Its roots appear to be in those entirely Spanish concepts of the bases on which the nation had rested during the centuries of its greatness and previous to the adoption early in the nineteenth century of a system based on the liberal parliamentary systems of Great Britain and France; broadly these bases can be said to be Christianity, monarchy, Cortes and a guild system, with the interests of the individual first and the state second.

On the other hand, the social part of the Falange program was a mixture of modern Catholic teaching and certain doctrines, such as the nationalization of the banks, belonging to modern political socialism.

As the years passed, the Falange began to take on more and more an aspect of state-worship or totalitarianism and became the pro-German section of Spain and often the instrument of the Germans. Contributory causes of this were that the left-wing elements, which had been Communist, Socialist and Republican during the civil war, had been gradually absorbed into the Falange and predominated it at the expense of the conservative elements; like people in other countries, they found little difficulty in passing from their Marxist totalitarianism into national-socialist and Fascist totalitarianism.

An interesting illustration of the spirit of the new Spain was provided by the new Nationalist coat-of-arms designed to replace the old Spanish coat-of-arms, a part of which had become an anachronism. The single eagle of Queen Isabella substituted the double-headed eagle of the Hapsburgs as a background, and the shield merely comprised the castle of Castile, the lion of Leon, the flag of Aragón and Catalonia and the chains of Navarre. The motto was perhaps most significant of the new Spain: "One, Great and Free."

On one side of the shield was depicted the yoke, and on the other the five arrows, the emblems of the Falange. Both these emblems are those adopted by the "Catholic Kings," as Ferdinand and Isabella are called in Spain. It was a courteous custom of those days, for a husband to have as emblem the initial of his wife's name, and vice versa. In accordance with this custom Ferdinand of Aragón adopted the *Yugo* or Yoke, which begins with the initial Y for Ysabel, as Isabel was then spelt in Spain, while Isabella of Castile adopted the *Flechas* or arrows beginning with F for Ferdinand. Both these emblems were signs of the establishment of a united Spain and of her great Empire, and consequently fall in aptly with the spirit of a new Spain, Catholic, traditionalist and monarchist.

One direction in which the policy of General Franco was obscure, probably intentionally so, was that of the monarchy.

Most Spaniards are as monarchist by tradition and character as are Britons; especially is this so as regards the Requetés or Traditionalists.

General Franco was said to be a monarchist in 1939 though most of his generals, especially Queipo de Llano, were strong Republicans at one time, and he himself in the time of the Republic had refused to identify himself with either creed. The only declaration he had at that time made on the subject was in July, 1937, when the Seville newspaper *A.B.C.* quoted him as saying: "Should the moment for a restoration arrive, the new monarchy would be very different from that of 1931, different in constitution, and in the person who should incarnate it."

XXII

REFUGEES AND EXILES

The exodus of refugees from Catalonia into France, fleeing before the advance of the victorious Nationalist armies and described in Chapter XIII, reached enormous proportions. Exact figures under the then existing conditions were impossible to ascertain, but it was stated that 500,000 souls crossed the frontier into France and that 200,000 of these were ex-soldiers of the defeated Republican armies. This presented the French government with a very difficult problem, and French soldiers under General Ménard took charge of the refugees and herded them into camps in Argèles, Le Boulou and other places in the south of France, but only after bands of them, starving and destitute, had roamed over the countryside destroying and robbing. The French authorities estimated that some 10,000 of the refugees were criminals liable to prosecution in any country.

Many of the refugees, who felt that they were not guilty of crimes liable to punishment in Spain, gradually filtered back into their own country, but the vast number that remained, many of them sick or wounded, endured unspeakable sufferings in the camps, where they were often without food, shelter or sanitation.

Charitable relief organizations abroad sent supplies, doctors, and ambulances, but in all too small a quantity to do anything but alleviate some of the suffering. The cost to the French government was enormous, and various foreign governments, including the British made monetary contributions.

Dr. Negrín and his colleagues had in their control very considerable supplies of food and money and several merchant ships, in reality the property of the Spanish republican government. At first, they appear to have done nothing to assist their unfortunate compatriots and followers, but at the end of March, 1939, they set up in Paris an organization called S.E.R.E. (*Servicio de Emigración para Republicanos Españoles*) to assist exiles and refugees. However, they only decided to give financial assistance to the higher officials of the late Republican government and the higher officers of the Republican army, who had sought asylum in

France, the rank and file were to be helped to emigrate; schemes for emigration to South America and Mexico were made, but only partly carried out. Mexico had at first agreed to receive 50,000 refugees, but the first instalments, chosen by S.E.R.E. and sent under the auspices of the British National Joint Committee for Spanish Relief, had a strong communist flavor, which probably was the cause of the Mexicans refusing to receive further remittances.

The close communist affiliation of Dr. Negrín and S.E.R.E. was proved and cost them dear for, when the Communist party went antiwar on the signing of the Hitler-Stalin pact, the offices of S.E.R.E. were raided by the French police and Dr. Negrín's fleet of merchantmen, purchased with Spanish Republican money, was confiscated.

The unfortunate refugees continued their miseries, in gradually decreasing numbers; many died, many entered French labor battalions or the French foreign legion, and others returned to Spain. After the fall of France, the Vichy government sent back to Spain various political refugees, and among them Señor Luis Companys, who was tried by court martial on his return and shot in October, 1940.

Thus disappeared one of the chief revolutionary figures of Catalonia, for Companys was the president of the Catalan government; he was imprisoned after the 1934 rising in Barcelona against the Republican government, but was released to become the nominal leader of Catalonia and collaborated with the Republicans throughout the civil war. During his regime there took place, first the assassinations and excesses by the mob in Barcelona, and later the abominations of the Popular Tribunals and the Cheka prisons, of which photographs appeared in English papers and of which the writer received accounts from English eyewitnesses. Thus, the execution of Companys offers one of those problems of criminal and political responsibilities which will perplex the world for many years after the end of the Second World War.

We will trace into their retirement or oblivion a few of the other Republican leaders.

Señor Álvarez del Vayo had retired to France on the fall of Dr. Negrín and went subsequently to the U.S.A.

Sr. Indalecio Prieto had gone to Mexico on his expulsion from Dr. Negrín's government in 1938, but he reappears in 1939 in a controversy with Dr. Negrín in Paris over the spoils controlled by the latter. This controversy was carried on by letters which were eventually published in Paris in 1939 (*Epistolario Prieto y Negrín*). From these letters and from other sources, and especially from a book called "Men and Politics" by Louis Fischer, an American agent and intimate of Dr. Negrín's, the following story emerges. Dr. Negrín had accumulated a fabulous wealth[7] in money and jewels to the estimated value of $50,000,000 in a villa at Deauville; this was shipped in February, 1939, in the yacht *Vita* to Mexico, where Señor Prieto was able to establish a claim to it, maintaining that it was public property and not the property of Dr. Negrín.

The latter went to Mexico to rescue the treasure and returned in the same ship with his opponent and the two proceeded to struggle for the ownership of the booty in Paris. Señor Prieto had on his side the remnants of the permanent committee of the Cortes, which still existed in Paris under the president of the late Republican Cortes, Señor Martinez Barrio. The Committee held a session on July 26th at which they passed a resolution to the effect that they were "neither at the end of their mandate nor dissolved," but that, pending the reestablishment of the Republic, they set up a committee to administer the national patrimony; this committee was called J.A.R.E. (*Junta de Auxilio a los Republicanos Españoles*, or committee for the assistance of Spanish Republicans). It was in fact a self-aid society to administer the funds and was composed of members of all parties except the Communist and excluding Dr. Negrín, who refused to acknowledge it. Since then a curtain has been drawn down on the fate of this enormous booty, which presumably not only maintained the emigres but also provided funds for Republican and Communist propaganda. The J.A.R.E. and the S.E.R.E. became the rival organizations of Señor Prieto and Dr. Negrín respectively and became political organizations in opposition to each other. This further aggravated the divisions already existing between the exiled politicians, and it appeared that Dr. Negrín still claimed to be prime minister of a nonexistent government and that the permanent committee still claimed to represent a nonexistent Cortes.

Subsequently, Dr. Negrín sought the asylum of England, while Sr. Prieto returned to Mexico.

Señor Aguirre, the President of Euzkadi (Basconia) also escaped to South America, as did Señor Martinez Barrio, the ex-president of the Cortes, and many other Republican politicians. Thence they carried on a ceaseless propaganda against the established regime in Spain with the

---

[7] This booty of Dr. Negrín's has nothing to do with the official funds of the Republic in Paris and Bordeaux, which were subsequently returned to Spain under the Bérard-Jordana agreement.

expressed intention of reopening the bloody conflict, which had cost their country so dear and had enriched many of them, but their irreconcilable differences had, after six years' exile, prevented any unity of policy and action.

Señor Prieto and Dr. Negrín reappeared at San Francisco in May 1945, when the conference was taking place, and doubtless aided in increasing the hostile atmosphere against the Spanish regime. In the previous November, another exiled politician, Señor Miguel Maura, who had been Minister of the Interior in the first Republican government, appeared on the scenes in Paris, proposing himself as General Franco's successor, but he soon faded into oblivion again.

Other prominent refugee politicians were Señor Salvador de Madariaga, perhaps the most distinguished politician, diplomat and historian among the exiles, who kept himself apart and appeared to dislike equally the Franco and the Republican regimes, and Señor Largo Caballero, described earlier in this history as predestined by Moscow to be the Lenin of Spain, who reappeared in Paris from a German concentration camp in May, 1945.

In that month General Franco offered freedom and repatriation to all Spanish refugees abroad provided that they had not committed murder or been willful accomplices of assassinations. He gave the assurance that if, after his arrival in Spain, a refugee were found to be guilty of judicial offences, he would not be detained but merely expelled from Spain and that exiles accused of looting during the civil war could return freely if they brought back their loot with them.

XXIII

END OF THE CIVIL WAR TO DECEMBER 1940,

INTERNAL AFFAIRS

With a view to clarity and to assist the reader in following events, from this point internal and foreign affairs are described in separate chapters.

Immediately after the entry of the Nationalist troops into Madrid and other recently surrendered provincial capitals, work began on the repairs to streets and public buildings and the "Auxilio Social," as the Falangist social welfare organization was called, followed in the wake of the army as it had done throughout the campaigns. This organization, which was served by women volunteers, immediately opened free dining rooms throughout Madrid and it was said that within a week some 1½ million food rations were being distributed daily from the supplies accumulated beforehand by the Nationalists preparatory to the fall of Madrid. Statistics published in the following November, showed that this remarkable organization fed daily 496,000 children in 2,847 centers and served 25 million meals in one month.

Immediately at the end of the war military tribunals were set up and all civil servants of the late Republican regime, inhabitants of houses where murders during the civil war were known to have taken place, and all persons having knowledge of crimes committed were summoned to give evidence. A similar system was instituted in the other towns that had been under Republican rule, and arrests, trials, executions, and imprisonments took place on a large scale throughout the next two years. As was unavoidable, though great efforts were made to avoid reprisals and the evil of professional informers, injustices were bound to occur, hatreds were kept alive and the prisons and labor camps were filled to overflowing. Much criticism was levelled at General Franco's government from abroad on this account, but it is difficult to think that any other system could have been followed. Feeling ran high after three years' fighting and the remembrance was green of the terrible atrocities that had taken place under the Republican-cum-Communist regime. It must be remembered that the figure of those killed in cold blood was put at 3,400,000 and official figures stated that 40,000 people had been assassinated in Madrid alone during the first three months of the civil war. There was hardly a single family of aristocratic or bourgeois position that had not the memory of relations murdered under the most horrible circumstances. Under those conditions and at that time any form of general government amnesty was impossible and would not have been endured by the people themselves, who would have taken reprisals into their own hands. It was to prevent this that General Franco established on March 14th, 1939, a special tribunal of political responsibilities to deal with all persons accused of subversive activities before and during the war and with those accused of opposition to the Nationalist movement.

On May 18th, 1939, there took place the great victory parade in Madrid. General Franco made a state entry into the capital and reviewed a sixteen-mile procession of troops from a stand in the Castellana Avenue, which was renamed General Franco Avenue. Portuguese, Italian, and German flags were flown, and German and Italian generals were on the stand. The parade was followed two days later by a religious ceremony in the church de las Salesas, in which the Primate of Spain laid General Franco's sword on the high altar before the Christ of Lepanto (this is a huge crucifix, which was carried on the ship of Don Juan of Austria at the great battle of Lepanto in 1571 and which usually rests in Barcelona Cathedral).

Great activity was shown by the educational authorities with a view to reestablishing the school system dislocated by the civil war; provincial and municipal committees, on which the Church was represented, were set up. There was also considerable activity in all matters concerning religion, culture and art, which were marked in June by the return of the Spanish Academy to Madrid and by a great procession throughout Spain of the Virgin of Covadonga, one of the most ancient and venerated of Spanish sacred statues, especially respected in parts of Spanish America; this image was found in the embassy in Paris, where it had apparently been taken as loot by the Republicans.

In a speech to the Council of the Falange on June 5th. General Franco outlined the disastrous financial situation of Spain as the result of the robbery by the Republicans of the gold reserves of the Bank of Spain, the civil war, and successive years of adverse trade balances. In the years subsequent to 1915–19, during which there was an annual surplus of seven hundred million pesetas, there was a yearly deficit in the balance of trade of six hundred million up to the year 1930. On the advent of the Republic, Spain's commerce was reduced by a half and the deficit fell to two hundred and fifty million. General Franco deprecated the obtaining of foreign loans and credits and preached that salvation could only come by production.

In July the Appeal Court of Poitiers ordered the return to Spain of 9,000 cases of valuables, being the booty robbed from private individuals and banks and sent to France by the Basque Republican government during the war.

General Queipo de Llano was removed from his command on account of an indiscreet speech. Ever since his dramatic capture of Seville in 1936, he had been an outstanding figure, in the capital of Andalucía on account of his command, and in this country on account of his picturesque broadcasts.

In August 1939, a double reorganization took place of the Falange and General Franco's cabinet. The latter consisted of the following fifteen members: General Franco (President), Colonel Beigbeder (Foreign Affairs), General Varela (Army), Admiral Salvador Moreno (Navy), General Yagüe (Air), Ramón Serrano Suñer (Home Office), Esteban Bilbao (Justice), José Larraz (Exchequer), Luis Alarcón de la Lastra (Industry and Commerce), General Muñoz Grandes (Secretary of the Falange Party), Alfonso Peña (Public Works), Joaquin Benjumea (Agriculture), José Ibáñez (Education), and two ministers without portfolio, Rafael Sánchez Mazas and Pedro Gamero del Castillo.

The reorganization of the Falange party was affected by a decree dated 31st July 1939. The new constitution extended considerably the faculty for membership: it placed the control in the hands of a National Council of 57 to 75 members and of a political committee of 12 members and it named General Franco as President of the National Council. From this time onwards General Franco adopted more and more the title "Caudillo."

The members of the National Council were partly elected on a functional basis and partly ex officio and the members of the political committee were all appointed by the Council or by General Franco. The Secretary was to be a member of the cabinet and the first to hold this office was General Franco's brother-in-law Señor Serrano Suñer.

These reorganizations of the cabinet and the Falange party marked an important tendency in General Franco's policy away from the more conservative-minded and monarchist traditionalists towards the more totalitarian and leftish Falangists. The conflict between these two elements had existed from the beginning and the official merging into one party had in no wise healed the breach, which was one of irreconcilable differences in ways of thought and life, and which became more and more irreconcilable as time went on and the Falange became more and more affected by totalitarian philosophy. It would seem that General Franco had now determined that in imitation of the one-party regime of the Axis powers and the making of the Falange all-powerful was the only way to realize his aim of Spanish unity; he failed, but the task was probably an impossible one; the characters of the people would not allow it.

However that may be, the reconstruction marked that ever-increasing power of the Falange, which later reached its apex under the pro-German Serrano Suñer and then began to decline as the power of the conservative elements, monarchists, Catholics and the army began to increase. But in the new cabinet seven Falangists replaced traditionalists, and among them General Jordana and the Conde de Rodezno, so that only one traditionalist remained.

In this same month, but before the government reconstruction, a law was passed by which all men between eighteen and fifty had to serve the reconstruction program either with personal labor or with money.

During September and October 1939, important financial transactions took place, which were a sign of the rapid recovery of the country. An issue of two billion pesetas of 3 percent treasury bonds was announced and doubly oversubscribed in one day and national bonds for two and a half billion pesetas were converted to 3 percent from higher rates of interest.

In September 1939, all the laws passed by the Catalan parliament were cancelled and the pre-Estatuto (Statute of Catalonia) situation restored. In this same month, the divorce law passed by the Republic in 1932 was annulled and the government announced the return to the payment of state stipends to the clergy. The reopening of the courses at the Madrid University began in October and the Minister of Education reorganized the museums and public libraries of Spain; one hundred annual scholarships were founded for Spanish-American students. In December 1939, Señor José María Pemán was elected Director of the Spanish Academy. On November 30th, amid great pomp and ceremony and with full military honors, the body of Jose Antonio Primo de Rivera, the founder of the Falange was translated from Alicante, where he had been imprisoned and murdered in 1936, and interred in the church of the Escorial. General Franco issued a decree in January, 1940, constituting in every province a commission to examine sentences passed by the military tribunals with a view to their modification and, in February 1940, a law was promulgated reducing all sentences not exceeding twelve years imposed for offences committed prior to April 1st, 1939, that is to say before or during the civil war.

Further legislation consisted of the law for the reestablishment of the Council of State, an ancient Spanish consultative institution, somewhat similar to our Privy Council, which had been abolished by the Republic. The new council was to consist of a president and six counsellors nominated by the head of the state from certain specified high officials such as ex-ministers of state. Other laws passed during February and March 1940, were, one making freemasonry and all secret societies illegal and making special mention of anarchists and communists in this respect, and another returning to their former proprietors all the lands confiscated by the Republic, in this latter law special reservation was made of those lands required by the state for their plans of peasant colonization and provisions were made to prevent injustice to the actual holders of the properties.

Six new members were elected to the Spanish Academy, an independent entity, whose membership is as great a distinction in Spain as is that of the Academie in France. Among those elected were the Cardinal Gomá, the Primate of Spain and the Duke of Alba, Spanish ambassador in London. In March 1940, a sign of returning normality and prosperity was the opening of the stock exchanges in Madrid, Barcelona, and Bilbao, which had been closed since the opening of the civil war in July 1936. A further sign of return to normality and Christianity was the celebration throughout Spain of Holy Week, which had been suppressed nine years before on the advent of the Republic. The celebrations showed unprecedented solemnity and enthusiasm especially in Seville, where the most renowned celebrations take place; they were attended by General Franco and his family.

On the occasion of the first anniversary of the end of the civil war, the inauguration took place by General Franco of the building of a great church to the dead in the Guadarrama Mountains, not far from the Escorial. A further decree of conditional liberty to prisoners over sixty years of age was announced, which gave a further sign of attempts at appeasement of the wounds of war.

A deficiency of supplies of foodstuffs and especially of bread had been increasingly evident for some time. In a speech made in April 1940, Señor Serrano Suñer stated that the shortage of wheat amounted to a million tons. It was estimated that it would be possible for the government to import 850,000 tons of wheat during the year, subject to their obtaining ships to carry it, and a purchase of 10,000 tons was arranged with Portugal. The British government gave facilities during the months of greatest scarcity for no less than thirty-four ships carrying wheat to arrive in Spain. The bread rations had been fixed at 250 grams per day and attempts were made to classify the ration so that the poorer families should receive more and the well-to-do receive less. However, there was in many quarters' great misery, and even starvation, and a great scarcity of tobacco, fuel, petrol, paper and other supplies.

In May 1940, it was estimated that, though only then out of the 450 churches in the diocese of Madrid had been fit for use on the capture of that city, 36 were then in use for worship.

Since its reorganization in the previous year, the Falange had been growing in power and a series of laws had put under their control the various vertical syndicates or corporations into which the national activities had been canalized. In August 1940, a new law was promulgated organizing a Falange militia with the expressed aim of training the Spanish youth and of forming four divisions of soldiers. Not only did this impinge on the functions of the army, but it had an unpleasant similarity to Nazi and Fascist measures, it naturally aroused rancor in the army and among the traditionalists against the Falange and aggravated the division among General Franco's supporters, and it became increasingly apparent that he was turning more and more towards extreme Falangism in the pursuit of the almost impossible task of Spanish unity and that the Falange in its turn was learning more and copying more from its axis models and taking to itself dictatorial powers, which were bound eventually to make it hateful to Spanish individualism. In September, 1940, there died in prison at the age of seventy, Señor Julián Besteiro, president of the Republican Cortes and member of Colonel Casado's Council of Defense, refused to fly from Madrid with his colleagues and was tried by the commission of political responsibilities and sentenced to thirty years' imprisonment.

This again aroused much criticism among partisans of the Republic in this country, but as already explained, it is difficult to suggest any alternative but a general amnesty, which was obviously impossible in the then state of mind of Spaniards. The criticisms came home to roost, as such things will, when the cry for the punishment of political leaders of the axis in the Second World War became almost universal. What is sauce for the goose is sauce for the gander!

In October 1940, a law was passed further extending the scope of conditional liberty for political prisoners; the numbers of those so released up to October amounted to 6,900.

Black marketing had arisen and flourished throughout Spain as the result of food shortage, and legislation was passed to curb it. Spanish hatred of discipline and order to a great extent nullified, as it was bound to do, the effectiveness of regulations and there grew up throughout Spain the profession of "estraperlista" or dealer in the black market, who quite openly, like any tradesman, provided his customers with goods from the black market. This word "estraperlista" was derived from the political scandal which took place in 1935 in connection with a gaming table called "straperlo" described in Chapter VII. The legislation fixing prices (*ley de tasas*) was however only partially flouted and enormous fines were imposed on industrialists for failing to observe the law. There was ever increasing evidence of official bribery and corruption.

In November, the Spanish universities began their new year. Besides the reconstruction and rehabilitation of the faculties in the University City of Madrid, this year saw the reopening of the destroyed university of Valladolid and of the Jesuit University at Deusto.

In an attempt to curb the Spanish tendency to waste time and the Spanish custom of dining late and sitting up all night, a law was passed in December, 1940, fixing the hours of work in government offices and private offices, limiting the hours at which meals could be served in restaurants and at which entertainment establishments should close.

On December 6th, a new law established the legal bases of the vertical syndicates or corporations, of which mention has been already made. These corporations were composed of employers, technicians, and laborers, who were conjointly to control their respective industry or profession. Lip service was given to the voluntary character of the syndicates and their freedom from bureaucratic control, but they were definitely subordinated to the discipline of the Falange party, which was a still further step towards totalitarian control by that party.

XXIV

END OF CIVIL WAR TO DECEMBER 1940,

FOREIGN AFFAIRS

On April 1st, 1939, the United States recognized General Franco's government; this completed the recognitions of the Nationalist government by all the countries with the exception of the U.S.S.R. and Mexico.

Spain signed the anti-Comintern pact in April, and the German and Italian troops, whose immediate repatriation had been promised by General Franco, were allowed to remain in Spain until after the victory parade in Madrid, which took place on May 18th, 1939. A few days later the German Condor Legion, which comprised German troops that had taken part in the civil war, left for Germany. On June 1st, the Italian troops likewise left Cádiz for Italy, and after a few days the Portuguese legionaries, who had fought for General Franco, were given an enthusiastic send off at Salamanca and returned to their own country. The return of the Italian troops was made an occasion of great celebration and publicity. Señor Serrano Suñer went in an Italian man-of-war to Naples and took part in the celebrations and the victory parades of Italian and Spanish troops that took place before King Victor Emmanuel and Signor Mussolini.

The signature of the Hitler-Stalin pact in August 1939 temporarily threw Spanish opinion out of gear because their feeling of hatred for Russia and communism made it difficult to digest simultaneously the friendship for Germany, Russia's ally. However, the apparently impossible digestive process was achieved, though Spain energetically denounced Russia's attack on Finland. On the other hand, the anti-communist actions taken by the French government improved the feeling between Spain and France.

On the outbreak of the Second World War, Spain's neutrality was proclaimed, and General Franco issued an order to all Spaniards to observe the strictest neutrality and to the press to abstain from comments.

In January 1940, the signature of a French-Spanish trade agreement indicated that the rapprochement between the two countries was progressing. In February, an Italian institute was opened in Madrid and there were demonstrations of Spanish-Italian friendship. At this time Spanish-Portuguese relations became increasingly close.

In March, an Anglo-Spanish trade agreement was signed covering the settlement of outstanding debts and balances by Spain and granting Spain credits in London for £4,000,000. In a debate in the House of Commons, Mr. Butler, under-secretary for foreign affairs, stated: "we have no cause to complain of the Spanish government's attitude, which has been one of strict neutrality."

On May 12th, 1940, on the occasion of the entry into the war of Holland and Belgium, General Franco again affirmed Spain's neutrality, and in that month Sir Samuel Hoare was appointed by the king as ambassador to Spain. At this time, a delegation of Catholics from England presented gifts for the destroyed Spanish churches and brought a personal present from Cardinal Hinsley to Cardinal Gomá, the primate of Spain.

On the entry of Italy into the war, General Franco changed the official attitude of Spain to one of "non-belligerency"; the difference between this and neutrality has never been defined. On June 14th, 1940, Spanish troops under Colonel Yuste marched into the international zone of Tangier; the Spanish Government declared that the occupation was of a temporary nature with the object of guaranteeing the neutrality of the zone. The occupation was the occasion for the pro-German and anti-British elements in Spain to organize street demonstrations in which the crowds shouted "*Viva Tánger Español*" and "*Gibraltar para España.*" It should be mentioned here that the Tangier question was not a new problem but was one of long standing, which always aroused a feeling of injustice in Spanish breasts. At this time, a decree was issued prohibiting any press propaganda by or on behalf of the belligerent nations.

The capitulation of France in June, 1940, brought the war and the danger of being involved in it much nearer to Spain, whose rulers saw the causes of the French collapse in the many years of social and political corruption, which culminated in communism and its instrument the Front Populaire. The German army was now on the Spanish frontier, and there were fears that it might be allowed to march through Spain to Gibraltar. Such was not the case, but friendship with the Germans was demonstrated by a reception at the frontier of high German officers and the German ambassador by General López-Pinto, who called for cheers for the German and Italian armies, the Führer and the Duce. This resulted in the almost immediate dismissal of the general from his post. In July 1940, General Franco offered the palace of La Granja as a residence for the duration of the war to the children of King Leopold of Belgium. The opening of a British institute in Madrid by the British Council with the object of furthering cultural relations and understanding between Spain and Britain was announced.

In July, an Anglo-Spanish-Portuguese imports agreement was signed, which facilitated the purchase and payment of wheat and other foodstuffs for Spain. This was followed in September by an agreement for supplying Spain with fuel oil.

The German ambassador, von Stohrer, a very able man, who gradually acquired through the pro-German section of the Falange complete control over the Spanish press and radio, in September, 1940, presented General Franco in the name of the Führer with the Grand Cross of Gold of the Order of Merit of the Eagle. General Franco in his speech of thanks referred to the friendship between the two nations and their strife against the common enemy (communism).

In the same month (September, 1940) Señor Serrano Suñer, at that time home secretary and president of the political committee of the Falange, left on a mission to Germany and Italy, where he had interviews with the Führer and the Duce and made flattering speeches about the identity of Spanish and Axis aims. His visit coincided with the Brenner meeting of Hitler and Mussolini, but it did not bring about the change in Spain's status that some people expected.

A few days later the prime minister in the House of Commons stated that Spain "has for some months past seemed to hang in the balance between peace and war" and after various friendly remarks he said: "British interests and policy are based on the independence and unity of Spain."

On October 20th, the replacement of the foreign minister, Colonel Beigbeder, by Señor Serrano Suñer indicated a bow to Germany and the Spanish pro-Germans. Then on October 23rd, 1940, came the surprising news of a meeting at Hendaye between the Führer and General Franco, who had so far succeeded in not paying a visit to either Hitler or Mussolini; evidently great things were expected of the visit, for Himmler had also recently been in Madrid; great pressure was brought to bear on General Franco to allow the German army passage through Spain, but he refused and Spain remained neutral. In November Colonel Yuste unexpectedly assumed the governorship of Tangier in the name of the

Spanish Government and abolished the existing legislative assembly and committee of control. As these proceedings altered the bases of the international agreements, protests were made by the British and U.S.A. ambassadors, and there were misgivings as to Spain's intentions, which were not quietened until February, 1941, when a temporary agreement was made between the governments. By this agreement British rights and interests in the zone were safeguarded, an undertaking being given that the zone would not be fortified and both countries consented to reserve their present position with a view to a final settlement.

On November 17th, 1940, the Council of Hispanidad was created to strengthen the racial and cultural relations between Spain and South and Central America, through the medium of cultural and economic affairs. Hispanidad is in its essence a nonpolitical and cultural movement, though at one time certain political elements tried unsuccessfully to convert it into a political instrument.

At the end of November, Señor Serrano Suñer had fresh interviews with the Führer and with Count Ciano.

In the same month, a new Anglo-Spanish financial agreement was signed by Sir Samuel Hoare and Señor Serrano Suñer, granting facilities for certain imports into Spain and safeguards against their delivery to Germany and Italy.

XXV

JANUARY 1941 TO DECEMBER 1943, INTERNAL AFFAIRS

The terrible consequences of the bread shortage in Spain received sympathetic help in January–February 1941, from Great Britain and the U.S.A. The former delivered wheat from her reserves in Canada and the American Red Cross sent various shiploads of flour which they distributed themselves in Spain. The shortage was so great that in Madrid the bread ration, already far too small, was halved in February and could only be doubled again in the following April. An epidemic of lice-born typhus broke out in Madrid owing to malnutrition and to the increase in the number of beggars.

On February 28th there took place in Rome the death of King Alfonso XIII.

On May 1st the council of Grandees of Spain assembled for the first time since the fall of the monarchy and the establishment of the Republic: the Duke of Berwick and Alba was elected life president of the council.

In May 1941, various events took place which indicated the "pull devil pull baker" situation between the Falange, the army, and the traditionalists. In the first place, at the beginning of the month, an order was issued exempting the press of the Falange from censorship, which was annulled fifteen days later by an order of Colonel Valentín Galarza, the newly appointed minister of home affairs. Simultaneously with various changes in General Franco's government a large number of changes and appointments took place in civil and military posts, of which some of the most outstanding were:

- ~ The removal from the civil governorship of Madrid of Señor Miguel Primo de Rivera, the Marquis of Estella, and his nomination as minister of agriculture.
- ~ The appointments of General Dávila to be chief of the general staff, and of General Martínez Campos to command the artillery reserve.
- ~ Generals Asensio and Kindelán, prominent figures in the civil war, returned from commands in Morocco and the Balearic Isles

to commands in the peninsula.

~ Señor Joaquín Benjumea, Minister of Finance. Señor José Antonio Girón, Minister of Labor.

~ Señor José Luis Arrese, Vice-Secretary of the Falange.

Ever since 1938 conversations had been carried on between the Vatican and General Franco with a view to a return to the broken concordat of 1851, or the negotiation of a new one. In 1940 Señor Serrano Suñer had been received by the Pope but no results had so far appeared. Now on June 12th 1941, an agreement was signed by the Spanish foreign minister and the papal nuncio in Madrid, settling the long outstanding and much disputed question of the appointments of archbishops and bishops, promising to respect certain clauses of the 1851 concordat and presaging negotiations for a new concordat.

On July 17th, 1941, the eve of the fifth anniversary of the outbreak of the civil war, General Franco made a speech to the Falange national council illustrating the glories and defects of Spain, outlining the causes and effects of the civil war, inciting his hearers to further efforts and sacrifices and stating that the military battle had been followed by the political battle. His references to foreign affairs are dealt with in the next chapter.

In September, the passing of a law was announced instituting benefits in reduction of taxes and in education facilities for families with no fewer than five children.

In October 1941, a new tribunal, set up to deal with the repression of masonry and communism, passed sentences of thirty years imprisonment and loss of civil rights on several prominent Republican politicians who were in exile; among them were Dr. Negrín, the former Prime Minister and Señor Álvarez del Vayo.

Progress in educational matters was shown in a review by the minister of education of the rebuilding of many school and university buildings throughout Spain and the institution of sixty-five new professorships during the past year. The minister of public works also announced the construction of many new roads and of large irrigation works on the Douro, Tagus, and Guadiana rivers and referred to the new afforestation works in progress.

The primacy of Spain left vacant by the death of Cardinal Gomá was filled by the appointment of Monsignor Enrique Pla y Deniel, Bishop of Salamanca; like his predecessor he was a Catalan.

In November, there took place the first official purge of the Falange to eliminate members who were not loyal to the party or its aims, which was a further sign of political conflict and opposition to the dominating position in the regime acquired by the extreme Falangists.

In January 1942, the budget estimates for 1943 were published; they gave receipts at 7.869 billion and expenditures at 7.880 billion of pesetas against the figures of 6.413 billion and 6.840 billion respectively for 1941.

The labor charter incorporated in General Franco's scheme for a New Spain envisaged measures of social security and in March 1942, the minister of labor announced that the following had been achieved in fulfilment of the promises of that charter:

~ Old Age insurance: The pension had been increased from one to three pesetas per day and the premiums received had increased from 45 million in 1935 to 145 million in 1941.

~ Maternity insurance: The premiums received were 5 million pesetas in 1935 and 7.25 million in 1941. The new scheme of clinics and outpatient wards was in full operation.

~ Accident insurance: Pensions paid in 1936 were 6.5 million pesetas and in 1942 45.75 million.

~ Family allowances: The figure for this new service were 834,495 families assisted, and 2,520,087 workmen insured.

~ Marriage insurance: In 1941, loans of 2,500 pesetas had been authorized to men and 5,000 pesetas to women, who gave up their work on marrying. Allowances were made for children resulting from these marriages.

In February, General Franco made the appointments of fifty members (*Procuradores*) to the new Cortes in accordance with its constitution; among them were three dukes, several bishops and archbishops, generals, and admirals.

On March 16th, the new Cortes consisting of 438 members began their sessions with an opening ceremony. The members comprised 13 ministers, 103 counselors of the Falange, the presidents of the supreme civil court, of the military courts and of the council of state, 142 representatives of the syndicates or corporations, 102 mayors and representatives of regional councils, 12 rectors of universities, 6 presidents of royal academies, 7 representatives of the colleges of lawyers, doctors and architects and the 50 members nominated by General Franco to which reference has already been made.

The president of the Cortes, Señor Bilbao, made a speech in which he condemned the liberal parliamentary regimes of the past as causes of Spanish decadence and told the members that they were returning to a system that represented the true Spain. The *Times* correspondent described the chamber of the Cortes as follows:

> The red upholstered seats of deputies (an unpopular color in Spain nowadays) have been altered to blue for the *procuradores*. Marble tablets or rolls of honor bearing the names of many outstanding Spanish leaders have been removed. Everything that recalls the liberal period from the time of the Cortes of Cádiz in 1812 has been obliterated. All paintings and inscriptions have gone from the walls, but the yoke and arrows, the emblems of the Falange carved in gold appear in the upper part of the chamber... There is no accommodation for the press or the public."
>
> It should be remarked that the yoke and arrows were originally the emblems of the Catholic monarchs (Ferdinand and Isabella), which had been adopted by Falange and that they denote much more than the modern Falangist spirit; they had a deep historical significance for the monarchists, traditionalists and other Spaniards, whose theory of the 'New Spain' was based on a return to a traditionally Spanish form of government to replace the Anglo-French parliamentary system, which they considered had proved itself unsuitable for Spain throughout a trial of more than a century.
>
> The day following the opening of the Cortes and after a mass sung by the primate of Spain in the church of San Jerónimo el Real, General Franco made a visit of state to the Cortes and delivered a speech in which he said: "With these Cortes has begun the collaboration of the people in the affairs of the state... the interests of the people are represented by the *procuradores*.

Other events of interest in January and February 1943, were the visit of the Duke of Alba to Prince Juan in Switzerland, the opening of the reconstructed colleges in the University City and the conclusion of the reconstruction of the naval shipbuilding yards at Cartagena, destroyed during the civil war. General Franco in announcing the religious services to be held on the anniversary of the death of King Alfonso XIII said that "the monarchy represented the final process of the unification and imperial expansion of Spain."

On April 1st, 1943, the fourth anniversary of the end of the civil war, General Franco announced a further amnesty to those suffering imprisonments for rebellion; all those serving sentences not exceeding twenty years were to have conditional liberty. There had been a progressive series of amnesties for those with smaller sentences throughout the past two years and some 15–20,000 of those under sentences of less than fourteen years had been released in the previous two months alone.

In May, 1943, an agreement was signed with the Argentine Republic for the supply of a million tons of wheat to Spain.

At Huelva on May 4th, General Franco, before an audience of 50,000 Falangists extolled the Spanish system of government in comparison with the liberal and Marxist systems. The liberal system he condemned as supporting neither freedom nor equality, and as converting men into chattels and he condemned the Marxist system for being worse than slavery for its state-worship and for its opposition to Christianity. He outlined the Spanish Falangist system as based on Christianity, the family, the municipality, and the syndicates.

The Spanish press received the news of the dissolution of the Comintern with the belief that it was a camouflage which should not deceive them.

Discontent with the regime and with the corruption of Falangist officials became increasingly evident and in July 1943, an important step was taken by the monarchists. Twenty-seven prominent monarchists, including members of the Cortes and high military, naval and civil officials signed a memorial to General Franco couched in respectful and laudatory terms, but requesting an immediate return of Spain to "the traditional Catholic monarchy" as the only method of gaining political stability and healing the rancor and differences existing in Spain. The two first signatories were the Duke of Alba, Spanish Ambassador in London and Señor Juan Ventosa, the prominent lawyer and political leader of Catalonia and a former finance minister of Spain. A few days later Señor Arrese, secretary of the Falange, announced that five Falangists were expelled from the party and had consequently lost their seats in the Cortes, because they had signed the memorial; they included such important figures as Señor Gamero del Castillo, ex-secretary general of the Falange, and Manuel Halcón, chancellor of the council of Hispanidad. General Franco made no public pronouncement on the matter and it was significant that only Falangist signatories to the memorial suffered any sanctions and nothing happened to the non-Falangist signatories. German radio commentary showed that German opinion was anti-monarchist.

On July 16th, at a full session of the new Cortes, the presidential speech was a eulogy of General Franco and a motion acclaiming his leadership was approved with applause. This was taken as intended as a set off to the monarchist memorial. On the following day General Franco, in a speech to the national council of the Falange, insinuated the possibility of a restoration of the monarchy, stating that their doctrine did not exclude the possibility that the established regime would one day take "the form which Spain possessed in the days of her glory"; he punctuated the necessity of party discipline and condemned, as he had done on many previous occasions, oriental freemasonry, which he qualified as one of the chief instigators of rebellion throughout the eighteenth century. This attitude of General Franco was a shock to the monarchists, but it must be noted that, as previously, General Franco showed that his regime was not rigid and he foreshadowed change; he did not make it clear whether he was firmly determined to continue to govern with extreme Falange as the chief pillar of the state or whether he was gradually turning away from them towards the more conservative elements.

At the end of July, the news of the bombardment of Rome by the United Nations was received soberly, notwithstanding the intense catholicity of Spain. Opinion appeared to understand that every care had been taken not to touch or damage the Vatican.

In August, it was reported from Mexico, where Señor Indalecio Prieto and other Republican politicians had taken refuge, that they were meeting in order to form a "government in exile" under Señor Martínez Barrio, ex-president of the old Republican Cortes.

General Franco inaugurated in Marín the new naval academy which had been constructed at a cost of 40 million pesetas.

In September 1943, Señor Arrese, secretary of the Falange, announced on the radio that Spain rested upon three pillars—the Caudillo, the Army and the Falange; that the Falange did not wish to establish a totalitarian state such as existed in Russia and other countries and that the Spanish system placed the individual first and the state second. This was no doubt a repercussion of the fall of Italy and Italian fascism and its identification in many countries with the Falange system. No doubt it was the intention of the speech to counter that idea and it cannot be denied that, though the systems are similar, they had considerable differences both of creed and practice; extreme Falangists had however much corrupted the creed and practice by directing them towards those of Nazism and fascism.

The occupation in September 1943, of the Vatican by German troops and the virtual imprisonment of the Pope created a great revulsion of feeling in Catholic Spain.

At the end of September, a large number of military promotions and changes in command were announced.

In November 1943, the publication of a letter from Señor Gil-Robles to General Asensio, the minister of war, created a sensation; the letter had been written in September and though couched in courteous and conciliatory terms it strongly advocated the immediate restoration of the monarchy, under the aegis of the army, that the king should be free from any one political party and independent of General Franco, and that the latter should be set aside. The letter painted vividly the dislike of General Franco and the Falange by the United Nations on account of their pro-German tendencies and the chaos and corruption existing under the Falange regime; it said that this regime must be changed immediately without waiting for the end of the war, so as to assure the cooperation and understanding of the victors, and pointed out that no revolution would be necessary as long as the restoration had the support of the army. Señor Gil-Robles at the time of writing the letter was in exile in Portugal; as described earlier in this history he was the leader of the right-wing C.E.D.A. party, which in 1934 had a majority in the Cortes, which his vacillation failed to use; for this he was much criticized, as it was thought he might have brought about the restoration at that time, prevented the advent of the Popular Front and saved his country from civil war. In 1938 he had attempted a rapprochement with General Franco but was rejected and obliged to remain in exile.

In October, 1943, five of General Franco's generals also addressed to him a letter in favor of a restoration and, though the Minister of War publicly announced a few days later that General Franco had the fullest confidence and loyalty of the army, these incidents showed which way the wind was blowing and that the army and the monarchists were becoming increasingly restless; a further indication of this was the dissolution by General Franco in December of the Falange militia.

At the end of the year 1943 activities were evident among the exiled Republican politicians. Señor Diego Martínez Barrio and General Miaja tried to assemble a committee in Colombia and failed, while Señor Indalecio Prieto formed in Mexico a Spanish committee of liberation composed of himself, Señor Álvaro de Albornoz and Señor Antonio María Sbert. In the meeting at which the committee was constituted, Señor Prieto stated that neither the Communists nor the Basque Separatist party would be admitted into the committee of liberation.

It was stated that in Mexico at that time there were 13,000 Spanish refugees and 130 deputies that belonged to the old Republican Cortes. There appeared to be no less than five distinct party leaders in Mexico, England, and other countries all on bad terms with each other; these parties were:

1. Republican Union under Martínez Barrio.
2. Socialists under Prieto.
3. Left Republicans.
4. Anarcho-Syndicalists.
5. Communists under Negrín.

The 1944 budget approved by the Cortes at the end of December, 1943, gave expenditures of 13 billion Pesetas, receipts of 10 billion, and a gold reserve of 1.1 billion. In the following February a supplementary budget was passed for the 3 billion gap.

Figures published in the *Financial Times* (22.12.43) gave the National debt at Pesetas 32,035,700,000, of which only 910,700,000 was foreign debt: the corresponding figures of 1934 were 21,263,700,000 and 917,100,000. This was a formidable figure of national debt, but the accumulation of foreign credits and of such a substantial gold reserve within a short period after the end of the civil war, during which the Republican government had got rid of all Spain's gold reserve, was a notable achievement and a sign of Spain's great recuperative economic ability.

XXVI

JANUARY 1941 TO DECEMBER 1943, FOREIGN AFFAIRS

In a speech in Madrid on March 14th, 1941, Señor Serrano Suñer congratulated Germany on the triumph of her arms, linked together the names of Germany and Spain, and concluded "Viva Hitler," and on March 17th, the Spanish Government reinstated the German consulate in its pre-1914 residence in Tangier, the Mendoubia, originally the residence of the representative of the Sultan of Morocco.

In March 1941, an Anglo-Spanish agreement was signed providing a credit of 2.5 million pounds for the purchases of raw materials and food, and in the same month there was signed a Spanish-Portuguese agreement bringing the countries into closer commercial relationship.

On June 24th, 1941, a demonstration by young Falangists took place outside the British embassy in Madrid, for which an apology was demanded and received from General Franco. The invasion of Russia by Germany gave a great impetus to German influence and propaganda in Spain, where the pro-Germans were able to forget at once the recent German-Russian alliance and re-acclaim themselves the companions of Germany in a renewed campaign against the common communist enemy. Señor Serrano Suñer made violent speeches in favor of Germany and against Great Britain and the U.S.A. One important result was the prompt recruiting and dispatch to fight against Russia of the 'Blue Division,' composed of volunteers from the ex-combatants of the civil war, under General Muñoz Grandes. This was an unneutral act and was a victory for the pro-German section of the Falange and their German instigators at the German embassy, but it was following the example set by the International Brigades, which went to fight in Spain in 1936. In a speech to the council of the Falange on July 17th, General Franco restated the Spanish hatred of the Soviet and of communism and stated that the Allies had already lost the war.

In July and August 1941, trade agreements were signed with Finland and Denmark, and in August an agreement was made for the dispatch of Spanish labor to work in Germany. On the entry into the war of the U.S.A. and Japan in December 1941, a decree was issued announcing that Spain would maintain her attitude of nonbelligerency.

In January 1942, further shipments of wheat under the Spanish-Argentine treaty brought the quantity of wheat imported from the Argentine to 500,000 tons. This could, of course, only have been released by the benevolence of the British blockade, and the British ambassador announced that still further facilities were to be given to relieve the food shortage in Spain.

In February it was announced that Spain took over German, Italian, and Japanese representation in the U.S.A. and in thirteen Spanish-American countries, who had broken relations with the Axis powers and whose representation Spain simultaneously took over in Berlin and Rome.

The entry of the U.S.A. into the war and the attitude of the Hispano-American Republics began at this time to exercise a visible effect on those Spaniards who had been convinced of a German victory. This effect was visible increasingly in the behavior of General Franco towards the extreme pro-German Falangists led by Señor Serrano Suñer.

In February, General Franco made another of his pro-German speeches which, after repeating the anti-communist credo that inspired him, concluded with the words: "If the road were open to Berlin, it would not be one division of Spanish volunteers that would go there, but a million Spaniards would offer themselves."

In March 1942, a new U.S.A. ambassador to Madrid was appointed in the shape of Professor Carlton J. H. Hayes. Being a Catholic and a historian, who had been a strong supporter of General Franco during the civil war, this appointment was looked upon as evidence of a friendly disposition on the part of the U.S.A. towards Spain and a sign of satisfaction and rapprochement.

In June 1942, Señor Serrano Suñer made the last of his sensational visits to the Axis countries. He went to Rome, where he had long conversations with Mussolini and Count Ciano, the Italian foreign minister; he also visited the king and was received by the Pope, who gave him a blessing for Spain and for General Franco.

Allegations having been made in the foreign press, the foreign office in Madrid denied that Spanish ships had provided German submarines with fuel oil or used their wireless to assist submarines to discover the position of merchant ships.

In July 1942, on the anniversary of the Nationalist rising, General Franco spoke reviewing the state of Spain and the progress of reconstruction and stated the supreme necessity of Spanish unity. In his comments on foreign affairs, he made no friendly reference to the Axis powers as in former speeches, though he stated his opinion that "in matters pertaining to war the totalitarian regime has clearly demonstrated its superiority." He repeated and emphasized that communism was the great peril for Europe and for Spain, who had already been fighting against it for six years.

A new treaty between Spain and Argentina was announced for the purchase of meat, tobacco and a million tons of wheat to be carried in Spanish ships.

At the end of August, 1942, there came the sensational fall of Señor Serrano Suñer, who was replaced as head of the Falange by General Franco and as foreign minister by General Jordana, who had been foreign minister and Vice President of the first Nationalist government in 1938. Señor Serrano Suñer's fall was due partly to internal and partly to foreign politics, and it marked a decline of the power of the pro-German section of the Spanish people.

At the end of September, the reorganized government made an announcement confirming their position of nonbelligerency, stating the continuation of their crusade against communism and their friendship with Spanish-American countries.

On the landing of U.S. and British troops in North Africa in November 1942, Sir Samuel Hoare notified the Spanish government that "the operations in no way threaten Spanish territory, metropolitan or oversea. Spanish territory will be fully respected, and Spanish interests will not be compromised." He also informed them that the existing trade agreements and the *modus vivendi* in Tangier were not affected, and he concluded that it was desired that Spain should "take her due place in the reconstructed Europe of the future." President Roosevelt addressed a similar message to General Franco on behalf of the U.S.A.

On his 50th birthday (December 5th, 1942) General Franco received congratulatory telegrams from Hitler and Mussolini, and in his acknowledgement to Hitler he expressed his wishes for the victory in his fight to free Europe from the Bolshevik terror. This like General Franco's and Señor Serrano Suñer's former speeches created a bad impression in the United Nations.

General Jordana visited President Carmona of Portugal, and friendly speeches were made emphasizing the complete agreement between the two countries. General Jordana also reiterated Spain's determination to remain neutral.

In January, von Stohrer, the German Ambassador to Madrid was recalled; he had shown great activity and ability in organizing and working a huge propaganda machine throughout Spain, and he had made many friends in Spain. His recall was considered as a mark of Germany's discontent at the failure of his extensive efforts to break down Spanish neutrality and to bring Spain into the Axis, and indicated a further step towards safety for Spain along the tightrope of neutrality.

In January 1943, the Tangier question again came to the fore; the High Commissioner in Morocco, General Orgaz, made the statement that Tangier was incorporated in the Spanish Zone. This was met by a reminder from Great Britain that she refused to recognize Spain's unilateral actions in the Tangier Zone and reserved her rights as previously defined in 1925 and 1928.

On the occasion of the new German ambassador, Herr Adolf von Moltke, presenting his credentials to General Franco, speeches were made which again emphasized that Germany and Spain were fighting in a common European cause against communism. In January Señor Arrese, the secretary of the Falange paid a visit to Berlin.

In February, a new trade agreement was signed with Portugal.

On February 26th, Mr. Hayes, the U.S. Ambassador, addressed the American Chamber of Commerce in Barcelona and referred to the part which the United States had played in the improving of Spain's economy. He stated that the supply of petrol and petroleum products had been considerable, and concluded his speech by saying:

> As long as the war lasts and is kept away from Spanish land, the United States stands ready to continue to extend any help she can to Spain, who is herself doing so much with obvious success to develop a peace economy that can and will carry this country safely into the future period of world peace... No nation is self-sufficient, and the United States policy of good neighborliness cannot be effective unless it is reciprocal. (Quotation from the *Times*, 27th February).

Mr. Sumner Welles, Under-Secretary of State of the U.S.A. wrote in March to the committee of foreign affairs that Spain had given adequate guarantees to the governments of the U.S.A. and Great Britain that petroleum imports into Spain would not leave Spanish territory. A similar assurance was given in the House of Commons.

On April 17th, 1943, General Jordana, minister of foreign affairs, declared in a speech in Barcelona that Spain was in a position to defend her independence, and stated that she would be ready to offer her good services for the reestablishment of peace. This speech called forth declarations from the British and U.S. foreign secretaries to the effect that the policy of the United Nations was that of unconditional surrender by their enemies, as previously stated.

On May 12th, 1943, in Almería, General Franco spoke in favor of peace, stating that it was madness to postpone making peace, because behind the scenes lay communism, which for 25 years had been sowing hatred, and that neither side was strong enough to destroy the other. This speech was badly received by the press and radio of both sides (the United Nations and the Axis), and was considered in England and the U.S.A. to be a peace feeler on behalf of the Germans, a supposition for which no evidence was ever produced.

The successful conclusion of the Tunisian campaign and especially the wholesale surrender there of the German army had a great effect on the pro-German section of Spanish opinion, and the effect was immediately noticeable in the press and radio.

On May 19th, 1943, Mr. Eden, in the House of Commons, stated that British rights in Tangier were duly protected pending a final solution, which could not be attained until after the war.

At the end of May there was a campaign in the Spanish press and radio against aerial bombing of towns, no doubt partly inspired by the question of the bombing of Rome, and probably also by German and Falangist propaganda. This called forth violent protests in the British press and parliament, and caused considerable irritation both in England and the U.S.A. Thus there was an exact reversal of the roles of the government press and public of the three countries over the same problem during the Spanish Civil War.

On June 1st, the British consul general in Tangier protested to the Spanish authorities against various recent steps taken to extend their authority in the Zone; satisfactory explanations and promises were received by the consul general. In the House of Lords, Lord Cranbourne stated that by virtue the *modus vivendi* of February 1941, the interests of Great Britain were fully safeguarded pending a final agreement, which could only be reached after the war.

The landing in Sicily and the rapid success of Allied arms still further reduced in Spain the belief in an eventual German victory and, as the pro-Germans became less vocal, the pro-British and pro-United Nations Spaniards were able to make their voices increasingly audible, and a marked change was noticeable in the press.

On the fall of Mussolini at the end of July 1943, which created a great impression in Falangist circles, General Franco emphasized the difference between Italian fascism and Spanish Falangism, which he pointed out was purely Spanish in its origin and not foreign.

On August 4th, Mr. Eden, in the House of Commons, gave of a combined warning on the part of the U.S.A., Soviet and British Governments to certain neutral countries requesting them to prevent asylum being given to Mussolini and other war criminals. In the same session Mr. Eden stated that the return of the monarchy was entirely a matter for Spain to decide.

Also in August, Sir Samuel Hoare had a long conference in Coruña with General Franco and General Jordana, about which Mr. Eden stated in the house of commons that General Franco's attention was drawn to various complaints of "discrimination against British interests," some of which had been remedied, but others had still to be remedied; that his attention was also drawn to the position of the Blue Division and "it was made clear to General Franco that, so long as it remained in the Soviet Union, it was a serious obstacle to the development of cordial Anglo-Spanish relations."

In the same session of the House of Commons Mr. Eden repeated previous statements about Tangier, and said:

> H.M. Government in the U.K. have always made it clear that the *modus vivendi* reached between them and the Spanish government early in 1941... was of a provisional nature pending the possibility of a final settlement... They have always maintained their protest against the original unilateral action of the Spanish Government. Under the *modus vivendi* British rights in that Zone have been and are fully safeguarded.

He went on to say that the Spanish government had been warned to put an end to abuses and to ensure the strict neutrality of the Zone.

The occupation of the Vatican and the virtual imprisonment of the Pope created a great revulsion of feeling in Spain, which was expressed in the Spanish press; it affected still further the relative sympathies of Spaniards to the belligerents.

The agreement between Portugal and Great Britain on October 13th, by which the United Nations were allowed the use of bases in the Azores for naval and military purposes, caused in the Peninsula the conviction that the danger of a German invasion was completely over. In view of the close relations between Spain and Portugal and the affinity of their political outlook and systems, the effect on bringing Spain nearer to the

United Nations and separating her from German influence and menace was notable; an illustration of this fact was the announcement that the Blue Division was to be recalled from the Russian front.

The chronicle of events between the outbreak of the Second World War and October, 1943, seems to bring out certain facts clearly.

General Franco had been well disposed to the Axis powers, bitterly hostile to anything connected with communism and Marxist socialism, and inspired with a dislike for what he considered to be the liberal and plutocratic systems of Great Britain and the U.S.A. But he was first and last determined in the interests of his country to remain out of the war, and in that he was successful. His speeches and those of his foreign minister, the sending of the Blue Division to fight with the Germans against Russia, and the pro-German attitude of the Spanish press caused disgust in this country, but without them it is very doubtful if Spain's neutrality would have been maintained. Had Spain been a member of the Axis or had she been an ally of this country, in fact had she been anything but neutral, a German invasion of Spain and Portugal could hardly have been avoided, with far reaching and disastrous consequences to this country in the dark days of 1940–41 and to the whole length and trend of the war. It is necessary to visualize what would have been the effect on our Mediterranean position or on the U-boat campaign, if Spanish, and perhaps Portuguese, coasts and ports had been in the hands of the enemy and the German army at the gates of Gibraltar and in North Africa.

The motives inspiring Spain's neutrality were first and last the interests of Spanish patriotism, and it is futile to look for them elsewhere. It was maintained by able statesmanship on the part of General Franco and his government which often displeased both sides. It was assisted and maintained by able diplomacy on the part of the U.S. and British governments and their representatives in Madrid, and on the part of the Spanish representative in London. They assisted friendly cooperation between the countries and refused to be diverted from their course by the uninstructed clamor of the press and propaganda on either side. Results justified them.

One of the great causes of misunderstanding was the inability to discriminate between friend and foe in Spain. Spain was split in two, as it was in the First World War, between pro-Germans and pro-Allies. The former were the more vocal because they controlled the press and radio, but it would have been a feeble diplomacy that overlooked the latter because it hated the former. It is certain that in the Second World War the Allies had more friends in Spain than they had in the First World War.

There was a tendency in this country to look upon the Falange as representative of Spain as a whole, and to overlook the fact that, though officially only one party, the Falange, which was theoretically a combination of all political parties, then recognized in Spain, the unity was fallacious and a failure. In reality, though not officially, the conservative elements in Spain—the traditionalists, the army, the Catholics, the monarchists, etc.—were all powerful representative bodies of opinion and all wholly or partially opposed to the Falange, which it must be remembered gradually absorbed most of the old left-wing elements and simultaneously became pro-German.

At the end of October 1943, there took place in Barcelona the first exchange of wounded prisoners of the belligerent nations; the exchange took place in the presence of the Spanish authorities and the diplomatic representatives of Great Britain, Germany, and Japan. It was stated that this was the first occasion since the end of the Spanish Civil War that the red ensign had been seen in the great port of Barcelona—a sad commentary on the once prosperous conditions of Anglo-Spanish trade and shipping.

At the end of November 1943, there was a welcome renewal of Anglo-Spanish trade in the purchase of large quantities of oranges and onions to the value of £2,000,000.

The placing of bombs in some of the orange cargoes by German agents called forth diplomatic protests, which resulted in explanations being given in London by the Duke of Alba to the foreign secretary, and in Madrid by the Spanish foreign secretary to Sir Samuel Hoare, and in a promise of investigation and punishment of the offenders. These incidents again awoke the hostility towards Spain of the British press, which in some cases sought in saddle the Spanish Government with deliberate responsibility for what was obviously German sabotage; it was pointed out that to do this would be analogous to considering the British government responsible for the I.R.A. bombs placed in British pillar boxes in 1940.

XXVII

MONARCHY AND THE INFANTE DON JUAN

In February 1941, King Alfonso published a declaration to the effect that he renounced his rights to the throne of Spain in favor of his son the Infante Don Juan. He had been ill for some time and on February 28th he died in Rome. Thus ended the life of a monarch who possessed outstanding qualities both as king and man. He undoubtedly made his mistakes like other mortals, but he always exhibited an outstanding personal courage, great patriotism, and a great personal charm. He was accused of being too much of a politician for a constitutional monarch, but it is probable that the unsuitability of the parliamentary system existing in Spain, which converted the Cortes into a talking shop and made political parties owe allegiance to persons instead of to programs, made it unavoidable for the monarch to take a hand in politics.

The day following the death of Alfonso XIII the Spanish government officially expressed their sorrow and proclaimed the day as a national day of mourning, which was observed with great fervor throughout the country. His body was buried temporarily in Rome with a view to eventual transfer to the royal mausoleum in the Escorial. The Infante Don Juan, Prince of Asturias, in a speech to the Spanish grandees assembled in Rome for the funeral, said:

> By his death the country loses the first and the most exemplary of her servants. His whole life was taken up by impassioned love of her and zeal for the increase of her greatness. When his dying lips kissed the crucifix for the last time, the word they uttered was 'Spain.'

The Infante then proceeded to quote a letter he had written to his father, when the later renounced the rights to the throne in his favor shortly before he died. In that letter after referring to his father's great record as King, the Infante said:

> The suffering endured by our people on the occasion of this great national crusade (the civil war), and the blood generously poured out

by so many glorious martyrs of God and the country, deepen the sense of responsibility with which I accept the claim to the throne of Spain, which falls to me by the inviolable law of history, which by the design of providence brings to an end the cycle of quarrels over the rights of succession, which were the main cause of the civil wars in the nineteenth century. I implore God to grant me the gifts of right judgment, firmness, and perseverance necessary to accomplish the objects of my destiny. And when it calls me to assume the crown of Spain, I shall do so with the grim determination to restore the traditional significance of our monarchy for the state and for the people, reviewing that warm and generous inspiration by which it lived, and which, on the foundation of our Catholic faith and of our consciousness of our united destiny made the country one and made it great.

With this as my fundamental object, when the hour comes to fulfil my duty, and my desire to save my country, I shall do my best to guarantee her spiritual unity and her historical continuity, to alleviate with a father's affectionate authority the recent happenings, and to give a real satisfaction to the longings of the great mass of Spaniards who hope for a juster and a better life.

The Infante Don Juan was the third son of King Alfonso XIII and Queen Eugenia, having been born on June 20th, 1913. He became heir to the Spanish throne on 11th June, 1933, when his two elder brothers, the Prince of Asturias and the Infante Don Jaime renounced their rights of succession on account of their physical disabilities. He then himself assumed the title of Prince of Asturias.

His mother was an English princess, the daughter of Prince Henry of Battenberg and of Princess Beatrice, the daughter of Queen Victoria. Thus he was half English by birth and his connection, with England was cemented and made closer because, in his own words, he "served for five exceptionally happy years in the British Navy."

He married in 1935 the Princess Mercedes, daughter of the Infante Don Carlos of Bourbon Sicily and of Louise, Princess of France, who was herself an Infanta of Spain. He had a daughter born in 1936 and a son, the Infante Don Juan Carlos born in 1938.

He was anxious to serve in the Spanish Civil War, but he was not allowed to do so and he expressed his regret in the following words:

> I greatly regret that the privilege of fighting for my country was denied
> me, first when acting under the impulse of my feelings I went to Spain
> at the beginning of the war, and later by Generalissimo Franco himself
> when I asked him to let me have a place in the Navy.

These quotations come from a foreword that he wrote to a book called *The New State* by Victor Pradera, a prominent traditionalist writer and politician who was assassinated in the civil war. In this foreword the Infante also stated that, owing to his English connections, "it is therefore very sad for me to find that my own countrymen are troubled and perplexed by the British attitude, and that the British do not understand the issues in Spain," and he went on to outline and refute many of the popular misconceptions and myths about the civil war held in England, which he rightly considered to be due to the fact that the British public had been misinformed by the press.

The fact that he wrote the foreword to *The New State* can be considered to indicate that that book outlined the regime that he would wish to see established in Spain. Broadly speaking that regime is based on the monarchy, the church, the council, the Cortes, the municipalities, and a guild system of representation; it is a system in which the individual comes first and the state second; it visualizes a return to the historical Spanish system existing previous to the adoption, at the beginning of the nineteenth century, of a liberal parliamentary system based on the foreign systems of England and France. It is in fact similar in many ways to the theory of the system of the Falange and of General Franco, but without the tendency towards socialism and totalitarianism into which that system had fallen.

Though they appear in their chronological sequence on other pages, yet, on account of their importance, it will be well to repeat here various declarations by General Franco as regards a restoration.

In July 1937, he said: "Should the moment for a restoration arrive, the new monarchy would be very different from that of 1931, different in constitution and in the person, who should incarnate it."

In February, 1943, he said the monarchy represented the final process of the unification and imperial expansion of Spain, and in the following July he said that the regime would one day take "the form which Spain possessed in the days of her glory."

The *Jornal de Genève* of November 11th, 1942, published a declaration by the Infante of which the following is a translation:

I am the head of no conspiracy, but I am the legitimate depository of the secular political inheritance of the Spanish monarchy. I am sure that it will be restored as soon as the interests of Spain demand it. When the Spanish people think the time has come, I shall not hesitate a moment to put myself at their disposal.

I have no intention of imposing on Spaniards on my own authority the forms and institutions of their national life. My highest ambition is to be king of a Spain in which all Spaniards finally reconciled to each other can live in common. If I succeed in reducing or suppressing the motives of dissension and improving the spiritual and material conditions in harmony and peace, monarchy will have carried out its historic and traditional mission. As a man of my time with direct knowledge of social inequalities, created by the economic system of the nineteenth century, I shall not fail to favor all measures likely to contribute to a more equitable distribution of wealth.

In foreign relations close friendship or rather fraternity with Portugal and Spanish America will be the unshakeable foundation of our policy. As regards other nations, I am convinced that there is no claim which Spain might advance, which is incapable of peaceful and mutually satisfactory settlement.

In the present conflict Spain, still bleeding from the effects of civil war, has the right to claim the greatest respect from all belligerents.

No attitude of a restored monarchy is conceivable except that of scrupulous and impartial neutrality, supplemented by firm resolution to defend it at all costs, even by arms, should any country attempt to violate it.

If the territorial integrity of Spain were unfortunately violated, I am sure that the Spanish people would, as ever, resist the invader with courage and bravery. Should God intend this trial for us, my sword, as a Spanish soldier, will be at the service of my country.

From 1942 onwards discontent with the regime in Spain had been growing and it became increasingly evident that General Franco's attempts to unify Spain under the one-party system of the Falange had failed. There was increasing friction between the extreme Falangists and the traditionalists, monarchists and conservatives, and the call for the return of the monarchy became accentuated, as a means of reconciliation and the establishment of a more popular regime. As described in Chapter XXV, in July 1943, a monarchist petition headed by the Duke of Alba was drawn up requesting, in the interests of Spain, an immediate return to "the Traditional Catholic Monarchy."

In his letter to his father quoted above, the Infante referred to the end of the succession conflict in Spain, for he had become by hereditary succession the legitimate heir of the Carlist claim to the throne. In July 1943, certain minor disputes between the traditionalists and the legitimists, who were both Carlists, came to an end with a common agreement to accept the Infante Don Juan as king.

The monarchist movement rapidly gathered force in the last half of 1943. On October 15th a petition in favor of a prompt restoration was presented to General Franco by a number of the most prominent generals and in November there was made public a letter in the same sense written in the month of September to General Asensio, the minister of war, from Señor Gil-Robles, the ex-conservative leader of the C.E.D.A. party, who was living in exile in Portugal.

In March 1944, some 100 university professors from all over Spain signed a monarchist petition.

No further monarchial moves were made for some time, but in November, 1944, General Franco spoke in an interview to *United Press* about a possible return of Spain to a monarchy at some future date, but he let it be understood that the time and the kind of monarchy to be established would be chosen by himself.

Then in March 1945, Prince Juan issued from Lausanne a manifesto to his country:

> Spaniards, I know well that you are sadly disillusioned, and I share your fears. Perhaps I feel them even more deeply than you do, since in the free surroundings of this watchtower in the middle of Europe, where God has set my lot, my eyes are not bandaged, nor my mouth gagged. Thus, I am able to hear and speak freely on what is being said about Spain.
>
> Since April 1931, when the King my father suspended his royal prerogatives, Spain has passed through one of the most tragic periods of her history. The state of insecurity and anarchy caused by numberless revolts, strikes and disorders of all sorts, during the five years of the Republic, let loose the civil war, which for three years desolated our country and drenched her in blood. Thus, the King's generous sacrifice in leaving his country, in order to avoid the shedding of Spanish blood, was useless.
>
> Today, six years after the end of the civil war, the regime established by General Franco, which was modelled on the totalitarian systems of the Axis powers and which is entirely contrary to the character and tradition of our people, is quite incompatible with the conditions prevailing in the world as a result of the present war. The future of our nation is compromised by the foreign policy of that regime. Spain is running the risk of seeing herself dragged into a new

fratricidal struggle and of finding herself isolated in the world. The present regime, whatever efforts it may make to adapt itself to the new situation, will only encourage both these dangers, whereas a republic, however moderate it may be in its beginnings and its intentions, is certain to swing towards one extreme or the other and inevitably provoke another civil war.

It is only the traditional monarchy that can be the instrument of peace and concord leading to reconciliation among Spaniards, that can obtain respect for Spain abroad by establishing an effective legal status, and that can call into being that harmonious combination of order and liberty, which forms the Christian concept of the State. Millions of Spaniards of the most varied ideologies understand this truth and see in the monarchy their only hope of salvation.

Ever since 1941, when, owing to the resignation and death of the King don Alfonso XIII. I assumed the duties and rights of the Spanish crown; I have shown my disagreement with the home and foreign policies of General Franco. In letters addressed to him and to my representative I have set forth my disapproval of the regime he represents, and I have twice declared publicly in the press my disagreement with him in certain fundamental policies.

For these reasons, I have resolved, in order to free my conscience from the ever-increasing burden of responsibility that afflicts it, to raise my voice and solemnly require of General Franco that he should recognize the failure of his conception of a totalitarian state, surrender his power and allow the restoration of Spain's traditional regime, which is the only one capable of guaranteeing religion, order and liberty.

Under the monarchy, which will favor reconciliation, justice and tolerance, many reforms will be necessary in the interest of the nation. Its foremost duties will be: the immediate approval by popular vote of a political constitution, which shall recognize the natural rights of the individual and guarantee political liberties; the establishment of a legislative assembly elected by the nation; the recognition of regional differences; a full political amnesty; a more just distribution of wealth and the suppression of unfair social inequalities, which are not only contrary to Christian precepts but are dangerously and flagrantly in conflict with the political and economic ideas of the age.

I am not raising the flag of rebellion nor do I incite anyone to sedition, but I must remind those who support the present regime of the tremendous responsibility that they incur by helping to prolong a situation which runs the risk of causing irreparable damage to the country.

Strong in my trust in God and in my age-long rights and duties, I await the moment when my most ardent desires may be realized namely, peace and concord among all Spaniards.

Long live Spain.

This manifesto was considered in many quarters to be inopportune and in others to be well conceived as a clarification of the situation. General Franco made no public reply but in a press interview in June 1945, on announcing the formation of a Council of State, he again indicated a return to monarchy at some indefinite time, saying that the Council of State would demand from the hereditary prince definite guarantees and the necessary prerequisites of fitness to ascend the throne.

Certain repercussions took place as the result of the manifesto and some monarchists in official positions considered they could no longer serve under General Franco. Among these was the Duke of Berwick and Alba who resigned his post of ambassador to England in April on the grounds of his tradition, his conscience and his conviction that his efforts to improve relations between Great Britain and Spain would be useless until there were a change in the regime, which was bringing Spain into disrepute and unpopularity abroad. Prince Juan's manifesto and the Duke's reasoning received confirmation in the outbreak against Spain in the San Francisco conference.

XXVIII

JANUARY 1944 TO AUGUST 1945, INTERNAL AFFAIRS

In January 1944, the Minister of Labor, Señor Girón announced a national health insurance scheme, which was shortly to be put into operation. It was to be a state insurance scheme in that the state would legislate, order, and organize the conditions of insurance and benefits, but already existing medical and insurance organizations were to carry out and administer the powers, which would be delegated to them by the state. The principal benefits were to be: (1) free medical treatment, free drugs and free hospital treatment for the insured and their families, (2) free and complete assistance in childbirth, (3) the receipt of from 50 to 90 percent of wages during incapacity for work.

In March 1944, some hundred university professors signed a petition for the restoration of the monarchy, for which four of them were arrested and exiled from Madrid to residences in the country.

In March 1944, the Minister of Justice made an announcement in reply to statements in the foreign press that a million political offenders were still in prison. He stated that the total number of people imprisoned since 1936 amounted to about 400,000, of which over 200,000 had been amnestied, and that there had never been more than 270,000 in prison at any one time, that during his term of office he had closed 23 prisons and that there were then 30,000 prisoners convicted of common crimes and a rather smaller number of political prisoners, most of whose sentences had been reduced.

In August 1944, occurred the death of General Count Jordana, the Minister of Foreign Affairs, who had been in 1936 president of the Nationalist junta, which preceded General Franco's first regular government; he was a traditionalist in politics and considered to be anti-Axis and pro-British; he was succeeded by don Jose Felix de Lequerica a conservative politician of the old regime and an ex-diplomat.

The liberation of Southern France from German occupation resulted in the freeing of the Spanish Republicans and members of the International Brigades, who had been in concentration camps in France since the end of the Spanish Civil War. Some of these formed into bands and took violent possession of Spanish consulates in towns of Southern France and penetrated into Spain, where they were soon dealt with by the Spanish army and frontier guards.

In November 1944, there was an excited flutter in the world's press over a declaration by Señor Miguel Maura, who was Minister of the Interior in the first Republican government in 1931 and was living in exile in Paris, to the effect that General Franco was about to resign, that he was ready to take his place and would shortly travel to the Spanish frontier to discuss the matter with representatives of Spanish political parties. He was a most unlikely person to succeed in such an enterprise, as he was discredited with most parties in Spain. His declaration was deservedly ridiculed in Madrid, where it was promptly and officially denied. The incident was unimportant except as an illustration of refugee republican activity.

Construction, buildings, university and education developments and economic and labor improvements were important throughout the year 1944 and Spain then appeared to be one of the best fed and most tranquil countries of Europe. An indication of this returning prosperity was a new issue of two billion pesetas of treasury bonds which was over-subscribed in two hours in January 1945. A further indication was given in April of the same year, when Spain purchased 80 percent of the stock of the Spanish Telephone Company from its owners, the Telegraph and Telephone Corporation of New York, for the equivalent of £14,250,000 payable partly in bonds and partly in cash.

In April 1945, the Infante Don Juan issued a manifesto to the Spanish people calling attention to his disapproval of the existing regime in Spain and the dangers threatening Spain internally and externally owing to its policies, and calling on them to restore the traditional monarchy; it caused no immediate repercussions except the resignation of various monarchist officials and among them the Duke of Alba, ambassador in London, and six prominent municipal councilors of Madrid. It appeared that within Spain, though there was a great desire in many quarters to return to a monarchy, there was a reluctance to force a change at a moment when prosperity had returned after a long period of trouble.

It was announced in June 1945, by the government that in future all prosecutions for purely political offences would be dropped and that Spanish consuls had been ordered to accept applications from exiles to return to Spain. This amounted to a general amnesty for all non-criminal offences.

In June 1945, General Franco announced the impending formation of a *Consejo de Estado* to decide the question of the monarchy and succession "when necessity arose." This did not alter the immediate monarchical situation, but the formation of the Consejo was another step towards the reestablishment of the traditional structure of Spanish government.

There was considerable corruption under the Falange regime, which added to its internal unpopularity. The black market had become an established fact of Spanish life, being as in other countries one of the inevitable results of excessive bureaucracy and food restrictions.

On July 17th, 1945, General Franco made a speech in which he outlined the great reconstruction and successes that had taken place under his regime and the completion of the Spanish bill of rights (Fuero de los Españoles), which had just been passed by the Cortes and the council of state; he repeated his former declarations of his intention to re-establish a monarchy in due time.

Three days later he announced cabinet changes and the cabinet then remained as follows: Martín-Artajo (Foreign Minister), General Dávila (War), Admiral Regalado (Navy), General Gallarza (Air), Señor Suances (Industry and Commerce), Señor Rein (Agriculture), General Landreda (Public Works), Señor Burín (Finance), Señor González (Interior), Señor Martín (Education), Señor Fernández-Cuesta (Justice).

In making these changes he dropped from the cabinet Señor Arrese, the strong secretary general of the Falange, and Miguel Primo de Rivera, Marqués de Estella, the brother of its founder, which indicated a further decrease in the Falange's influence.

As was to be expected the religious persecutions between 1931 and brought the usual fruits of religious revival to the Christian church in Spain. In July 1945, a visitor[8] to Spain, whose observation and knowledge must be respected, wrote:

> Today the churches in Spain are full. In the great cities for six hours
> on Sunday morning there is a constant filling and emptying. It seemed
> to me that those were right who said that the passion of the civil war
> has led to a great revival of faith.

The unpopularity of Spain and the international left-wing hostility to her government, as illustrated by the demonstrations at the San Francisco and Potsdam conferences, gave great encouragement to the exiled

---

[8] Mr. Douglas Woodruff, editor of *The Table*.

politicians, who, notwithstanding their internecine quarrels, got together in Mexico and in August elected Señor Martínez-Barrio as president of a Spanish Republican government in exile. They acted as if the small rump of the old Cortes, existing of the exiled deputies in Mexico, had some constitutional and legal basis, a thesis which a survey of the stipulations of the constitution showed to be quite untenable, even if the legitimacy of its birth in 1936 were conceded.

XXIX

January 1944 to August 1945, Foreign Affairs

Allied diplomatic activity had increased, as the probability of the Germans crossing the Pyrenees receded, and increasing pressure was brought to bear on Spain to settle to the satisfaction of the United Nations certain matters in which they were giving assistance to Germany. Sir Samuel Hoare and Mr. Carlton Hayes were constantly reported as interviewing the Spanish Foreign Secretary, while the Duke of Alba was as constantly active both in London and Spain. The culmination of Allied pressure was ultimately reached by the application to Spain of sanctions in the form of the cessation of oil shipments.

The principal questions between Spain and Great Britain were:
1. The tungsten shipments from Spain to Germany.
2. The question of Italian ships, which had taken refuge in Spanish ports on the surrender of Italy.
3. The repatriation of the Blue Division.
4. The question of the activities of German agents in Spain. Tangier and Spanish Morocco.

The first of these questions—that of tungsten shipments to Germany—was highly important to both sides in the war, because Germany obtained from the Iberian Peninsula a very high percentage of her total requirements of this all-important mineral for her war industries, which she could not obtain elsewhere. Spain was of course entirely within her rights as a neutral to sell her products to Germany, just as other neutrals, Turkey and Sweden were within their rights in selling Germany their chrome ore and iron ore, and the United Nations were within their rights in trying to stop them. The matter was complicated by the fact that our ally Portugal was in a similar position to neutral Spain and was selling large quantities of tungsten to Germany at the fantastic prices per ton to which this mineral had climbed from its insignificant peacetime level.

The United Nations' blockade was useless for stopping this traffic, which went overland, but they determined to make every effort to restrict it, either by themselves purchasing the metal or by diplomatic and economic pressure.

The second of these questions was concerned with some 11 Italian ships of war and merchant ships which had taken refuge in Port Mahón and other Spanish ports, either from lack of fuel or some other reason, at the time of Italy's surrender. The Spaniards alleged their obligation as neutrals to intern any ships of war, which remained more than a certain number of hours in their ports, and they laid claim to some of the merchant ships as recompense for Spanish ships previously sunk by Italian submarines. On the other hand, the United Nations claimed the ships as having been surrendered to them by Italy.

Both of these questions brought into play the legitimate and recognized rights of neutrals, but the third question was of a different category. The Blue Division was composed of Spaniards who with the open assistance and consent of the Spanish government were fighting for the Germans against one of the Allies. It was argued by Spaniards that they were volunteers and they compared them to the English volunteers who fought on the Republican side in the civil war as members of the International Brigades. The cases were similar but not analogous, because in the Spanish case there was open government assistance and consent and in the English case there was merely government myopia.

Throughout the last half of 1943 drafts from the Blue Division had been repatriated to Spain without being replaced by new drafts, as had been the case before, and the strength of the division had consequently been decreasing rapidly, not only from lack of drafts, but also by reason of their heavy casualties. In December it was announced in Spain that all the Blue Division had been recalled, but Soviet news alleged that this was not the case and that the remaining men had merely incorporated themselves with the German army. The matter in dispute was, in the event of the truth of the Soviet allegation, to what extent the Spanish government had cognizance or gave any consent to such action on the part of its citizens.

These questions and the oil sanctions caused in the English and American press the usual outbreak of abuse of Spain and her government, to which the public was accustomed. It was especially significant of the mysterious press campaign against everything Spanish, merely because it was Spanish, that the similar policies of Turkey and Sweden in respect of their chrome ore and iron ore were passed over without abuse of those countries.

However, patience, common sense and goodwill on the part of the foreign secretaries and ambassadors of Spain, U.S.A. and Great Britain, eventually prevailed over the ignorance and abuse of the anti-Spanish campaign and, on May 2nd, 1944, Mr. Eden, the foreign secretary, announced in the House of Commons the conclusion of an Anglo-American agreement by which all the four outstanding questions mentioned above were satisfactorily settled. Tungsten shipments to Germany, except for a small monthly token shipment, ceased; German agents were to be expelled; Italian merchant ships with the exception of two were to be released and the fate of the Italian warships was to be settled by arbitration. As regards the Blue Division, it was announced that the remaining Spanish units had been withdrawn and that the survivors of the Blue Division and Blue Air Squadron had returned to Spain. On the other side of the balance sheet of the agreement the renewal of oil shipments to Spain was granted.

This happy solution of the relations between Spain and Great Britain was punctuated on May 25th by Mr. Winston Churchill, the Prime Minister, in a speech in the House of Commons on foreign affairs. As this speech is in accord with the historical facts as set forth in this history and is completely condemnatory of the false legends to which attention had so often been called, an extract of that part which refers to Spain is here given, for the speech marks an important milestone in Anglo-Spanish relations and is a great tribute to the vision and statesmanship not only of the Prime Minister but of General Franco, General Jordana and the Duke of Alba.

This is the extract from Mr. Churchill's speech taken from Hansard:

> From Italy one turns naturally to Spain, once the most famous empire in the world and down to this day a strong community in a wide land, with a marked personality and distinguished culture among the nations of Europe. Some people think that our foreign policy towards Spain is best expressed by drawing comical or even rude caricatures of General Franco, but I think there is more to it than that. When our present ambassador to Spain, the right honorable gentleman the member for Chelsea (Sir S. Hoare) went to Madrid almost exactly four years ago to a month, we arranged to keep his airplane waiting on the airfield, as it seemed almost certain that Spain, whose dominant party were under the influence of Germany because Germany had helped them so vigorously in the recently ended civil war, would follow the example of Italy and join the victorious Germans in the war against Great Britain. Indeed, at this time the Germans proposed to the Spanish government that triumphal marches of German troops should be held

in the principal Spanish cities, and I have no doubt that they suggested to them that the Germans would undertake, in return for the virtual occupation of their country, the seizure of Gibraltar, which would then be handed back to a Germanized Spain. This last feature would have been easier said than done.

There is no doubt that if Spain had yielded to German blandishments and pressure at that juncture our burden would have been much heavier. The Straits of Gibraltar would have been closed and all access to Malta would have been cut off from the west. All the Spanish coast would have become the nesting place of German U-boats. I certainly did not feel at the time that I should like to see any of those things happen and none of them did happen. Our ambassador deserves credit for the influence he rapidly acquired, and which continually grew. In his work he was assisted by a gifted man, Mr. Yencken, whose sudden death by airplane accident is a loss which I am sure has been noted by the House. But the main credit is undoubtedly due to the Spanish resolve to keep out of the war. They had had enough of war and they wished to keep out of it. (An Hon. Member: 'That is a matter of opinion.') Yes, I think so, and that is why my main principle of beating the enemy as soon as possible should be steadily followed. But they had had enough, and I think some of the sentiment may have been due to the fact that, looking back, the Spanish people, who are a people who do look back, could remember that Britain had helped Spain to free herself from the Napoleonic Army of 130 years ago. At any rate the critical moment passed: the battle of Britain was won; the island power, which was expected to be ruined and subjugated in a few months, was soon that very winter not only intact and far stronger in the homeland but also advancing by giant strides, under Wavell's guidance, along the African shore, taking perhaps a quarter of a million Italian prisoners on the way.

But another very serious crisis occurred in our relations, with Spain before the operation designated 'Torch,' that is to say the descent of the United States and British forces upon northwest Africa, was begun. Before that operation was begun Spain's power to injure us was at its very highest. For a long time before this we had been steadily extending our airfield at Gibraltar and building it out into the sea, and for a month before zero hour, on 7th November, 1942, we had sometimes 600 airplanes crowded on this airfield in full range and in full view of the Spanish batteries. It was very difficult for the Spaniards to believe that these airplanes were intended to reinforce Malta, and I can assure the House that the passage of those critical days was very anxious indeed. However, the Spaniards continued absolutely friendly and tranquil. They asked no questions; they raised no inconveniences.

If, in some directions, they have taken an indulgent view of

German U-boats in distress, or continued active exportations to Germany, they made amends on this occasion, in my view, so far as our advantage was concerned, for these irregularities by completely ignoring the situation at Gibraltar, where, apart from aircraft, enormous numbers of ships were anchored far outside the neutral waters inside the Bay of Algeciras, always under the command of Spanish shore guns. We should have suffered the greatest inconvenience if we had been ordered to move those ships. Indeed, I do not know how the vast convoys would have been marshalled and assembled. I must say that I shall always consider a service was rendered at this time by Spain, not only to the United Kingdom and to the British Empire and Commonwealth, but to the cause of the United Nations. I have, therefore, no sympathy with those who think it clever, and even funny, to insult and abuse the government of Spain whenever occasion serves.

I have had the responsibility of guiding the government while we have passed through mortal perils, and, therefore, I think I have some means of forming a correct judgment about the values of events at critical moments as they occur. I am very glad now that, after prolonged negotiations, a still better arrangement has been made with Spain, which deals in a satisfactory manner with the Italian ships which have taken refuge in Spanish harbors, and has led to the hauling down of the German flag in Tangier, and the breaking of the shield over the consulate, and which will, in a few days, be followed by the complete departure of the German representatives from Tangier, although they apparently still remain in Dublin. Finally, it has led to the agreement about Spanish tungsten, which has been reached without any affront to Spanish dignity and has reduced the export of tungsten from Spain to Germany during the coming critical months to a few lorry-loads a month.

It is true that this agreement has been helped by the continuous victories of the Allies in many parts of the world, and especially in North Africa and Italy, and also by the immense threat by which the Germans conceive themselves to be menaced, by all this talk of an invasion across the Channel. This, for what it is worth, had made it quite impossible for Hitler to consider reprisals on Spain. All his troops have had to be moved away from the frontier, and he has no inclination to face bitter guerilla warfare, because he has got quite enough to satisfy himself in so many other countries which he is holding down by brute force.

As I am here today speaking kindly words about Spain, let me add that I hope she will be a strong influence for the peace of the Mediterranean after the war. Internal political problems in Spain are a matter for the Spaniards themselves. It is not for us—that is, the government—to meddle in such affairs.

The months following the Allied invasion of France in June, 1944, were marked by a great decrease in German influence and activities in Spain and by a great change in the tone of the Spanish press, so long under the influence of German propaganda. In August, the Vichy Ambassador to Spain, M. Pietri, notified that he considered his mission at an end owing to the end of the Vichy regime. In September, the Spanish government placed 100 lorries and large quantities of food and clothing at the disposal of the Red Cross for Belgian relief.

The foreign secretary announced in the House of Commons on September 27th, 1944, that the German consulate in Tangier had been closed and that some of the German agents had been expelled from Tangier and Spanish Morocco. In October, Spain gave assurances to the U.S. and British ambassadors that they would not provide asylum for war criminals. On October 31st, General Franco recognized the government of General de Gaulle, thus regularizing French-Spanish relations. General Franco through the press, suggested that Spain and other neutral countries should take part in the peace settlement but, in reply to a question in the House of Commons, the foreign secretary said he could see no reason why any country, which had not made a positive contribution to the United Nations war effort, should be represented at the peace conference.

In December 1944, Lord Templewood (Sir S. Hoare) and Mr. Carlton Hayes resigned from their posts as ambassadors of Great Britain and the U.S.A. respectively; both had shown statesmanship under difficult circumstances, refusing to be unduly influenced by the press campaigns against Spain in both their countries; they undoubtedly contributed to the essential business of keeping Spain on the difficult course of neutrality.

On his return to England Lord Templewood recounted his difficulties in face of the pressure brought to bear on Spain by Germany in the early years of the war and described how thousands of British soldiers had been able to escape through Spain from the time of Dunkirk onwards. Lord Templewood was succeeded after a few months by Sir Victor Mallet.

Spain severed relations with Japan in April 1945, owing to atrocities committed in the Philippines against Spanish citizens. In the previous February, the Japanese had burnt the Spanish consulate-general and were said to have assassinated all the consulate staff. In the same month landings of all German planes were forbidden in Spain and shortly afterwards all German assets in Spain were frozen, the German embassy and consulate closed, and diplomatic relations were severed.

In May, Laval, the French collaborationist leader, in an endeavor to escape his punishment, arrived in Barcelona in an airplane; the Spanish authorities requested him to leave again at once, but he refused, and he was then arrested and interned in the prison castle of Montjuïc. The French thereupon demanded that Spain should expel or extradite him, which Spain could not do under international law, because Laval was a political offender and as such claimed the right of asylum usually conceded by all countries to political refugees. Spain for her part and in accordance with her undertaking not to give refuge to war criminals offered to surrender him to the representatives of the U.S.A. and Great Britain, who refused to take him, as he was not technically a war criminal in accordance with the United Nations definition laid down in Moscow in 1943. This situation, which was quite correct as far as Spain was concerned, was misunderstood and misrepresented by the left-wing press and caused a renewal of that abuse of Spain, which the prime minister's speech the previous May had curbed for the time being. It did not occur to the critics of Spain that, if she consented to deliver Laval to France, she would cause the destruction of other extradition treaties and that Spanish Republican politicians like Dr. Negrín, who had been tried and condemned for political offences in Spain and had been given asylum in England, would also have to be given up. On August 2nd this apparently insoluble diplomatic problem was settled by the very simple expedient of expelling Laval from Spanish territory without delivering him to any specified country. The German airplane, in which he had arrived, took off from Barcelona for an unspecified destination with Laval on board and landed in the zone of Austria occupied by the Americans, by whom Laval was at once handed over to the French.

As was anticipated, the end of the war with Germany resuscitated the question of Tangier, which had remained, as is set forth in previous pages, with the acceptance by Great Britain of Spanish occupation as a temporary measure. In May 1945, discussions began between Great Britain, France and U.S.A. as regards the reestablishment of the international regime. In July, the Soviet government unexpectedly notified the participants in the conference that they wished to be represented in the conference. This demonstration of Russian imperialism in a quarter in which she had no interests of any sort, unless it were the desire to retrieve her defeat by Spain in 1939, further complicated a problem which had been a running international sore for so long and of which a solution seemed imminent.

No invitation to attend the San Francisco conference held in May 1945, to set up an international charter or new League of Nations was issued to Spain or other neutral countries. The unpopularity abroad of Spain, General Franco and the Falange had become increasingly acute and the main reasons were these. First of all, General Franco's pro-German speeches, the pro-German actions, and words of the Falange and the sending of the Blue Division to help Germany were not forgotten. Secondly, foreign public opinion did not appreciate that the Falange was more left-wing than it was right-wing or Fascist, comprising not only the pro-Nazi but also the pro-communist elements of Spain, and that General Franco had progressively decreased their power. Thirdly, the left-wingers and left press of the whole world refused to forgive General Franco for proving them to be wrong about the civil war and wrong about his maintenance of Spanish neutrality, which had been of such inestimable value to the United Nations. The majority of people all over the world were convinced, however unjustly, that Spain had been the tool of the Axis and the curious negligence of Spain to deny, through her official embassies, and agents, the many false accusations made against her, were much to blame for this state of public opinion.

The hostility to the Spanish regime was demonstrated at San Francisco on June 20th, in an impassioned speech by the Mexican delegate who proposed that Franco's Spain should be excluded from membership of the new world organization.

A motion to include this proposal in the charter was defeated by 17 votes to 5, but it was unanimously decided that the original proposal should appear on the official records, thus giving a grievous rebuff to Spain.

This unpopularity had been demonstrated on May 25th, when the foreign affairs committee of the French National Assembly unanimously recommended the French Government to ask the Allies to request Franco to abandon power; General de Gaulle's government however refused to support the recommendation, but it illustrated how far towards the left France had gone that such an attempt to intervene in the internal affairs of another country should take place.

In June, another incident took place when a trainload of Spaniards, who were being repatriated from various European countries, was attacked by a mob at Chambery, several of its members being seriously injured and only rescued from murder by the military and police. Anti-

Spanish feeling was exploited by the press in France and the situation between the two countries appeared dangerous. As a result of these two incidents Spain closed her frontier to France, thus stopping the passage of French repatriates and food, both of which were much desired by the latter country. In early July the French government apologized for the Chambery incident, the frontier was reopened, and a commercial agreement was negotiated.

While describing the unpopularity of Spain, which was augmented by her being qualified as "Fascist," it is interesting to refer back to the communist origins of the civil war and the plot to set up a soviet in Spain in 1936, in which was laid down the project to start "the worldwide agitation to be named anti-Fascist."

The culmination of the hostility to Spain took place in August at the Potsdam conference, when it was announced that Spain under the Franco regime was excluded from membership of the security organization of the United Nations. This declaration stated that the Spanish government, "having been founded with the support of the Axis Powers, does not, in view of its origins, its nature, its record, and its close association with the aggressor States, possess the qualifications necessary to justify such membership." To this the Spanish government replied with dignity that they were being unfairly treated, stating that "on being now so unjustly referred to, she sees herself obliged to declare that she does not beg admittance to international conferences and would not accept anything inconsistent with her history, her people, or the services that Spain rendered to peace and culture."

Continued, "Spain proclaims once more her peace-loving spirit and her good will towards all peoples, and trusts that, once the passions exacerbated by war and propaganda are allayed, the present excesses will be corrected."

XXX

1945 TO 1947

Seldom, if ever, in history can there have been such a striking case of collective injustice and bad reasoning, in which politicians and statesmen throughout the world have taken part or acquiesced, as the treatment meted out to Spain successively at the conferences of San Francisco (United Nations, June, 1945). Potsdam (the Big Four, August 1945), Hunter College (United Nations, April, 1946), and Lake Success (United Nations, 1946, 1947 and 1948). It is fair to say that certain statesmen have disassociated themselves in part from this treatment, which appeared to be openly directed by the conductor's baton of the Muscovite Marshal; among them can be cited Mr. Churchill, Mr. Byrnes, Mr. Van Kleffens, Mr. Bevin and Sir Alexander Cadogan, but even these politicians thought it necessary to pay tribute to popularity by expressing their "detestation" of the existing Spanish regime. During the last phases of the discussions in the meetings of the U.N. the refusal on the part of certain Latin American republics to obey the conductor's baton was both courageous and marked; the representatives of Columbia, Cuba, Ecuador and Argentina were especially notable in this opposition.

The injustice and hypocrisy of the discussions in the U.N.O. were demonstrated because they failed to measure other nations by the same "yardstick" that they applied to Spain. As regards Spain but not as regards her accusers, the U.N.O. laid on one side the principle of the Atlantic Charter, that the internal affairs of a country were exclusively her own concern. The quintessence of injustice was reached when the plaintiffs at Hunter College became both prosecutors and judges, a procedure which must eternally discredit any court.

The situation became a mixture of farce and tragedy. It was a farce that the U.N.O. should seriously treat as a potential government for a nonmember country a group of that country's exiled politicians, elected by the rump of an unconstitutional parliament, itself elected by fraudulent processes, many of whom were living on spoils stolen from Spain during the civil war and guilty in the eyes of the majority of Spaniards of the blood of thousands of their fellow countrymen; it was a tragedy because Spain stands, and throughout history has stood, for the same Christian Western civilization to which Britain and America belong, which is threatened today with destruction. The powerful, intelligent, and active campaign of Soviet Russia and communism to revenge themselves on Spain for the defeat of 1936–39 bore its magnificent harvest in the debates and motions of the U.N.O.

At the San Francisco conference, on June 20th, 1945, the Mexican delegate proposed that Francoist Spain should be excluded from membership of the new world organization; a motion to include this proposal in the charter was defeated by seventeen votes to five, but it was unanimously decided that the original proposal should appear on the official records; this was a strange and alarming example of lack of principle and resort to camouflage.

In the previous month, on May 25th, the Foreign Affairs Committee of the French National Assembly unanimously recommended the French government to ask the Allies to demand that General Franco should abandon power; this was a demonstration of Soviet-Communist power in France, but General de Gaulle's government refused to support the recommendation. This, and later French action on U.N.O. showed how justified were the fears of Spain that frontier incidents or even an invasion of Spain by International Brigades of Communists from Southern France were dangers that had to be foreseen and provided against. Spain visualized a possible repetition of French and Russian armed intervention, such as had taken place in 1936–38, and it was a grave menace until the French elections of May 1946, broke the Communist domination of French politics. Spain's action of reinforcing her army on the frontier to meet the menace was justified by the various incursions of armed bands across the Pyrenees, to which little or no publicity was given in the press. This prudent action on the part of Spain. which would have been approved if it had been taken by any other country faced by a similar danger, was seized upon by her enemies and their propaganda cohorts as proof of her aggressive intent, though no sane person could visualize Spain invading an allied country.

After San Francisco, the next Soviet attack and victory over Spain took place at the Potsdam conference in August 1945, when the following declaration was made:

> The three governments feel bound to make it clear that they for their part would not favor any application for membership put forward by the present Spanish government. which, having been founded with the

support of the Axis powers, does not in view of its origins, its nature, its record, and its close association with the aggressor states, possess the qualifications necessary to justify such membership.

At the beginning of April 1946, the question of Spain was brought before the Security Council of U.N.O. for discussion on a motion proposed by the delegation of Panama, which was adopted with forty-five votes in favor, two against and two abstentions. It is only possible here to give the merest outline of the main motions and events that took place in the long discussions during the following months; the protagonists against Spain were the Soviet and Polish delegates, generally supported by the French delegate, while the British delegate, Sir Alexander Cadogan, refuted many of the accusations against Spain, though he seemed to think it necessary to express his detestation of the Spanish regime. Poland moved a resolution calling on all members of U.N.O. to break off diplomatic relations with Spain and to declare that the Spanish situation "endangers international peace and security." A subcommittee consisting of Australia, Brazil, China, France, and Poland was then appointed to examine the statements and to report to the Security Council by May 17th. During the examination no attempt of any sort was made to hear the plaintiff or obtain Spain's own evidence, but evidence was taken from many of Spain's accusers and even from Señor Girál, the premier of the so-called Spanish Republican government in exile; the most violent of the accusers was Dr. Lange the delegate of Poland.

The report of the subcommittee was presented to the Security Council on June 2nd, and stated (the *Times*, June 3rd, 1946):

> ...that the Franco regime is a 'potential menace' to such peace and security, but not an existing threat, and it is proposed that the case be referred to the General Assembly on September 3rd, with a recommendation that, unless the Franco regime is withdrawn and other conditions of political freedom are met; the Assembly call on the fifty-one members of the United Nations to break off diplomatic relations.

The report was signed by Dr. Evatt, the delegate of Australia and chairman of the subcommittee, but before presentation to the Security Council the following words were added: "or alternatively such other action be taken as the General Assembly deems appropriate and effective in the circumstances prevailing at the time."

On June 13th, the debate on the report began in the Security Council and a clear-cut clash of opinions was shown. Mr. Gromyko, the Soviet delegate, made a long speech repeating the identical accusations made by Dr. Lange; he challenged the legality of the findings of the sub-committee and threatened that, if stronger action against Spain were not taken, he would exercise the veto.

On June 17th, in the resumed debate, Sir Alexander Cadogan for Britain moved the recommendation that the Assembly call for the collective severance of relations with Franco Spain should be deleted; he expressed the grave doubts of the British government about the juridical right to interfere in the internal affairs of a country unless there was a clear threat to peace and he added that "the British government had shown over and over again its detestation of the regime and had shared in every declaration condemning it." Sir Alexander Cadogan's amendment was negatived and the motion was adopted, Mr. Gromyko voting against and Dr. Van Kleffens (Holland) abstaining.

The Polish delegate then notified his intention to move his original resolution (see above).

The long debates continued at subsequent sessions with the same division of opinions—Russia and Poland versus other delegates and perpetually obstructing any unanimous decision. The Security Council rejected the original Polish resolution and the issue was narrowed down to finding the right form of words to express the desire voiced by various members to keep the question on the agenda of the Council and to leave the General Assembly free to discuss it in September. Against the ruling of the President of the Council, Mr. Gromyko announced at the meeting of June 27th, that he exercised his veto against the question being submitted to the General Assembly. The discussion then became confused and acrimonious and was described by the *Times* correspondent in the following words: "the confusion was such... that it is not certain what was voted and what was not."

In spite of the evident confusion regarding what had or had not been decided in the meetings of the U.N.O. at Hunter College in April, and the large number of matters which should have been discussed, the Spanish question mysteriously received preferential attention both in the debates and in the press throughout the subsequent sessions of the General Assembly of the U.N.O. held in October to December 1946, at Lake Success.

On October 24th, 1946, the opening day of the Assembly, Mr. Trygve Lie, the secretary general, again demonstrated his anti-Spanish and pro-Soviet bias by stating that "the Franco regime would remain a constant source of mistrust and that he hoped that those who gave us victory and peace may also find the ways and means whereby liberty and democratic government may be restored to Spain." As in the previous session, Dr. Lange, the Polish delegate, led the attacks on Spain and it was decided to refer the matter to the political committee. Debate in that committee began on December 2nd, with a proposal by Dr. Lange for the rupture of diplomatic relations with Spain. In general, the discussion was a gramophone record of previous debates with more or less the same protagonists on either side. The U.S.A. presented a motion for the exclusion of Spain from international organizations and repeated the general accusations against the Spanish government, while Colombia proposed postponement. The Spanish government at once protested to the U.S. Chargé d'Affaires in Madrid, refuting the statements made in the political committee and stating:

> The Spanish people repels energetically the interference in their internal affairs, the attack from abroad on their institutions, the incitement to revolution and revolt and foreign dictation as to what they should do.

On December 3rd, the U.S. delegate qualified his statements of the previous day stating that he wished to see a democratic regime and would intervene if there were a threat to peace, but that he was at present against coercion, which would consolidate the regime or lead to civil war. The British delegate declared that nothing should be done that might lead to bloodshed and opposed economic sanctions. At the end of two days' debate and the presentation of ten different motions by different delegates, a Cuban motion to name a subcommittee to coordinate the motions were put to the vote and passed by twenty-six against eight, with nine abstentions. The U.K. delegate opposed the inclusion in the subcommittee of any delegates whose motions proposed intervention in Spain, but, nevertheless, a subcommittee of eighteen was named which included Soviet Russia, Yugoslavia and White Russia.

On December 5th and 6th, the subcommittee debated the preamble of a resolution, which was opposed by the U.S. and U.K. delegates but was ultimately passed without opposition; this preamble repeated the old accusations against the Franco regime, that it was imposed by force on the Spanish people with the help of the Axis, that it did not represent the Spanish people and made impossible Spanish participation with the United Nations, and that it was a danger to international peace.

Meanwhile in Madrid on December 6th, the Spanish government had issued a public declaration of the "firm determination of the government to maintain the country's independence completely free of foreign intervention" and protesting against the "iniquitous action" of the great majority of the members of the subcommittee by their insults, and the repetition of calumnies already denied by the government. On December 9th, a monster public demonstration took place in Madrid, when the crowd, said to have numbered 300,000 cheered General Franco for three hours in front of the Royal Palace. In his speech to the crowd General Franco said:

> We Spaniards must not be surprised at what has happened in the U.N.O., for a wave of communist terror is devastating Europe and violations, crimes, and persecutions, of the same order as many of you suffered or witnessed, preside, unpunished, over the life of twelve nations, independent till yesterday... As long as the concert of the nations of the world continues to stand on a respect for the sovereignty of every nation and until there shall exist some international Fascist body to dictate to and unify us, no one can have any right to mix in the private concerns of any other nation.

It was dramatic that on the previous evening (December 8th), the subcommittee of the U.N.O. had already approved by eleven votes to six, against the opposition of the U.S.A. and Great Britain, a motion recommending the members of the U.N.O. to sever their diplomatic relations with the Spanish government and passing a further motion to cease buying from Spain. The matter then passed from the subcommittee to the political committee, which rejected the recommendation for the rupture of diplomatic relations, but thereupon approved a Belgian motion for presentation to the General Assembly, of which the first part was approved by twenty-six to eight votes with sixteen abstentions including the U.S.A. and Great Britain, while the second part was ap-proved by twenty-seven votes to seven with sixteen abstentions; in the latter case Great Britain voted in favor and the U.S.A. abstained.

From all of the available sources of information it was difficult to extract a completely clear account of events, but there appeared to be no difference in essence between the motion approved and the motion rejected by the political committee, which, together with the incongruity of the voting, gives an impression of the confusion and unreality existing in the debates. Colombia, Argentina, Peru, Ecuador, Costa Rica, and Cuba notably opposed the motion as contrary to justice and existing international conventions, and the Cuban delegate suggested that the supporters should simultaneously withdraw their representatives from Poland, Yugoslavia, and Russia.

The passing of these motions a roused further mass demonstrations in Spain, in Madrid, Barcelona, Valencia, and other centers, while organizations all over the country sent protests to the government against foreign intervention. Spanish opinion as to the origin of the campaign against their country was again clearly indicated by the slogan of the demonstrators, "*Franco sí, Rusia no!*"

On December 12th, the motion came for discussion before the General Assembly, where by thirty-four votes (including the U.S.A. and Great Britain) to six and with twelve abstentions a resolution was passed stating:

> That the Franco government of Spain be debarred from membership in international agencies established by, or brought into relationship with, the United Nations, and from participation in conferences, or other activities which might be arranged by the United Nations or by these agencies, until a new and acceptable government was formed in Spain.
>
> If within a reasonable time there was not established a government which derived its authority from the consent of the governed, committed to respect freedom of speech, religion and assembly, and to the prompt holding of an election in which the Spanish people, free from force and intimidation and regard less of party, might express their will, the Security Council should consider the adequate measures to be taken in order to remedy the situation.
>
> That all members of the United Nations immediately recall from Madrid their ambassadors and ministers plenipotentiary accredited there, and that members report to the secretary general and to the next session of the General Assembly, what action they have taken in accordance with the recommendation.

Both officially and unofficially great indignation was expressed in Spain and a collective protest against "foreign interference and infamous attacks" was made by the Cortes and read out by its president, Don Esteban Bilbao; the protest concluded with a message of homage and adherence to General Franco.

The practical result of this monopoly of the time and energies of the representatives of fifty-five nations in the U.N.O. whose supposed objects and duties were world reorganization and the establishment of peace. was a "ridiculous mush" and negligible except for the ill feeling it aroused and the discredit it brought on the U.N.O. Few nations had at the time either ambassadors or plenipotentiary ministers in Madrid, but only chargés d'affaires, and the work of the foreign missions in Spain, which had not been included in the U.N.O. resolution were able to continue their normal functions without interruption.

There was no U.S. Ambassador, but Sir Victor Mallet, the British ambassador, left Madrid and Don Domingo de las Bárcenas, the Spanish ambassador, left London, leaving their missions with chargés d'affaires; the only other heads of missions to be withdrawn were those of Turkey and Holland.

The *Times* newspaper made an inexcusable blunder on December 16th, when they stated that "governments are asked to withdraw their diplomatic missions from Madrid." With a similar inaccuracy, the U.N.O. bulletin in March 1947, stated that "forty-four nations had notified action," thereby giving the impression that that number had withdrawn their representatives, whereas what had actually occurred was subsequently published in the printed report of the secretary general of the U.N.O. That report stated that on December 20th, he requested all the member governments to notify what action they had taken in accordance with the resolution of December 12th, and that, out of fifty - five replies received, three States had recalled their ambassadors or minister, thirty States had no diplomatic relations with Spain, and nineteen States had no ambassador or plenipotentiary in Madrid; on the other hand Argentina merely acknowledged receipt of the notification and almost immediately sent an ambassador to Madrid, where they had none at the time.

It will be well to quote here paragraph 7 of Article 2 of the United Nations Charter: "Nothing in this charter shall authorize the United Nations to intervene in matters which are within the domestic jurisdiction of any State."

It is also pertinent to the matter that this Spanish regime, which was being attacked and boycotted by the nations in the U.N.O. was the same regime and the same government which the very same nations, except the U.S.S.R., had unanimously recognized as the legal government of the Spanish people in 1937–39. Not one of these countries then expressed any reserve, not one alleged that the Spanish government was not free and independent, and the recognitions were based on international law and the custom of civilized nations.

The government was recognized *de facto* and *de jure* and it had suffered no change since. To try and alter these facts by alleging the help received from the Axis powers previous to the recognition, is to deny the meaning of diplomatic recognition, which is a principle of international law, fully and categorically respected in Article I of the Charter of the United Nations.

When the session of the U.N.O. opened in Lake Success in November 1947, the Spanish question was taken up where it had been left in December 1946, with the resolution of boycott and the withdrawal of the heads of three diplomatic missions. Soviet Russia and her satellites led the attack as in the former sessions of the U.N.O. in an attempt to obtain a new resolution reaffirming the boycott and of applying further sanctions to Spain. The lengthy debates showed an increase of supporters for Spain among whom Argentina, the Dominican Republic, Costa Rica, Peru, and El Salvador were prominent. The U.S.A. attitude was also more friendly to Spain and constituted a notable *volte-face*.

On November 12th, the Political Committee approved the following resolution for submission to the General Assembly, the voting being twenty-eight in favor, including Britain and the U.S.S.R., six against, and twenty-three abstentions, including the U.S.A.:

> In view of the fact that the Secretary-General in his annual report informed the General Assembly of the steps taken by the States members of U.N.O. in conformity with the latter's recommendation of December 12th, 1946, the General Assembly [reaffirms its resolution passed on December 12th, 1946, with regard to relations between the United Nations members and Spain and) expresses confidence that the Security Council will do its duty in accordance with the charter in so far as it will deem that this is required by the situation as regards Spain.

On November 17th, 1947, the paragraph of this motion included in brackets was presented separately to the General Assembly and defeated, for it failed to get the necessary two-thirds majority. Twenty-eight countries including Great Britain and the U.S.S.R. voted in favor, sixteen countries including the U.S.A. against, and thirteen abstained. The remainder of the motion, not included in the brackets, was then presented and approved, the voting showing that thirty-six countries including Great Britain, the U.S.A. and the U.S.S.R. voted in its favor, five voted against, and sixteen abstained or were absent. Features of the debates were an important pro-Spanish speech by Dr. Arce, the Argentine delegate, and the extraordinary procedure which allowed Sr. Álvaro de Albornoz, the pretender to the title of premier of the government of the Spanish Republic in exile, to take part in the debate, while the Spanish government, which had been recognized by almost all the members nations, was not even heard.

This session of the U.N.O. was closed on November 30th, and marks the end of a long campaign, which brought discredit to the U.N.O. and did small damage to Spain except to try her pride and her patience.

In July 1947, there was achieved in the Paris Conference of ambassadors a major disgrace in international politics, when that conference decided to issue invitations to economic cooperation to all the states of Europe with the exception of Spain. This was a resounding victory for Mr. Molotov and for the exceedingly clever communist campaign conducted against Spain, because by it Spain was categorically ostracized from association with the rest of the world, while the bitter enemies of Christianity and the British Empire—Soviet Russia and her satellites—were considered worthy to be members of the unhappy family.

The eclectic condemnation of Spain by the U.N.O. for offences completely condoned when they were committed by members of the United Nations was very clearly exposed by Professor Carlton Hayes, U.S. Ambassador to Spain from 1942–45, in his book "Wartime Mission in Spain." Mr. Hayes was professor of modern European History at Colombia University and consequently adequately prepared for accurate observation and authoritative description of events in a European country; on pages 297–300 and 303 of his work he says the following:

> Let me now set forth certain conclusions from my wartime experience and reflection in Spain. Throughout my entire residence there, from May 1942, to January 1945, I had constant evidence that the large majority of the Spanish people greatly desired (1) to stay out of the international struggle, (2) to avoid recurrence of civil war, and (3) to be friendly with the English-speaking democracies, especially with the United States. These desires have been common, not only to the mass of 'Leftists' (Republicans and Socialists), but also to most of the 'Rightist' groups which supported General Franco in the Spanish Civil War (Liberal Monarchists, Traditionalists, and the Conservative following of Gil-Robles) and consequently to members of these groups who held office in the existing government (which was essentially a coalition rather than a single-party government).
>
> General Franco is in a curious position. He is a cautious politician with strong military backing, and, though doubtless the large majority of Spaniards, 'Rightist' as well as 'Leftist,' would ideally prefer another chief of state (if it could be arranged in an orderly fashion),

many of them recognize. with varying degrees of gratitude, that by virtue of his cautious policy he succeeded in keeping Spain free from foreign and domestic war during an extraordinarily trying period.

So long as Axis victory seemed to him inevitable, so long as almost the whole continent of Europe was at the mercy of Germany, with German armies massed near the Pyrenees and German submarines infesting the seas adjacent to Spain, General Franco let Hitler and indeed the world believe that he was pro-Axis. Nevertheless, whatever may have been his inmost thoughts and personal fears in the matter, the fact remains that at least from the date of his dismissal of Serrano Suñer from the foreign office and the leadership of the Falange, in September 1942. General Franco guided or backed the responsible officials of his government in approximating Spain's official position to the pro-Allied position of the large majority of the Spanish people.

From September 1942, to June 1943, while the Spanish government was still ostensibly 'nonbelligerent' and hence technically 'unneutral,' it not only placed no obstacle in the way of our landings and military operations in North Africa and Southern Italy, but gave us significant facilities. such as de facto recognition of the French Committee of National Liberation at Algiers and of its official representatives in Spain; free transit through Spain of over 25,000 volunteers (chiefly French) for active service with our armed forces in North Africa; non-internment of several hundreds of our forced-landed military airmen and their evacuation through Gibraltar; immediate delivery to us, quite uncompromised, of secret equipment on forced-landed planes, and freedom and full opportunity to carry on economic warfare with the Axis on Spanish territory by means of preemptive buying of tungsten, mercury, fluorspar, skins, woolen goods, etc… and blacklisting of Spanish firms doing business with the Axis.

From July 1943, to May 1944, the Spanish Government shifted its declared position from 'nonbelligerency' to 'neutrality,' and gradually increased the facilities it was according us to the detriment of the Axis. It not only curbed the discrimination against us in the Falangist controlled press of the country, withdrew the Blue Division and Blue Air Squadron from the Eastern Front, and replaced pro-Axis with pro-Allied diplomatic representatives in countries of Europe and Latin America, but it permitted the commercial sale of American propaganda magazines, granted us control of all passenger traffic, by Spanish airplanes as well as by ships, between Spain and Spanish Morocco, and withheld recognition of Mussolini's 'Social Republican' government in North Italy.

Moreover, it speeded up the evacuation of Allied refugees and forced-landed airmen, arranged for the escape to Spain of a considerable number of Jews from Hungary, Germany, and the Low

Countries, and tolerated, even to the point of abetting, the very important clandestine activities of our secret espionage services directed toward obtaining from across the Pyrenees invaluable military information about German troop movements and dispositions in France. Finally, as the result of a series of negotiations, pressed by us and vehemently opposed by Germany, Spain embargoed all exports of tungsten to the Axis from February to May and agreed to allow thereafter only token shipments (which stopped altogether after our landing in France in June, 1944). Simultaneously, the Spanish Government agreed to submit to arbitration the question of the internment of Italian warships which had been held for several months in the Balearic Islands, to close the German Consulate at Tangier, and to expel its staff and other Axis agents suspected of espionage or sabotage against us.

Actually, the Franco regime owes its origin only in part to military aid it received from Italy and Germany during the civil war. This aid has been much exaggerated, as that of Russia and France to the 'Loyalists' has been minimized. The civil war was primarily a Spanish affair, in which a half of the Spanish nation and more than half of the Spanish army supported General Franco.

…Nor, as I have previously explained, has General Franco's dictatorship been inspired by Nazi ideology or directed solely by Fascists; it has been more in the nature of a military dictatorship traditional to Spanish-speaking peoples.

Mr. Hayes also emphasizes in his book the falsification of facts and history not only by the press but also in the State Department and says (p. 138):

Unfortunately in other important agencies of our government and within the department itself, there were individuals who had only a partial, if any, picture of what was really happening and who substituted for it the caricatures provided by journalists.

The truth of this was at this time convincingly illustrated by two parallel mistakes made by the State Department. These two mistakes consisted of the publication throughout the press of the world of two documents, parallel as regards their injustice, partiality, incompleteness, and their abandonment of the usual language and courtesy customary in diplomatic international communications; one was the incomplete and ex parte publication of documents discovered in Germany concerning German-Spanish relations in the early years of the war, and the other, the

U.S. blue book on Argentine affairs, meant to hinder the election of Colonel Peron as President, but actually giving his cause the very greatest assistance and increasing feeling in Argentina against the U.S.A. The Spanish documents had an analogous effect in Spain and materially strengthened the position of General Franco, which it was their object to weaken.

At the end of 1945, the *Sunday Chronicle* published a series of letters from Hitler to Mussolini, which had been produced at the Nuremberg trials. One of these had such an important bearing on the accusation that Spain was the tool of the Axis that it is worthy of quotation. This letter, dated December 31st, 1940, says:

> Spain, highly disturbed by the situation... has turned down the collaboration with the Axis powers... I am sorry because on our part we had completed all preparations to cross the Spanish border on January 10th and attack Gibraltar at the beginning of February.

A further bit of evidence in the same direction came from General Jodl's trial at Nuremberg. In a lecture given by the General on November 7th, 1943, he gave three reasons for Germany's failure to attain victory by that date; the third of these reasons was the failure to draw Spain into the war on Germany's side and thereby create the chance of seizing Gibraltar; this was due, he said, to the resistance of the Spanish.

On the other hand, the publication of his memoirs by Lord Templewood, British Ambassador to Spain from 1940–45, created much ill feeling in Spain towards Great Britain owing to their unfairness and inaccuracy. Lord Templewood's book commits serious sins of omission and among them that of not emphasizing the important help given to the Allies by Spain in aiding and abetting the passage and escape of thousands of Allied combatants to rejoin the forces of their countries fighting against Germany. But the similarities of the two stories in impersonal matters are greater than the differences, which are probably caused by the distinct backgrounds of the authors. Lord Templewood is a politician, his book is subjective, and he seems curiously to believe that he was the *deus ex machina* who kept Spain out of the war, while Dr. Carlton Hayes book is objective, as would be expected from the pen of a trained historian and professor. But Lord Templewood's book contains very valuable material in the publication of notes exchanged between him and Generals Franco and Gómez-Jordana. The Spanish notes demonstrate a surprising and often a prophetic vision of the state of

Europe and the intentions and actions of Soviet-Russia both before and after the defeat of Germany, whereas the British notes were equally wrong in their prognostications. These notes provided interesting and revealing reading in 1947, when first Canada, then the U.S.A. and then the rest of the world began gradually to comprehend through their own experience what Spain had learnt ten or fifteen years before, a knowledge that they had refused to gather or use to their own advantage. It appeared, strangely enough, that the British Foreign Office were still reluctant to acknowledge their mistake.

XXXI

1947 AND 1948

Owing to the tendentious and unreliable quality of much of the press news from Spain, caused by the anti-Spanish campaign already described in these pages, it became necessary in September, 1946, for the present author to make an extensive tour of some of the most important cities and agricultural regions of Spain, with a view to studying, with his own observation and past experience of the country, the actual conditions, political, social and agricultural of Spain and he satisfied himself that the picture painted by her critics of a country of famine, want, and terrorism was a complete illusion. Many things were faulty and others were inefficient, as in other countries; Spain is ever a country of contradictions and Spanish character and methods are the same throughout the centuries, but no observer could deny that the vast majority of all classes in Spain were well fed, well clothed, and happy, with money to spend on the favorite recreations of bull ring, football, and the cafes.

It was soon evident that the stories of a tyrannous police state, which were rife abroad, were quite unreal and that the Spanish citizen was enjoying a greater freedom of life and speech than that existing in many other countries, saving only that he must not engage in communistic activities. This does not mean that in Spain all things were perfect and rosy, for there were undoubtedly abuses, as in other countries, and above all the universal curses of inflation and excessive bureaucracy with the corruption that always follows in the train of this last. There was a dangerous inflation with the accompanying spirals in prices and wages. Spanish statistics must be treated with discrimination, but official figures stated that the note circulation in 1945 was 18 billion pesetas against 4.3 billion in 1936.

At the same time the increase over 1936 in the cost of living was about 300 percent and the increase in wages over the same period about 100 percent. This fact taken by itself would mean universal want and poverty, which was not the case, for wages were supplemented by a compulsory system of cheap meals and supplies provided by employers,

211

family allowances, special rations for workmen, and the well-organized social welfare institutions of the state, and the religious institutions with their canteens and free meals. There was evidence of excessive expenditure in the nation's budgets and in the nationalization by purchase of the telephone company and other foreign investments, which were said to have exhausted Spain's foreign credits and made it necessary for her to obtain foreign loans.

In August, 1946, Sr. Martinez Barrio was elected in Mexico as president of a Republican government in exile; at the same time a government composed of other of the exiled politicians was named with Sr. Girál as prime minister. This government was acclaimed by the persecutors of Spain in the U.N.O. as the legal and constitutional government of Spain without the smallest respect for truth or history, as is clearly shown in these pages and in Sr. de Madariaga's history 'Spain.' In addition to other legal and constitutional defects, this government and president were elected by a minority of 94 members out of the old fraudulently elected parliament of 473, which according to the clauses of its own constitution of the Spanish Republic had ceased legally to exist several years before. Such was the status of the Republican Spanish government in exile, which subsequently the governments of Mexico, Panama, Venezuela, Guatemala, Yugoslavia, Poland, Romania, and Czechoslovakia thought fit to recognize officially and which was acclaimed as legal by 101 members of the mother of Parliaments in London. The names of the countries were adequate proofs of the all-pervading power of Soviet Russia.

Spain, however was not likely to forget so soon that the origin of the civil war, the reign of terror and the Cheka tortures were inspired by that same power and that Sr. Girál was the Minister of Marine when the red mutineers of the lower deck of the Spanish navy murdered all their officers in Cartagena in 1936, and went unpunished and unreproved. Nor did she forget that these same exiles who presumed to elect themselves as a government had sent Spain's gold reserves to Russia and taken with them in their flight an enormous booty robbed from the banks and their fellow citizens, and that they were directly or indirectly guilty of the blood of tens of thousands of their compatriots. It was these men with whom the U.N.O., foreign secretaries, parliaments, and the press of the greater part of the world were prepared to negotiate, while they boycotted the legal government of Spain, which they had all previously recognized.

Sr. Girál's government lasted until January 1947, when disputes broke out anew among the exiled politicians. Señor Girál resigned and was succeeded as premier by the almost unknown Señor Rodolfo Llopis. On August 6th his government resigned owing to the withdrawal of those socialists who looked to Indalecio Prieto as their leader; after attending a socialist congress in Toulouse, the latter had made a broadcast stating that he aimed at forming a compromise government of all parties except the Communists, which he said would meet the requirements of the U.N.O. Señor Prieto was considered as the most intelligent of the Republican politicians in exile; in April, 1938, during the civil war he was excluded from the Republican government as he was not sufficiently subservient to the Soviet, who had kept him in power as long as he was useful, and then discarded him in favor of Dr. Negrín. He had so far been outside the governments in exile and he might well be the cleverest of the exiles, but his political record and his control of or connection with the booty taken in 1939 from Spain to Mexico was not forgotten, and he was not likely to be welcomed in Spain.

In September 1947, Señor Prieto was received by the British foreign secretary and it was generally but erroneously reported in the daily press that the Spanish government had protested against his presence in England. This was not so; the Spanish protest was against Señor Prieto's political activities in England and the public and official character given to his reception; there was no question of any protest against the accepted and traditional right of asylum for political exiles and the Spanish Embassy issued a démenti to that effect.

Señor Prieto's efforts were abortive and on August 27th a new government in exile elected itself in Paris under Señor Álvaro Albornoz, one of the members of the first Republican government after the revolution of 1931 and the departure of King Alfonso, but since then not prominent in Republican politics. In August 1947, there appeared to be various groups of Republican exiles respectively following Albornoz, Prieto, Negrín, and Álvarez del Vayo, the most intimate friend and agent of Soviet Russia both before and during the revolution; these were all disunited but all inspired with the common objects of intrigue and disruption in Spain. In October it was reported that Señor Prieto and Señor Gil-Robles, a prominent monarchist and Conservative leader, had met in London and had been received by Mr. Bevin with a view to obtaining his support to a combination destined to replace General Franco's regime. This called forth an energetic protest from the Spanish government stating that "political machinations against the Spanish government have recently taken place in London with the connivance of the British foreign minister constituting an intolerable attempt on his part to interfere with Spain's internal affairs."[9] It was also reported in the press that Don Juan had sent a note to the Spanish government deauthorizing Señor Gil-Robles as his spokesman. On November 15th, Mr. Bevin answered Spain's protest in a peremptory manner and gratuitously repeated his disapproval of the Spanish regime and his hope that it would shortly be replaced by one with which Great Britain could maintain friendly relations. This grave discourtesy was keenly felt in Spain and caused public manifestations in protest.

Don Juan continued to reside in Lisbon surrounded by a court of Spanish monarchists, who spoke and thought of him as their king. Both Don Juan and General Franco had, during the period 1946–47, maintained their previous positions, while the persecution and abuse of Spain by the U.N.O. and the press of the world had consolidated Spaniards of all political color (except the communists and some extreme monarchists) behind General Franco and obliged them to come to the conclusion that any change of the regime under foreign pressure must be avoided at all costs.

One of the principal and unanswerable objections to a dictatorship is its lack of continuity, and, with a view to meeting this criticism to General Franco's regime, a succession law was drafted and published in March, 1947; on June 7th, it was passed by the Cortes after discussion and amendment and in its final form was presented on July 6th, for a plebiscite or referendum of the whole nation. The principal clauses of the law state that:

1. Spain is a Catholic and social state and is a kingdom in accordance with tradition. The head of the state is General Francisco Franco.
2. A council of the kingdom is set up presided over by the president of the Cortes and composed of the primate, the commander-in-chief, the president of the council of state, the chief justice, the president of the Spanish Institute (for education and culture) and elected members of the Cortes, the universities, the professional colleges, the syndicates and the municipalities.
3. In case of death or incapacity the head of the state shall be succeeded by the person of royal blood who shall be chosen by the combined council of the kingdom and government and accepted by two-thirds of the Cortes. In the event of no suitable

---

[9] *Daily Telegraph*, October 25th, 1947.

person being found a regent shall be named.

4. The head of the state must be a male of over thirty years, Spanish and Catholic.
5. The head of the state must swear to observe the fundamental laws—the Spaniards, charter, the labor charter the constitution of the Cortes and the laws of referendum and succession.
6. As soon as the headship of the state is vacant, a regency council shall assume power composed of the president of the Cortes, the primate and the captain general of the forces, who shall within three days arrange for the nomination of a ruler under clause 3.

The publication of the conditions of the law of succession brought out into the open the position regarding the conflict between General Franco and Don Juan. Both made speeches and declarations to the Spanish people and both gave interviews to the British press setting forth their aims.

Don Juan in an interview with the correspondent of The Observer on April 13th, made it clear that he confirmed his attitude as set forth in his manifesto of March, uncompromisingly insisted on a complete and unconditional transfer of power to himself and forbade monarchists to cooperate with the Franco regime.

On April 7th, 1947, Don Juan issued a manifesto to the Spanish people in which he stated that:

> The succession law, which declares Spain to be a kingdom, visualizes a system completely opposed to the laws which have throughout history regulated succession to the throne... which cannot be modified without the joint action of the king and a legitimately representative parliament of the nation. The hostility, with which the country finds itself threatened abroad is chiefly the result of the presence, as chief of the State, of General Franco, who wishes to make his dictatorship a life tenure... In view of this attempt it is my inescapable duty to make a solemn and public declaration of the supreme principle of legitimacy which resides in me, which I cannot abandon... I am and have been disposed to take any steps which will bring about the normal and unconditional transmission of power but I cannot give my consent to acts which impinge not only the rights of the Crown but the spiritual possessions of the nation.

That is the outline of Don Juan's attitude and we now come to that of General Franco.

In a broadcast speech coinciding with the publication of the draft of the succession law, he stated that its object was to give the fullest development to the regime and its achievements and to give it stability for the future.

On May 27th, an interview with General Franco by its correspondent was published in the Sunday Times, in which he stated that:

> The unjust attacks of the United Nations resulted in the Spanish people expressing categorically and unequivocally its unity and adherence to the Head of the State... the law of succession serves to remove any impression that the Spanish regime might be considered as only an interim one and does no more than give an official status to what during ten years I have been announcing... the reason for opposition by the pretender is that we are faced with an example of absolute ignorance of the situation and of the necessities of Spain... and to the deception and maneuvering of those who advise the pretender.

In May 1947, General Franco made visits to Catalonia, Valencia, and the Balearic Islands, which had the aspect of triumphal processions. After discounting the effect of government staging and propaganda and the fact that able propaganda can make the masses in any country applaud almost anybody or any slogan, no spectator or reader of the local press could possibly deny the genuine support of General Franco manifested not only by the proletariat but by people in all walks of life, whether professional, educational, industrial, or religious.

On July 6th, the succession law, after amendment by the Cortes, was submitted to a referendum of the whole nation; the ballot was secret and obligatory for all Spanish citizens over twenty years of age, the only exceptions being those incapacitated by the old electoral law of August, 1907. According to the press and British eyewitnesses the ballot was secret, fair and orderly throughout Spain and resulted in a sweeping majority of fourteen million votes out of fifteen million cast. As was natural, the whole government machinery of press, radio, and propaganda was brought into play without any possibility of equivalent methods for opponents of the regime. The public and press abroad, sadly accustomed to reading about electoral majorities in Russia, Yugoslavia, etc., were unimpressed by this overwhelming majority. But when all is said the comparison is an unfair one for the ballot was genuinely secret and it could not be known how individuals voted. In Spain, the referendum was looked upon as a vote of confidence in General Franco, as it was intended to be, as well as an approval of the succession law.

One of the fears expressed by monarchist opponents of General Franco was that the succession law of July 1947, was framed with a view to establishing him as a life tenant of dictatorship and possibly of founding in himself a new dynasty. The law reestablishing old titles, which had theoretically been abolished since the revolution of 1931, and gave General Franco power to confer new titles, was also looked on by them with suspicion. These fears and suspicions would appear groundless because the succession law stated that Spain was to be a kingdom ruled by a monarch of "royal blood."

In November 1947, the *Consejo del Reino* (Council of the Kingdom) was constituted partly by election and partly by nomination as established in the law of succession. This Council was a revival of the historic advisory council, which had assisted the Spanish monarchs throughout previous centuries; among its fourteen members were the president of the Cortes, the highest prelate, the captain general of land, sea and air, the head of the general staff, the president of the Supreme Court, the president of the Spanish Institute, the patriarch of the Indies, and a representative of the municipalities. On February 26th, at the Pardo Palace the councilors, including General Franco, duly took the oath on the crucifix and the Holy Gospels.

The law reestablishing titles (*titulos del Reino*) which has been referred to, states that the prerogative of granting and rehabilitating titles belongs to the head of the state, recognizes traditionalist titles granted by the Carlist pretenders and the use by Spaniards of foreign and Vatican titles.

Thus, at the end of 1947, it appeared that General Franco and Don Juan were far apart, though the majority tendency was towards the eventual reestablishment of the monarchy. Both the army and the Church, the two great powers of Spain, had strong monarchist tendencies though they appeared equally strongly attached to the regime of General Franco, which had brought peace and prosperity to their country. There were, however, a number of extreme and powerful monarchists who abhorred General Franco and his regime and appeared to desire to return to the old constitution of 1876, and the old system of personal political parties, though history had shown they were unsuitable to Spain and perpetual causes of disruption. In the 55 years under that constitution (1876–1931) there were 56 governments, a seven-year civil war (Carlist), various local revolutions, four prime ministers assassinated, three attempts on the life of the king and finally a revolution, which led to the terror and civil war of 1936–39.

The Franco regime had its serious defects, the most serious of which was excessive bureaucratic control. Foreign interest and criticism were focused on its effect on labor and social conditions and the fact had been overlooked that the burden of increased wages, the labor charter, family allowances, and social welfare had fallen in increased charges on industry. This burden fell exceedingly heavily on public utility companies, but industry in general was prosperous and profitable owing to the increased prices caused by demand exceeding supply. Theoretically there were strict controls and legislation governing prices, but Spaniards refused to accept the necessary discipline without which controls must be frustrated and they were observed as much in the breach as in the keeping. Thus, there was seen, as in other countries, the picture of black market, rising prices, rising wages, inflation, shortage of foreign currency, and excessive bureaucratic regulations, which hinder business and industry without compensating advantages.

It must be stated, however, that whatever may be the abuses of which the regime had been guilty, at the basis of Spanish fundamental laws are the improvement of the conditions of the working classes, the limitation of the abuses of capitalism, and the more equal distribution of wealth. These objects were being realized, as any comparison between conditions in 1948 and those ruling in 1936 must show.

Notwithstanding the power of the bureaucracy, nationalization had been restricted to the railways and the telephone company. Existing industries had not been nationalized and General Franco had given lip-service to private enterprise as the mainspring of national prosperity; but his regime was increasingly engaged in enormous new industrial enterprises centralized under an organization called I.N.I. (National Institute of Industry); the enterprises constructed or under construction comprised factories for airplanes, for liquid fuel, lubricants, etc. from coal, for aluminum, for mining, for textiles, for trucks and motor cars, for agricultural machinery, and for many other articles. In the middle of 1947, three companies, which were nominally independent but all having a government majority-holding of capital, had a combined nominal capital of 4.84 billion pesetas (£968 million) of which 1.17 billion pesetas (£234 million) had already been subscribed. The general opinion held at this time was that some of these industries were inefficient and extravagant owing to their management by the Falange bureaucracy.

The progress of hydroelectric development, on which Spanish prosperity so much depends, was remarkable during the recent years and statistics gave a production in 1946, of 5.466 billion of kilowatt hours against 3.271 billion in 1935, with further large projects in the course of construction at the beginning of 1948. At that time Spanish industries appeared to be prosperous in general though handicapped by the restriction of imports of raw materials owing to lack of foreign exchange.

Negotiations were proceeding for private loans and credits in the U.S.A. and it was expected that Spain would be admitted ultimately into the Western bloc and into participation in the E.R.P. of the United States. But in April 1948, the financial situation was changed owing to the Spanish-Argentine agreement, which was signed in Buenos Aires on April 9th. Under this agreement Argentina provided credits for 1.75 billion pesos, the equivalent of 4.5 billion pesetas, for the purchase of food stuffs and raw materials over the following four years. Spain undertook to repay into a peseta account to be applied by Argentina to the purchase of Spanish products and to the construction of ships in Spanish yards.

An important feature of the agreement was the establishment of a free port at Cádiz, to be leased to Argentina and used as a distribution center for Argentine products exported to Spain and Europe.

A strong spirit of spiritual, artistic and scientific renaissance and activities had gone hand in hand with the reconstructions and material developments since the end of the civil war; of this there had been evidence in the reconstruction of the University City in Madrid and in the construction and development of educational institutions in many centers. Among the events of 1947 was the establishment under the Ministry of Education of a Council of Scientific Investigations, which, through the medium of sixty institutes, coordinated and fomented the teaching of the sciences. There took place in May a congress of the Spanish Association for Scientific Progress, largely attended by the most prominent professors, at which matters and papers concerning the faculties of all the sciences were discussed; the importance given to the sciences of philosophy and theology indicated the Christian tendency of Spanish culture and education.

The renaissance of Spanish culture and its importance to the rest of the world was taking place, not only in the Peninsula but throughout Spanish-America and forming an increasing bond of sympathy throughout the Spanish speaking world. Exhibitions of Spanish books were held in 1947 in places as far apart as Amsterdam and Rio de Janeiro and at the end of that year there was celebrated with worldwide enthusiasm the fourth centenary of Cervantes.

Throughout 1947 and 1948 the international position of Spain continued to improve *pari passu* with the decline of the prestige of the U.N.O. and with the exhibition of Russia's imperialist and communist activities. This improvement was illustrated by a series of international acts of friendship and agreements; among which were trade agreements with Great Britain, Holland, Ireland, Mexico, Portugal, Switzerland, Italy, Uruguay, Chile, Sweden and Turkey, and the establishment of diplomatic relations with various countries. The development of friendly relations with Argentina were especially marked. In defiance of the 1946 resolution of the U.N.O., Argentina had sent an ambassador to Madrid: a mission of planes and their crews of the Argentine air force visited Spain and also an Argentine military mission, while General Franco and President Perón exchanged compliments and presents; the culminating point was the Spanish-Argentina trade agreement already described.

The relations with Portugal showed an ever-increasing friendliness, and a further improvement in relations took place with France. The unfortunate situation of the closed frontier between Spain and France, which had lasted for two years, came to an end in February–March, 1948, amid general satisfaction on both sides of the Pyrenees and negotiations began for a general trade agreement between the two countries. The first closing of the frontier in 1946 came from Spain and not from France, as was popularly thought, and it was far more harmful to the latter than the former. It was the Spanish reply to the anti-Spanish agitation of French communists, who then dominated the French government; this agitation was worldwide on the part of communists and their fellow travelers and the momentary excuse used to foment it was the execution in Spain of one man, Cristino García, represented by them as being wickedly executed for his political opinions. The true story of Garcia is that he was an Asturian fireman, who served as a sergeant in the Red Army in the civil war, after which he fled to France and served in the resistance. At the end of the war he joined the communist-terrorist school in Toulouse and was sent to Spain, where he formed a terrorist band to carry out revolution and sabotage. He was captured in October 1945, tried in the Spanish courts under the usual procedure with his own legal defenders, and was condemned to death on several counts of murder, assault, and robbery.

The Cristino García incident together with the myths about vast numbers of Spanish prisoners, was used to flog the unpopular Spain. The matter of prisoners has been dealt with in previous chapters and it would appear that by the end of 1947, owing to successive amnesties, the official figure of prisoners in Spain was 40,000 of whom 4,000 were the result of the civil war and most of these had been sentenced for ordinary and nonpolitical crimes.

During the latter half of 1948 there was no change in the official attitude of the U.N.O. towards Spain, which continued to be one of boycott, but there was a marked change in the attitude towards her of many countries and of their public opinion, which began with the gradual appreciation of the Russian danger and of the fact of the immense strategic importance of the Iberian Peninsula to any western union and to any anticommunist block. To this were added the appreciation of the failure of the U.N.O. owing to the Soviet veto and obstruction, and the progressive flouting of the decisions of the U.N.O. by various South American countries in sending plenipotentiary representatives to Madrid in defiance of the resolution of December 1946. The hypocrisy of the boycott of Spain was illustrated by the number of trade and other agreements made with her, among which can be cited:

~ Commercial and payments agreement with Sweden.
~ Spanish-French commercial agreement.
~ Agreement with the occupying powers of western Germany regarding commerce and the expropriation of German properties in Spain.
~ Commercial and payments agreement with Great Britain.
~ Treaty with the Philippines.
~ Agreement with the U.S.A. for the removal of financial controls and the unfreezing of Spanish assets in the U.S.A.
~ Extension for a further ten years of the treaties of friendship of 1939 and 1940 with Portugal.

In the debates in the U.N.O. and in their relationships with Spain, South American republics, and especially Argentina, took the lead in doing justice to Spain; they were followed by the U.S.A., who sent official missions to Spain, and authoritative opinions were expressed in the U.S.A. in favor of the admission of Spain to the U.N.O. and the extension to her of the benefits of the Marshall plan. The British Foreign Office, however, lagged behind and shewed no change of heart or any appreciation of the justice and expediency of friendship with Spain, whom they continued to treat as a pariah, though all the defects they unjustly attributed to her were condoled when practiced by other nations—some of them ex-enemies. Those nations, led by the Soviets were openly engaged in a bitter warfare (called cold) against every nation of the western world, utilizing the large staffs of their embassies in subversive intrigue against the governments to which they were accredited, whereas Spain showed no disposition in word or deed to interfere in the affairs of any nation and desired friendship with all who were not communist.

The economic situation of Spain became increasingly difficult during this period and she urgently required the E.R.P. assistance, which was denied to her, but granted to ex-enemy countries; her need was increased by the serious droughts which caused, not only a lack of rain and water for the crops, but a serious shortage of hydraulic power for her industries.

At the end of December, 1948, the finance minister announced the approximate result of the year's ordinary budget as showing a deficit of 1,253,000,000 pesetas; he also gave the estimates for the year 1949, showing expenditure at 16.821 billion pesetas and a deficit of only 39 million, but small reliance could be placed on the realization of this estimate in view of the notable discrepancy between the estimated and actual deficits shown in the past.

Two especially important events took place during the latter half of the year: one was the rapprochement between Don Juan and General Franco, the other the holding of municipal elections.

The first of these events was revealed to the public by two meetings, which took place at sea, between Don Juan and General Franco. No official statements were issued by either party, but the effective result was that Don Juan Carlos, the eldest son and heir of Don Juan, was sent to school in Spain. In an interview with a correspondent of the *New York Times* General Franco stated, regarding his conversations with Don Juan, that "we only spoke about the education of his son, Juan Carlos, who has come to school in Spain. We had a general exchange of views on Spanish matters, on which Don Juan is just as much interested as am I."

The municipal elections, which took place in November–December were looked on with expectation of internal trouble by Spain's socialist critics, but they took place in complete tranquility and order and showed a true democratic spirit. The percentage of voters amounted to 80–85 percent of the electoral rolls and the system under which they took place was a novel one, which had been laid down in a law approved by the Cortes a few months previously; throughout the law there ran the same spirit of functional representation and the avoidance of horizontal party politics, which had characterized the fundamental laws of the Franco regime. The principal features of this system were:

~ Election of municipal councilors on the basis of population, the
  number of councilors being scaled according to the number of
  residents of each town or village.
~ One-third of the councilors to be elected by the heads of families,
  one third by the syndicates established in the municipality and the
  final third elected by the two-thirds already elected, from among
  the commercial, cultural and professional people in the
  municipality.
~ Voting by secret ballot had to take place on three consecutive
  Sundays; for the first third, by all male and female heads of
  families over twenty-one years of age or over eighteen, if they
  were married; for the second third, by all males and females of
  those same age limits, who were inscribed in their respective
  syndicate; for the final third, by the successful candidates of the
  first two-thirds.

In October, the Republican politicians in exile again made a flutter. It
took the form of a supposed agreement, signed between Sr. Indalecio
Prieto for the Socialists and Sr. Gil-Robles for the Monarchists, to
oppose and upset the existing regime; the agreement was said to have
been handed to the British and other governments, but it was
categorically denied by Sr. Gil-Robles that he had ever signed such an
agreement and the affair passed into oblivion in an atmosphere of
mystery.

The year 1948 witnessed some important religious and cultural
celebrations of centenaries. There was that of Santiago de Compostella,
the goal of millions of pilgrims throughout the centuries, that of the
Ejercicios Espirituales of St. Ignatius Loyola and those of the
philosophers Balmes and Suárez. In considering the political structure
and practice of the Spanish regime, it is absolutely necessary to take
these things into account, for Spanish thought and institutions are so
saturated with Christian principles and Catholic philosophy that no true
appreciation of things Spanish is possible without them. Materialism and
secularism are not the backgrounds of Spanish culture and civilization,
but theology and philosophy are. It is this that made inevitable Spain's
repudiation of Marxism and freemasonry and instigated the international
persecution that took place from 1936 onwards. Spain understood in
1936 what the rest of the world began to learn ten years later.

The new law reestablishing titles, abolished by the Republic in 1931,
gave to General Franco the faculty of creating new ones, and in July

dukedoms were conferred posthumously on Don Jose Antonio Primo de Rivera, Don José Calvo Sotelo and General Emilio Mola, while General Moscardo was given the title of Conde del Alcázar de Toledo, in recognition of his great and glorious defense of the Alcázar in 1936. These honors gave recognition to the two men, who, together with General Franco, had inspired the policies on which the Spanish regime was built, and to two generals, who were the incarnation of the spirit in which the civil war was fought.

ARTICLE FROM *MORNING POST* OF OCTOBER 20th, 1931

CHURCH ISSUE IN SPAIN
Cross v. Hammer and Sickle
Catholic Feeling Running High
Counterrevolution Nearer

Barcelona,
October 20th, 1931

When the self-appointed government of the new Spanish Republic took control of Spain in April last they proclaimed "freedom of religion" as a part of their program.

Many unwary or ill-informed but well-intentioned persons who did not realize that the Roman Catholic faith is the only Christian religion in Spain with the exception of a few small foreign sects and chaplaincies, hailed this with joy as meaning only that all Christian sects were to have a free and equal field for their activities.

They were speedily undeceived when there took place the burning and sacking of churches and convents all over Spain, at which the soldiers and police looked on without interfering; when religious instruction was banned in the state schools, and when the cardinal primate of Spain and the bishop of Vitoria were obliged to fly the country.

DOCTRINES OF MARX

It then became evident that the spirit guiding the revolution was not one of liberal tolerance for the opinions and beliefs of others, but one with an anti-Christian bias determined on persecuting the established Church and the religious orders in Spain. The demands for the expulsion of the orders and especially of the Jesuits, with the confiscation of their possessions became clamorous.

This state of affairs should have caused no surprise when it is remembered that the vast majority of the government ministers and of

225

the new Cortes were all members of the parties of the extreme left, deeply imbued with the doctrines of Karl Marx and consequently bitterly anticlerical and strongly anti-Christian.

On the other hand, the hierarchy of the Roman Catholic Church, which always takes a hand in politics, and the majority of the priests were conservatives and the natural opponents of the parties of the left. Again, a factor—so often repeated in history—must not be forgotten; that the ever-accumulating power and riches of the religious orders incites their spoliation.

ABUSES IN THE CHURCH

It is also undeniable that, though many of the orders are composed of men and women spending self-denying lives in ameliorating the lot of their fellow men in hospitals, orphanages, and so forth, there are many abuses and an ever-increasing body of lazy and unemployed regular clergy, who bring the religious orders into disrepute and provide an efficient weapon to their opponents.

When the Cortes began to discuss the new Spanish constitution, it was anticipated that one of the most difficult points to settle would be that of the relations between church and state, and it has not falsified expectation, for it caused a series of wild and stormy sessions in which the opponents sometimes came to blows and has resulted in the acceptance of Article 24, containing clauses which have the approval of the extremist majority but have caused the resignation of Señor Alcalá-Zamora, the prime minister and the minister of the interior, Señor Maura, both of them professing Christians.

It is likely that the chances of the passing through parliament of the constitution have been wrecked by the approval of these clauses.

The outstanding features of Article 24 of the constitution as passed by the Cortes are:

~ Neither the state nor local authorities may support or help financially the Church or the religious institutions.
~ Stipends of the clergy cease being paid by the State within 2 years.
~ Certain religious orders to be dissolved; the others to be subject to stringent regulations and among them a prohibition to take part in teaching.
~ The faculty of the government to confiscate the possessions of the religious orders.

COUNTER-REVOLUTION

The approval of Article 24 does not mean that it has immediate effect, for it cannot come into force until the whole constitution is approved or a special decree-law promulgated by the government, but it has raised a storm of protest from religious societies all over Spain, and one can feel a growing indignation among the people, of whom a great number of all classes are ardent and professing Christians.

There can be no doubt that the right and clerical parties have been and will be extraordinarily strengthened by the feelings raised. It is in Navarre and the Basque provinces, which are also intensely monarchist, that feeling runs especially high in favor of the church and against parliament. It would appear that a counterrevolution has been brought appreciably nearer and, should it occur, there is reason to believe that it will be a fight led by the cross on one side and by the hammer and sickle on the other.

TRANSLATION OF SECRET DOCUMENTS DETAILING THE PLAN FOR THE ESTABLISHMENT OF A SOVIET SPAIN

The documents consist of two confidential reports and a secret report, which were obtained surreptitiously from the files of the communist headquarters in Spain, and were received in England in June 1936, by the author of this book. No less than four other copies of the two confidential reports were subsequently found in different parts of Spain; the five copies are almost identical, but in the interests of accuracy the slight variations that occur are printed in italics and in square brackets, though the variations are unimportant.

These four copies were found as follows:

1. At Palma, Majorca, among the papers of Commander Bayo, who was in command of the Barcelona-Valencia expeditionary force to Majorca, which was defeated in August 1936.
2. At the communist headquarters in Lora del Río, a small town in the province of Seville.
3. At the Communist center in a village near Badajoz.
4. At the Communist headquarters at La Línea.

All these documents were published with the permission and full authority of the Nationalist government. Translation of the documents mentioned above:

DOCUMENT NO. 1
CONFIDENTIAL REPORT NO. 3.

INSTRUCTIONS AND COUNTERSIGNS:

In order to control duly the final details of the movement, from the 3rd May next only liaison agents shall transmit orders, and they shall communicate with one another by cypher "E.M. 54-22."

The local chief officers shall give orders to their committees verbally. The general countersign is:

1-2 in 1:   Order to begin mobilization [the revolution]

2-2 in 2:   Order to begin the movement.

2-2 in 1:   Order to begin the attack on the spots specified.

2-3 in 5:   General arrest of counterrevolutionaries

2-4 in 3:   Trade union mobilization

[1-1 in 10]

1 to 10:   Order for provisionment

10-0:   The organization is ready

0-0:   Closure of frontiers and ports.

1-1:   Executions of the people named on the black lists.

All these orders will be given on the eve of the movement between [on] the 10th May and [or] 29th June at midnight from the wireless station in the Casa del Pueblo (Socialist headquarters) of Madrid, the wavelength of which is practically the same as that of "Union Radio" of Madrid.

MADRID ORGANISATION.

Madrid is divided into the following "Radios": [Sections:]

A & B: Chamartín de la Rosa. Depot at the Casa del Pueblo.

C & D: Cuatro Caminos. Depot at the Socialist Club.

E & F: Palacio District. Depot at the "Mundo Obrero" printing works.

G & H: University District. Depot at the offices of "El Socialista."

I & J: Latina District. Depot at the Socialist Club.

K & L: [Hospicio District]. Depot at the Casa del Pueblo, Secretarial offices, 1, 2, 5 and 7.

M & H: Inclusa District. Depot at the Socialist Group.

N&O: Pardiñas District. Depot at the garage at Calle Castello 19.

P&Q: Southern District. Depot at the Socialist Association of Vallecas.

R&S: [Upper and Lower]. Carabanchel. Depot[s] at the Socialist Club[s].

T-V, X-Z: Center of Madrid. Depot at the Casa del Pueblo, Secretarial offices, 2, 4, 6, 8 and from 10 to 20 and in the hall on the terrace.

PLAN TO BE FOLLOWED IN MADRID: The signal for beginning the movement will be the bursting of five small bombs at nightfall. Immediately thereafter a pretended Fascist attack on the Club of the C.N.T. (National Confederation of Labor) will be staged, a general strike will be declared, and the soldiers [and officers] implicated will rise in the barracks. The 'radios' will begin to act, the T.U.V. undertaking to seize the General Post and Telegraph Office, the prime minister's office, and the Ministry of War. The district 'radios' will attack the police stations and the X.L.Z. (? X.Y.Z.) the police headquarters. A special 'radio' composed solely of machine gunners and bombers will attack the Ministry of "Gobernación" (Interior) from the following streets: Carretas; Montera; Mayor; Correos; Paz; Alcalá; (*Arenal*); Preciados; Carmen and San Gerónimo. The 'radios' will act with fifty cells of ten men [100 *men*] each [*and in the streets of secondary and tertiary importance, and with only two cells in the streets of first importance and avenues*].

The orders are for all anti-revolutionaries [*who are arrested*] to be immediately executed. The revolutionaries of the Popular Front will be called upon to second the movement and, should they refuse to do so, will be expelled from Spain.

DOCUMENT NO. 2.
CONFIDENTIAL REPORT NO. 22 [11].

The dates of 11th May to 29th June are confirmed as the dates for starting the subversive movement (*according to the result of the elections for the presidency of the Republic, as stated in the former report*).

NATIONAL SOVIET.

PRESIDENT: Largo Caballero.

COMMISSAR FOR THE INTERIOR: Hernández y Zancajo (Socialist).

Do. EXTERIOR. Luis Araquistáin (Socialist).

Do. LABOR: Pascual Tomás (Socialist) (Communist).

Do. EDUCATION: Eduardo Ortega y Gasset (of the International Red Relief).

Do. AGRICULTURE: Sabalza [Zabanda] (Socialist).

Do. POST, TELEGRAPH & TELEPHONE: Pestana (Socialist).

Do. FINANCE: Julio Álvarez del Vayo (Socialist).

Do. WAR: (Lieut.-Colonel) Mangada.

Do. MARINE: Jerónimo Bujeda (Socialist)].

Do. RED ARMY: Francisco Galán (Communist).

Do. RAILWAYS: Álvarez Angulo (Socialist).

Do. INDUSTRY: Baraibar [Baraida].

Do. TRADE: Vega (of the International Red Relief).

Do. PUBLIC WORKS: José Diaz [Vealana] (Communist).

Do. PROPAGANDA & PRESS: Javier Bueno (Socialist).

Do. JUSTICE: [Luis] Jimenez Asua (Socialist).

ADVISER TO THE PRESIDENT: Ventura (Delegate of the Third International).

The Staff of the movement will consist of Largo Caballero, Hernández y Zancajo and Francisco Galán. The liaison officers will be the following:

SUPREME OFFICER: Ventura (of the U.S.S.R. and of the Third International).

OFFICER FOR EUZCADIA (Basque): Rafael Pérez (United Marxist Youth).

Do. FOR CATALONIA: Pedro Aznar (Catalan Proletarian Party) [Arnaez (Proletarian Group)].

Do. FOR LEVANT REGION: Escandell (Socialist).

Do. BALEARIC ISLES: Jaume (Socialist).

Do. CANARY ISLANDS: Mitge (Communist).

Do. ANDALUSIA: Boliva (Communist)

Do.CASTILLE: José Luis Andrés y Manso.

Do. ARAGÓN: Pavón (of C.N.T.).

Do. GALICIA: Romero Robledano (Communist).

Do. ASTURIAS: Belarmino Tomás.

Do. ESTREMADURA: Margarita Nelken.

MILITIA ORGANIZATIONS: The Militia is divided into three classes according to the task entrust to each. Assault Militia for the offensive; Resistance Militia for supplementary tasks; and Trade Union Militia for the general purpose of general strikes.

The approximate strength of these forces in the whole of Spain is: Assault Militia: 150,000 men; Resistance Militia: 100,000 men. Trade Union Militia, their number is not known (200,000).

The approximate number of arms they possess is: rifles, muskets, shotguns, etc: 25,000. Portable machine guns—30,000. Machine guns—250. Dynamite—sufficient for 20,000 men. The Resistance Militia only have (a great many) pistols.

SUPREME COMMAND OF THE MILITIA.

CHIEF OFFICER IN COMMAND: Santiago Carrillo.

OFFICER IN COMMAND IN EUZCADIA: Fulgencio Mateos of Bilbao.

Do. OLD AND NEW CASTILLE: Luis Azcasaga [Aceaya] and Bruno Alonso.

Do. EXTREMADURA: Nicholas de Pablo.

Do. ANDALUSIA: Fernando Bolaños.

Do. ASTURIAS: Graciano Antura [Antuna].

Do. CATALONIA: Miguel Valdes.

Do. LEVANTE: Sapi[n]a. GALICIA: Fernando Osorio.

Do. ARAGÓN: Castillos [Castilla and]

Do. BALEARIC AND CANARY ISLANDS: No officers (appointed yet, they will be communicated).

RADIOS AND CELLS. 'Radios' are composed of 1,000 men, and cells of 10 and the officer in command).

ZONES OF ASSAULT: These are: Madrid, Asturias, Extremadura [Catalonia, Andalusia], Galicia, Alicante, Santander, the mining and manufacturing zone of Vitoria [Vizcaya], Pasajes, and Mondragón in Guipuzcoa [Eibar], Murcia, Barrvelo, Reinosa and Logrono. The rest of Spain is a zone of resistance.

ARMED ORGANIZATION. Approximate numbers of each organization:

	Assault	Resistance	Trade Union
Madrid	25,000	25,000	25,000
Extremadura	15,000	10,000	20,000
Catalonia	30,000	20,000	40,000
Andalusia	15,000	12,000	15,000
Galicia	15,000	10,000	20,000

(Attention to the countersigns. Show blind obedience to officers and liaison agents and be sure that our triumph is a matter of hours and the soviet will be established).

DOCUMENT NO. 3
SECRET REPORT

On the 16th May a meeting took place in the Casa del Pueblo at Valencia. This meeting was attended by the delegate of the Third International, Ventura, and, on behalf of the Central Body of the Revolutionary Committee for Spain, Messrs. Aznar, Rafael Perez and several others. The three persons mentioned by their names have just arrived from France, where they exchanged views with the delegation of the French Communist Party and the C.G.T., at which meeting comrades Garpius, Thorez, and Freycinet attended, and it was decided to carry out a joint revolutionary movement in the two countries about the middle of June, by which date they presumed that the French Popular Front would have taken over power and Leon Blum would be prime minister. The full meeting at Valencia was also attended by Lomovioff and Tourochoff of the U.S.S.R. The following decisions were taken:

1. To transfer the central propaganda organization to Marseilles, 85, Rue de Montpelier, to the premises called "Etudes Internationales"
2. To start, on the same day as the said movement, the worldwide agitation to be named "anti-Fascist" so as clearly to express that the whole proletarian class is behind the movement.
3. For these purposes to appoint a liaison committee, composed of the abovementioned Ventura and also of Comlin, Magne, Lupine or Supovine, Basternier and Aznar, to whom should be added the abovementioned Lomovioff and Tourochoff.
4. To cause strikes systematically of an economic and social nature in all the larger towns of Spain so as to try out the preparation of the trade unions for revolution and the degree of resistance of the organization. Several of these strikes have been already declared in Madrid and the provinces.
5. To remove Casares Quiroga from power, either by an adverse vote in parliament or by any other means. An attempt on his life, it appears, is not considered, owing to the careful way in which he has himself guarded.
6. To discredit the leading members of the Socialist Party marked down as Reformists or Centrists, such as Prieto, Besteiro, etc. This must be done in such a way as to make it public and notorious.

Should the party congress be adjourned, as is the wish of Prieto's faction of the party, then the rupture of the U.G.T. (General Workers' Union) with the party should be provoked early in June and an official recognition given to their separation.

7. To provoke strikes in Asturias, Huelva and Bilbao particularly, as those are the places where the above-mentioned persons and also Gonzalez Pena have influence over labor circles.

8. To hold a meeting at Madrid on the 10th June next at the premises of the International Library at Calle Pablo Iglesias No. 11 Chamartín de la Rosa, to which the following are invited: Thorez, Cachin, Auriol, Fonchaus, Ventura, Dimitrov, Largo Caballero, Diaz, Carrillo, Guillermo, Anton, Pestaña, Garcia Oliver and Aznar.

9. To entrust one of the Madrid "radios"—No. 25—composed of active members of the police force, with the task of eliminating the prominent political and military men likely to play an important role in the counterrevolution.

10. To appoint the following liaison officers: Eguidazu and Mateos of Vizcaya, with Rafael Perez, of Navarre, for Irun-Hendaye-Aranda de Duero. Azcoaga and Sertucha of Madrid, for Madrid-Aranda. Valdés, Fronjosá and Carballido of Barcelona for Marseilles-Barcelona. Rodriguez Vera and Jaume, for Barcelona-Madrid.

PROGRAM OF THE NEW SPAIN

THE 26 POINTS OF FALANGE

COUNTRY—UNITY—EMPIRE

1. We believe in the supreme reality of Spain. To strengthen it, elevate it, and improve it, is the urgent collective task of all Spaniards. In order to achieve this end, the interests of individuals, groups and classes will have to be remorselessly waived.
2. Spain is a destined unity in the universe. Any conspiracy against this unity is abhorrent. Any form of separatism is an unpardonable crime. The existing constitution, in so far as it encourages any disunity, commits a crime against the destiny of Spain. For this reason, we demand its immediate abrogation.
3. We have a will to empire. We affirm that the full history of Spain implies an empire. We demand for Spain a preeminent place in Europe. We will not put up with international isolation or with foreign interference. With regard to the Hispano-America countries, we will aim at unification of culture, of economic interests and of power. Spain claims a preeminent place in all common tasks, because of her position as the spiritual cradle of the Spanish world.
4. Our armed forces, on land, on sea and in the air, must be as efficient and numerous as may be necessary to assure Spain's complete independence at all times and that world leadership which is her due. We shall restore to the armies on land and sea, and in the air, all the dignity which they deserve and, following their ideal, we shall see to it that a military view of life shall shape Spanish existence.
5. Spain will seek again her glory and her riches by means of the sea. Spain must aspire to become a great maritime power for her defense and for her commerce. We demand for our motherland an equally high standing for our navy and our air force.

THE STATE—THE INDIVIDUAL—LIBERTY

6. Our state will be a totalitarian instrument in the service of national integrity. All Spaniards will take part in it through their family, municipal and syndical functions. No one shall take part in it through any political party. The system of political parties will be implacably abolished, with all that flows from them—inorganic suffrage, representation by conflicting parties, and parliament of the familiar type.

7. Human dignity, the integrity of man and his liberty, are eternal and untouchable values. But only he is really free who forms part of a strong and free nation. No one will be allowed to use his liberty against the unity, strength, and liberty of the country. A rigorous discipline will prevent any attempt to poison, disunite or influence Spaniards against the destiny of the motherland.

8. The National-Syndicalist state will permit every private initiative which is compatible with the collective interest of all and will even protect and encourage beneficial enterprises.

ECONOMY—WORK—CLASS—WARFARE

9. In the economic sphere we imagine Spain as one gigantic syndicate of producers. We shall organize Spanish society in a corporative manner by means of a system of vertical syndicates with branches of production in the service of national economic integrity.

10. We repudiate any capitalist system which ignores popular necessities, dehumanizes private property, and huddles workers into shapeless masses ripe for misery and despair. Our spiritual and national sense also repudiates Marxism. We shall organize the impulses of the working classes, led astray today by Marxism, by exacting their direct participation in the great task of the national state.

11. The National-Syndicalist state will not cruelly ignore economic conflicts, and therefore will not stand unmoved in face of a domination of the weakest class by the strongest. Our regime will make class war radically impossible, in as much as all those who cooperate in production will be part of an organic whole. We abhor, and will prevent at all costs, the abuse of one partial interest by another and anarchy in the field of work.

12. The first object of wealth—and our state will affirm this—is to better the people's conditions of life. It is intolerable that great masses of people should live miserably whilst the few enjoy every luxury.
13. The state will recognize private property as a lawful means of fulfilling individual, family and social ends, and will protect it against the abuses of the great financiers, speculators and moneylenders.
14. We uphold the tendency towards nationalization of the banking services and also, through the medium of corporations, that of the big public services.
15. Every Spaniard has a right to work. Public bodies will, as a matter of course, assist those who are unable to find work. Until we have built up the new structure, we will maintain and intensify all the advantages which have been afforded to the worker by the existing social laws.
16. Every Spaniard who is physically fit has the duty of working. The National-Syndicalist state will not extend the slightest consideration to those who do not engage in any definite employment and aspire to live like invited guests at the cost of the effort of others.

THE LAND

17. At all costs, the standard of life in the country must be raised. It is the permanent spring of the life of Spain. To this end, we bind ourselves to carry out without hesitation the economic and social reform of agriculture.
18. We shall enrich agricultural production (economic reform) by the following means:
    a. By assuring for all products of the soil a remunerative minimum price.
    b. We shall insist that a great part of what is today absorbed by the towns in payment of their intellectual and commercial services shall be returned to the land so that it may be sufficiently endowed.
    c. By organizing a real national agricultural credit scheme which, by advancing money at low interest to the laborer on the security of his goods and harvests, will save him from usury and the domination of political bosses.
    d. By spreading the teaching of agriculture and cattle breeding.

e. By arranging the allotment of land according to its conditions and with regard to the possible disposal of its products.

f. By arranging tariffs so that they shall protect agriculture and the cattle industry.

g. By the acceleration of irrigation works.

h. By rationalizing the units of agriculture in order to suppress both the large neglected estates as well as small properties which are non-economic because of their poor return.

19. We shall organize agriculture socially by the following means:

a. By redistributing cultivable land in order to set up family properties and energetically stimulate the syndication of laborers.

b. By ending the misery of the human masses who today wear themselves out in ploughing sterile land, and who will be transferred to new cultivable land.

20. We shall embark on an untiring campaign to increase the importance of raising cattle and reforestation, taking severe measures against any persons who may place obstacles in the way, going so far as the temporary compulsory mobilization of the whole of Spanish youth for this historic task of reconstruction of the national wealth.

21. The state will be empowered to expropriate without compensation any property which has been illegitimately acquired or enjoyed.

22. The reconstruction of the communal land of the villages will be one of the first objects of the National-Syndicalist state.

23. It is the essential task of the state, by means of a rigorous discipline in education, to build up a strong and united national spirit and to instill into the souls of the future generations' happiness and pride of country. Every man will receive a pre-military education in order to prepare him for the honor of being incorporated in the National and Popular Army of Spain.

24. Culture will be organized in such a form that no talent shall run to seed for want of economic means. All those who deserve it will have easy access to the university.

25. Our movement will incorporate the Catholic spirit—of glorious tradition and predominant in Spain—in the national reconstruction. The church and the state will arrange a concordat defining their respective spheres. But the state will not permit any interference or activity which might lower its dignity or the national integrity.

NATIONAL REVOLUTION

26. The Spanish Traditional Phalanx of the J.O.N.S. desires a new order of things, which has been set out in the principles announced above. Its methods are preferably direct, ardent, and combative. Life is a battle and must be lived with a spirit alight with service and sacrifice.

THE LABOR CHARTER OF SPAIN

(Enacted by Decree on March 9th, 1938)

THE LABOR CHARTER

PREAMBLE

Reviving the Catholic tradition of social justice and the lofty sense of humanity that inspired the laws of the Empire. The state—which is national by reason of being an instrument wholly at the service of the entire nation, and syndical in so far as it represents a reaction against nineteenth century capitalism and communistic materialism—embarks upon the task of carrying out, with a disciplined constructive and soberly religious demeanor, the revolution that Spain is achieving to ensure that Spaniards may once more possess, for good and all, their country, bread and justice.

To attain this end and at the same time put into practice the motto of the unity, greatness and freedom of Spain, it enters the social field with the determination that the common wealth shall be at the service of the Spanish people and that the country's economy shall be subordinated to that policy. Basing itself on the postulate that Spain is one and indivisible as regards her destiny, it hereby declares its aim to make Spanish industry—in the fellowship of all its components—one and indivisible, so that it may minister to the needs of the country and uphold the instruments of its power.

The recently established Spanish State, in these declarations of what is to be the inspiration of its social and political economy, is putting faithfully into a concrete form the desires and demands of all who are fighting in the trenches and who compose, through their honor, valor and labor the most progressive aristocracy of this era in the nation's history.

Be it known, therefore, to all Spaniards, who are united in sacrifice and in hope, that WE DECLARE:

I. WORK FOR ALL

Firstly: Work is man's participation in production by means of the willingly given exercise of his mental and manual abilities, according to his personal vocation, that he may live a more seemly and comfortable life whilst assisting in the development of the national economy.

Secondly: Work, being essentially personal and human, cannot be lowered to the merely material idea of a merchandise, nor be made the subject of any transaction incompatible with the self-respect of him who lends it.

Thirdly: The right to work is a consequence of the duty to do so that God demands of man for the fulfilment of his individual ends and the prosperity and greatness of his country.

Fourthly: The State values and exalts work—the fertile expression of man's creative spirit and, as such, will protect it with all the force of the law, showing it the greatest consideration and making it compatible with other individual, family and social ends.

Fifthly: Work, being a social duty, will be universally demanded in some form or other of all Spaniards who are not cripples, as it is deemed a tribute all must pay to the wealth of the country.

Sixthly: Work is one of the noblest attributes of rank and honor and is sufficient justification for demanding the assistance and guardianship of the State.

Seventhly: Service is that work which is given with heroism, disinterestedness, and abnegation with the object of helping towards the supreme good which Spain represents.

Eighthly: All Spaniards have the right to work. The satisfaction of this right is one of the main concerns of the state.

II. HOURS AND CONDITIONS OF WORK

Firstly: The State undertakes to exercise constant and effective action in defense of the worker, his living, and his work. It will set proper limits to the working hours to prevent them being excessive and will grant labor every safeguard of a defensive and humanitarian order. It will specially prohibit night work for women and children, regulate homework and free married women from the workshop and the factory.

Secondly: The state will keep Sunday as a day of rest, as a sacred condition for the lending of labor.

Thirdly: Without loss of pay, and taking into account the technical requirements of the industry, the law will enforce the recognition of the religious holidays tradition demands, civil holidays which have been so declared and attendance at such ceremonies as the national leaders of the movement may ordain.

Fourthly: July 18th, the date of the beginning of the Glorious Rising having been proclaimed a national holiday, will be celebrated as the Feast of Homage to Labor.

Fifthly: Every worker will have a right to paid yearly holidays in order to enjoy a deserved rest, and the necessary machinery to ensure the better fulfilment of this order will be prepared.

Sixthly: The requisite institutions will be created so that, in their leisure hours, the workers may have access to all means of culture, happiness, health, sport and volunteer training.

III.   REMUNERATION AND SECURITY

Firstly: The minimum basis of payment for work shall be sufficient to provide the worker and his family with a worthy, moral living.

Secondly: Family subsidies will be established through suitable bodies.

Thirdly: The standard of living of the workers will be raised gradually and inflexibly in proportion as the higher interests of the nation permit.

Fourthly: The state will fix rules for regulating work, in accordance with which relations between workers and employers will be arranged. The principal contents of the said relations will be both the giving of labor and its remuneration and the reciprocal duty of loyalty, assistance and protection in the employers and faithfulness and obedience on the part of the workers.

Fifthly: Through the guild the state will be at pains to learn whether economic and all kinds of conditions in which work is being done are fair to the workers.

Sixthly: The state will see to the security and continuity of work.

Seventhly: The employer shall inform his personnel of the progress of production sufficiently to strengthen their sense of responsibility in the same, and in the terms to be laid down by law.

IV. THE ARTISAN

The artisan, who is a living heritage of a glorious guild past, will be fostered and efficiently protected, as being a complete embodiment of the human person in his work and presenting a form of production equally distant from capitalist concentration and gregarious Marxism.

V. AGRICULTURAL WORK

Firstly: Regulations for agricultural labor will be adapted to its special characteristics and the seasonal variations which nature ordains.

Secondly: The state will pay special attention to the technical education of the agricultural producer thus enabling him to perform all the work demanded by each unit of development.

Thirdly: The prices of the chief products will be regulated and fixed in such a way as to ensure a minimum profit in normal conditions to the agricultural employer, and consequently such as to make him pay his laborer wages that will enable them to improve their living conditions.

Fourthly: The aim will be pursued of giving every peasant family a small holding of family land sufficient for its own needs and to provide work during periods of unemployment.

Fifthly: Rural life will be enhanced by the improvement of peasants' dwellings and of the sanitary condition of the villages and hamlets of Spain.

Sixthly: The state will guarantee to tenants' continuity in cultivating their land by means of long-term contracts to safeguard them around unjustified evictions and to ensure for them the extinction of debt for any improvements they may have made in the period. The state aspires to find ways and means to cause the land to pass, on fair terms, into the hands of those who work it directly.

VI. TOILERS OF THE SEA

The state will look after the toilers of the sea with the utmost solicitude, giving them proper institutions to prevent depreciation of their wares and helping them to acquire the necessary equipment for carrying on their profession.

VII. LABOR MAGISTRACY

A new labor magistracy will be created based on the principle that this function of justice is a matter for the state.

VIII. CAPITAL AND ITS ROLE

Firstly: Capital is an instrument of production.

Secondly: The enterprise (employer or firm), as a producing unit, will arrange the members composing it in such a way that those of an instrumental nature shall be subordinate to those of a human category, and all alike to the common good.

Thirdly: The head of the firm will take on himself its management and be responsible to the state for the same.

Fourthly: After allotting a fair interest to capital, the profits of the firm will be firstly applied to the reserves necessary for its sound position, the improvement of production and the betterment of working conditions and the living of the workers.

IX. CREDIT FOR DEVELOPMENT

Firstly: Credit will be so ordered that, besides attending to its tasks of developing the country's resources, it may assist in creating and supporting the small farmer, fisherman, industrialist and businessman.

Secondly: Honorable conduct and confidence, based on skill in work, will comprise effective security for the granting of credit. The state will implacably suppress all forms of usury.

X. SOCIAL INSURANCE

Firstly: Savings will give the worker the certitude of being protected when in misfortune.

Secondly: There will be an increase in the social insurance against old age, disablement, maternity, work accidents, professional sickness, consumption and unemployment, the ultimate aim being the establishment of total insurance. A primary aim will be to devise means for providing a sufficient pension for superannuated workers.

XI. PROTECTION AND PRODUCTION

Firstly: National production constitutes an economic unit at the service of the country. It is the duty of every Spaniard to defend, improve and increase it. All factors combining in production are subordinate to the supreme interest of the nation.

Secondly: Individual collective acts that in any way disturb normal production or attempt to do so, will be considered as crimes of treason against the country.

Thirdly: Unjustifiable slackening in output will be the subject of appropriate punishment.

Fourthly: In general, the state will not be a business concern, except to compensate for the absence of private initiative or when the higher interests of the nation so require it.

Fifthly: The state itself, or through the guilds, will prevent all unfair competition in the field of production as well as such activities as obstruct the normal establishment or development of the national economy, but will encourage, on the other hand, all initiative that tends to its betterment.

Sixthly: The state recognizes private initiative as being a copious source for the economic life of the nation.

XII. PROPERTY AND THE FAMILY

Firstly: The state recognizes and protects private property as a natural means for fulfilling individual, family, and social functions. All forms of property are subordinate to the supreme interests of the nation, whose interpreter is the state.

Secondly: The state assumes the task of multiplying and putting within the reach of all Spaniards those forms of property vitally bound up with the person, the family health, the ownership of land and the instruments or goods of labor for daily use.

Thirdly: It looks on the family as the prime natural unit and foundation of society and, at the same time, as a moral institution endowed with an inalienable right superior to any positive law. As a greater safeguard to its preservation and continuance, the immunity of family patrimony from attachment will be recognized.

XIII. PRINCIPLES OF THE ORGANIZATION

Firstly: The National Guild organization of the state finds its inspiration in the principles of unity, totality and hierarchy.

Secondly: All factors of economy will be incorporated, by branches of production or services, in vertical guilds. The liberal and technical professions will be similarly organized as the law may prescribe.

Thirdly: The vertical guild is a corporation by public law, which is formed by combining into one single organism all elements that devote themselves to fulfilling the economic process within a certain service or branch of production, arranged in order of rank, under the direction of the State.

Fourthly: The officials of the guilds will necessarily be chosen from the active members of the Spanish Traditionalist Phalanx.

Fifthly: The vertical guild is an instrument at the service of the State—through which it will chiefly carry out its economic policy. It is the duty of the guild to know the problems of production and propose solutions subordinating them to the national interest. The vertical guild may intervene through specialized bodies in the regulation, supervision, and fulfilment of the conditions of work.

Sixthly: The vertical guild may initiate and maintain bodies of investigation, moral, physical and professional education, savings and assistance, as well as other bodies of a social character of necessity to the elements of production.

Seventhly: It will establish employment bureaus to find work for the worker properly adapted to his ability and merits.

Eighthly: It is a duty of the guilds to supply the State with exact data to work out the statistics of their production.

Ninthly: The law of guild organization will decide the way in which the existing economic or professional associations shall be incorporated.

XIV. PROTECTION OF THE SPANISH WORKER

The state will issue the opportune measures to be taken for protecting national labor in our territory; and through labor treaties, with other powers, it will see to the protection of the professional position of Spanish workers residing abroad.

XV.   RESTORATION OF SPAIN

On the day of the promulgation of this Charter, Spain is engaged in a heroic military struggle, in which at the cost of heavy sacrifice she is saving the riches of the soul and the civilization of the world.

To the generosity of the youth in arms and of Spain herself, national production with all its component factors must respond.

In this charter of rights and duties we therefore set down as most urgent and necessary those of the elements of production which co-operate with their just and resolute contribution to the restoration of the soil of Spain and the foundations of her power.

XVI.   FUTURE OF THE COMBATANTS

The state undertakes to incorporate in the posts of work, honor and command to which they have a right as Spaniards and which they have won like heroes, the young men who are fighting.

APPENDIX V

FOREWORD BY THE INFANTE DON JUAN

TO *THE NEW STATE* BY VICTOR PRADERA

(Messrs. Sands and Co., London, 1939,
reproduced by courtesy of the publishers).

It is with a certain diffidence that I have agreed to write the preface of this book. I greatly regret that the privilege of fighting for my country was denied me, first when acting under the impulse of my feelings I went to Spain at the beginning of the war, and later by Generalissimo Franco himself when I asked him to let me have a place in the navy. I feel that I should have had more hope of acquitting myself with credit in this simpler form of controversy than in dialectical argument. Nevertheless, perhaps one who is half English may be allowed to say a few words to help Englishmen to understand Spain when presenting them with the English version of the last work of Victor Pradera. He was one of Spain's greatest modern thinkers, and he died for the ideals for which he lived and for which he had worked.

My mother is a granddaughter of Queen Victoria, and my uncle, Prince Maurice of Battenberg, was killed serving as a second lieutenant in the 60th Rifles in October, 1914. I myself served for five exceptionally happy years in the British navy, and it is therefore very sad for me to find that my own countrymen are troubled and perplexed by the British attitude, and that the British do not understand the issues in Spain.

I personally am convinced, and am always telling my Spanish friends, that the British have an ingrained sense of fair play, and that their misconceptions of the Spanish War are due to the fact that they have not been properly informed. There is a homely English proverb: 'What is sauce for the goose is sauce for the gander.' Let me try and apply it to recent events in Spain.

I.   So-called Rebellion: In 1934, when Russia subsidized an armed rebellion in Asturias, the very people who in England today are denouncing Franco for rising against the legal government, applauded the rebels and denounced the government for suppressing the rebellion.

II.   Foreign Intervention: Russia intervened in 1934, two years before an Italian or a German landed in Spain. In August 1936, whilst the French 'Front Populaire' was busily engaged in sending troops and ammunition into Spain, Franco was carrying on without any help.

III. Air Bombardment: Great Britain was greatly stirred by the air bombardment of the military objectives in Barcelona and Valencia. Admittedly the whole question of how far one is entitled to bomb a military objective, knowing that civilians will probably be killed, is a difficult one. As one who is half English, I can quote from the official 'The War in the Air'

"The policy intended to be followed is to attack the important German towns systematically... It is intended to concentrate on one town for successive days, and then to pass to several other towns, returning to the first town until the target is thoroughly destroyed, or, at any rate, the morale of the workmen is so shaken that the output is seriously interfered with. Long distance bombing will produce its maximum moral effect only if the visits are constantly repeated at short intervals, so as to produce in each area bombed a sustained anxiety. It is this recurrent bombing, as opposed to isolated spasmodic attacks, which interrupts industrial production and undermines public confidence" (Appendix 6, Vol. VI).

Mr. Winston Churchill on civil casualties (Appendix IV): "our air offensive should consistently be directed at striking at the bases and communications upon whose structure the fighting power of his armies and his fleets of the sea and of the air depends. Any injury which comes to the civil population from this process of attack must be regarded as incidental and inevitable" (October 21st, 1917).

May I be forgiven for pointing out that in the earlier period in the war, when the Republicans had supremacy in the air and systematically bombed open towns with no military objectives in Nationalist territory, there were no protests from England or from English ecclesiastics.

May I, in this connection, deal with the traditional British view that, so far as atrocities are concerned, it is "six of one and half a dozen of the other."? Surely there is a universe of difference between accidentally killing civilians while attacking military objectives, and deliberately murdering men, women, and children in cold blood. The Badajoz and Guernica myths have been analyzed and refuted in Mr. Robert Sencourt's admirable book, *Spain's Ordeal.* I need deal no further with those points.

It is important to insist that the atrocities on the Republican side are not a question of opinion, but of admitted fact, since the Spanish Embassy in London did not deny the Burgos Report, and, indeed, explicitly admitted that the report was correct. Their defense was that they could not control these excesses; and yet the people who back this government, which on its own admission has been unable to prevent the massacre of hundreds of thousands of civilians. Men, women, and children claims the sympathy of Britain as a representative, democratic government. Fortunately, the truth is beginning to prevail. The simple device of labelling communists, socialists, or even liberals, has succeeded for some considerable time, but English people are beginning to discover that Spanish socialists are different from English conservative trade unionists who describe themselves as socialists. Mr. Attlee and Mr. Lansbury would certainly not feel at home if they stayed longer than a few days in Red Spain.

The *Times*, which throughout the war has scrupulously refrained from reproving either side, has maintained its high reputation for objectivity in its news services, and has summed up the situation in a memorable leading article which appeared on May 3rd, 1938:

> Loudly as the Barcelona government may denounce the unprovoked aggression of General Franco's rebels, their mentors in Moscow have already claimed the instigation of the civil war as a triumph of their own subversive diplomacy. For this is one of the essential stages of the desired revolution, which must, it is dogmatically asserted, follow the same course in every country. These steps to the compulsory millennium are four in number: The first is the 'united front' the second, strikes and disorders, the third, civil war, and the fourth, Soviet government.

The verdict of the *Times* was confirmed from an unsuspected source. Mr. John McGovern, M.P., representing the Independent Labour Party, an honest and convinced opponent of our cause, paid a special visit to Barcelona, and confirmed the view that the controlling power in Red Spain is the Russian Cheka.

The so-called Black Legend, which has done so much to harm our cause in England, is composed of three factors: the Spanish Inquisition, bullfighting, and the conquistadores. As to the Spanish Inquisition, on the evidence of Llorente, a bitter opponent and ex-secretary of the Inquisition, it put to death 32,000 people in three centuries. On the evidence of the Manchester Guardian, a paper which has been favorable to the Reds, 40,000 people were killed in Madrid in the first three months of the war. Therefore, the Red Terror was a thousand times more destructive of life than that much-hated institution, the Spanish Inquisition.

As to the conquistadores, I, as a Spaniard, am proud to feel that the spirit of a Cortes or a Pizarro, who conquered a continent with a handful of men, has been reborn in those young leaders who are fighting today for the true and everlasting Spain. Nationalist Spain, as the *Times* now fully admits, is fighting the battle of Christian civilization against communism and deserves the support of all fair-minded Englishmen.

It is therefore my pleasure and privilege to sponsor this publication. The "Old" State for which Victor Pradera died is now revealed to us in all its truth as the New State which, under God, will be the salvation of Spain after the most terrible experience that can befall a nation.

JUAN DE BOURBON
Rome, December, 1938.